Meetings with Remarkable Animals

Meetings with Remarkable Animals

MARTIN CLUNES AND JO WHEELER

MICHAEL JOSEPH

PENGUIN MICHAEL JOSEPH

UK | USA | Canada | Ireland | Australia
India | New Zealand | South Africa

Penguin Michael Joseph, Penguin Random House UK,
One Embassy Gardens, 8 Viaduct Gardens, London sw11 7BW

First published 2024

003

Copyright © Martin Clunes, 2024

The moral right of the author has been asserted

Set in 13.5/16pt Garamond MT Std
Typeset by Jouve (UK), Milton Keynes
Printed and bound in Great Britain by Clays Ltd, Elcograf S.p.A.

The authorized representative in the EEA is Penguin Random House Ireland,
Morrison Chambers, 32 Nassau Street, Dublin D02 YH68

A CIP catalogue record for this book is available from the British Library

HARDBACK ISBN: 978–0–241–72378–4
TRADE PAPERBACK ISBN: 978–0–241–72379–1

www.greenpenguin.co.uk

Penguin Random House is committed to a
sustainable future for our business, our readers
and our planet. This book is made from Forest
Stewardship Council® certified paper.

With Special Thanks to Jim, Penny, Dodger, Arthur Colin, Tina Audrey, Mary Elizabeth, Maisie Anne, Chester, Bee, Timmy, Tommy and Jemima.

Contents

Guide dog Laura, who joined our pack when she retired in spring 2023.

Introduction

In the autumn of 2021 I heard a programme on the radio which caught my attention. It also sort of changed my life. Funnily enough the show itself was called *Life Changing*. A woman called Jaina Mistry was talking about how her life had been changed by a kind and lovable black Labrador retriever cross called Laura. When she was a teenager Jaina had lost her sight suddenly after a devastating and unexpected illness. As a result she had also lost a lot of her independence. At first, the idea of getting a guide dog to assist her had not really been an option for Jaina. She had been afraid of dogs ever since she was chased by one as a child. After several years of being unable to do so many of the things she wanted to do independently, Jaina decided the only way to get her freedom back would be to get over her fear of dogs and get a guide dog. And that's what she did: she got over her fear of dogs and that's when Laura came into her life.

Jaina spoke on the radio movingly about how she and Laura had formed the most remarkable bond of trust and love. With her dog at her side Jaina had got back so much of her independence. She had seen her health and fitness improve and gained the confidence and independence to launch a whole new career. Through it all Laura had been her comfort, her buddy and her champion. After ten years together, the terrifying and heartbreaking moment had come: it was time for Laura to retire. Jaina had put herself on the waiting list for a new guide dog and now had a tough decision to make about what to do with Laura. After some soul searching, Jaina eventually decided she could not in all good conscience leave Laura on her own at home all day, while she went to work with a new guide dog. So by the time I heard her talking on the radio she had made the difficult decision for Laura to move in with another family and she was searching for the perfect canine retirement home.

My first thought was that we could give that dog a nice retirement. I called my wife and she had heard the programme too and the idea had sort of flitted through her mind as well, so I emailed the programme and asked to be put on the list as I imagined I wasn't the only one enquiring after Jaina's glowing radio commercial. We love dogs in our house and at that time we had four of them. There was my Jack Russell Jim, my number-two, who went everywhere with me. There was Penelope Jennifer or Penny, our Jackahuahua, half Mexican half Cornish, who we got from our friend Naomi in Cornwall. Then there was Heidi Mae, our blue roan cocker spaniel, who gave us a litter of seven beautiful puppies; there were six black girls and one golden boy the same colour as Mary Elizabeth, our first cocker, so we kept the boy and he's called Bob Jackson. So that was four dogs, plus two cats, my Clydesdale horses Ronnie and Bruce, along with three other horses and a rehomed Shetland pony, not to mention a handful of cattle. So what possible harm could it do to add another dog?

I think all children are born with an innate curiosity about other animals. Disney knew it, didn't he, and I was no different. I have a clear memory as a toddler of pushing an earwig into some plasticine to make him a home, but it turns out that earwigs don't thrive in plasticine, a lesson that I'm glad I learned so early on. Then I had a newt who we took on the train in a jam jar to stay with my aunt in Essex; we got him there and home again and I think he enjoyed himself, but not long after we came home he buggered off. I don't know where to, maybe back to Essex. When it comes to more official pets, my sister had the usual succession of hamsters. My dad, Alec, had a ginger-and-white cat called Timmy, which gave him a lot of joy. I don't remember paying that cat all that much attention. He was definitely my dad's cat.

My childhood became a bit trickier when my father died. I was eight. From then on Timmy gained a new meaning in the household. It was as if he became a kind of representative for my father. He was treated with a lot of respect and was more than a little bit spoiled. He also got quite eccentric and would perform magnificent leaps across the kitchen counter tops. There was a little shelf by the side of our table in the kitchen where he would sit for ages washing his paws without looking at you. Then all of a sudden he would eye up what was on your plate and just sort of reach for whatever took his fancy.

When my dad died there was pressure from my mum's family to put me into boarding school. Apparently they were scared I would turn gay if I lived with only my mum and my sister. Times were different then and the decision was doubly regrettable as I learned when I was an adult that my dad had always wanted me to go to a state school, but then the minute he died the family decided this would better my chances. So at nine years old I was packed off to a prep school in the Surrey countryside. It wasn't a bad little school really. There were only about twenty boarders out of a hundred and thirty or so pupils. But all the other students had done a lot of

Latin and French and stuff that I didn't know anything about as a state-school kid. This meant I was behind in lessons and had to stay back a year, which was a kind of agony. I wasn't exactly cherished in the dormitory either. I had become a massive bedwetter. So to add to my own humiliation and the annoyance of the other pupils, I was given a kind of electric warning system under the plastic bedsheet, which made a terrible noise in the night. To everyone's relief I was eventually moved out of the dorm and put in a room, which belonged to matron, on my own downstairs. What made it all a bit more bearable was that the school had a small menagerie in the grounds where they kept all kinds of animals. There were hens and a turkey, a sheep, some ducks and geese, chipmunks, quail and an occasional visiting donkey. As a stab at doing something with me, the kindly biology teacher gave me the responsibility of going out in the morning before everyone was up and letting them all out and feeding them. I loved the routine of heading into the fresh morning air while it was still quiet, opening the door to the barn and letting the light in. There they all were, blinking back at me. The sheep, standing with a turkey on its back. The hens and ducks quacking and clucking away. It was a great source of comfort to be part of this gentle wholesome scene and it's a memory from that difficult time that I cherish to this day.

Ever since then I have always had a great attachment to and affection for animals. Over the years our little family has acquired quite the collection. We've had eight dogs, at least twelve horses, three cats and a thriving colony of sea monkeys. I'm always pleased when Max Peter the cat chooses to sit on my lap, even if it is only to dry himself off from the rain. I love the nuzzle of a horse's nose in my hand and the feel of our dogs' fur on my face. I've probably wept more for the pets who are no longer with us than I have for some humans. Of course any pet owner will waste no time in telling you how much they love their animals. But there really is something special about bridging the species divide, in having another creature acknowledge you and look you in the eye with what seems to be a look of total trust and understanding. It's hard to beat the strong bond you build up with a dog over years of simply walking and hanging out together. My life has been enriched by spending time with animals of all kinds over the years. I once met a pack of wolves, which was thrilling and terrifying in equal measure. One of the bigger females almost knocked me over with an enthusiastic greeting. But I relished the chance to give her a good old ruffle around the neck after I sensed there was trust.

Animals have helped us as a species in so many ways. We've harnessed the powers and skills they have to do things that we can't do for ourselves. We teamed up with those wild wolves and turned them into dogs of all shapes and sizes to guard and protect us, herd our livestock, keep us company, pull sleds and sniff things out that we could only dream of finding with our own noses. We tamed and tethered horses to help us carry things and travel the world. They allowed us to jump on their backs and kit them out to go into battle with us. Animals have become our best friends and companions. We've rewarded and honoured them for their loyalty, service and courage, for what they've done during wartime and how they've assisted and accompanied us in times of need.

Human attributes like bravery, valour and courage are often used to describe cats, pigeons and horses. I don't think that's quite right. I don't think that they know that they are risking their lives to save us and help us, and yet they do time and time again. But as an animal lover who has spent a lot of time with a lot of animals, I have no doubt that what they do for us is truly remarkable. I've been discovering stories of people across the world whose lives have been changed and saved by animals, to find out more about what's going on when these incredible partnerships develop. From therapy horses and life-saving dolphins to mine-detecting rats, disease-sniffing dogs and the award-winning pigeons who have helped us win wars, what lies at the heart of our connection with these extraordinary creatures? Where better to start than with the animal who has done more for us throughout history than any other, my pal the horse.

My daughter Emily and my first horse, Chester.

1. Dawn Horse

Taming Equus

It's hot and humid in the forest. A group of animals about the size of foxes are munching their way through the leaves of a primitive type of tree. They could be mistaken for a herd of small deer, maybe with a hint of tapir somewhere around the eyes. They might look relaxed but they're on high alert. These plant-eating forest dwellers are definitely not at the top of the prehistoric food chain. They're the first equids, among the earliest members of the family which today includes horses, asses, donkeys and zebras. Eohippus, the 'dawn horse', would not have looked much like any horse we know today, at dawn or otherwise. At around twenty inches tall they are also thought to be an ancestor of the tapir and the rhinoceros. They had an odd number of toes and their flexible mouth parts were perfect for chewing the lush forest leaves. Eohippus lived around fifty-five million years ago during the balmy Eocene epoch. Another fifty million years later, global temperatures had plummeted. Different equids had come and gone, most unable to cope with the dryer cold conditions. Some lucky survivors with stronger teeth were able to graze the rough grasslands on the flat plains of what is now North America. They developed strong, agile legs for running away from predators. They also lost a few toes along the way and developed a single hoof. We call them *Equus*. They were not quite as tall as most modern horses but would be very recognizable to us today. Several thousand miles away our own ancestors were beginning to ponder whether or not to climb down from the trees. It would be another few million years before our paths would cross.

My first real encounter with a horse came not via the wilderness of the North American plains but the Wimbledon rag and bone man. As a child I loved the sound of his big hairy Gypsy Cob as he clipped past our house pulling a wagon. A bell would ring and the familiar call would bring people out with all their scrap metal to be loaded on to the flatbed. Then the old man would click his tongue and the giant horse would start up again down the road and out of sight. I can't say I took loads of notice of this horse, but it was a comforting remnant of a time when these stately creatures would have been everywhere in our towns and cities.

Horses are actually still quite common in Wimbledon even today. Mounted Keepers, uniformed rangers on horseback, have been patrolling Wimbledon Common from dawn to dusk for over seventy years. I'm not entirely sure what their duties to 'protect people on the common' mean in practice. Most likely shooing away up-to-no-good youths. I was once one of those up-to-no-good youths. Me and my mates used to hang about on the common a lot, catapulting acorns and smoking Player's No. 6. I don't remember the mounted guards ever catching hold of us but they were an impressive and intimidating sight, towering over us as they rode past on horseback. There's also a village stable yard in Wimbledon, another remnant of a bygone time. My sister used to take riding lessons there when we were growing up. I confess I never took that much interest in those horses either. I was more about jumping into hay bales while she followed the purpose-built horse tracks around the common. The horses on those tracks seemed like a bit of a nuisance to me too, especially when I was whizzing around them with my mates on my bike. So, all things considered, I never imagined growing up that horses would come to play such a central role in my life.

I have always been drawn to animals so it's no surprise that when my wife Philippa and I got together we began to build our own animal family. Our first dog was a cocker spaniel called Mary Elizabeth. When our daughter Emily was born we encouraged her to engage with creatures of all kinds. I was involved with the Born Free Foundation so she was often surrounded by the piles of cuddly endangered species which furnished her cot. The first horse in our life was an old Shetland pony called Scooby-Doo; we used to take Emily to ride on him in Richmond Park. That little horse must have launched the riding careers of many young people as he stoically walked around the park with a succession of small humans on his back. Scooby-Doo was approaching thirty years old. Perhaps he's no longer with us or maybe he is; ponies can live for years and years . . . out of spite some say.

I knew Philippa had always wanted a horse ever since she was a little girl but she had never had the chance, so one year on a whim I bought her a retired racehorse called Prince. He wasn't easy to handle and at one point Philippa got seriously injured. In the end we had to give him up and it turned out the poor thing had a brain tumour. It was a lesson in taking care when choosing a thousand-pound animal to bring into your life. Eventually we got Philippa another horse called Bee, a beautiful and kindly mare who we kept at an equestrian centre. It was a pleasure to watch as Philipa bonded with this majestic creature, and it got me wondering, how did we ever gain the trust of these huge, shy animals?

*

About two to three million years ago some of those early horses crossed from North America into Eurasia. Fast-forward to 32,000 years ago, it's the Palaeolithic, the Stone Age. Early humans have begun to document the world around them on the walls of the caves where they hang out. In charcoal and red ochre they depict wild cattle, rhinos, reindeer, aurochs, buffalo and horses. The oldest picture of a horse that we know of is in a cave in southern France. The so-called *Panel of Four Horses* depicts, you guessed it, four horses. Drawn from the neck up in charcoal they're extremely beautiful and moving to look at, even 30,000 odd years later. We don't know whether they had any spiritual significance or whether they are just very good doodles, but the images are remarkably sensitive and alive. The four heads are partially layered over one another, which gives the impression as your eye drifts down the rock of an early moving picture. The horse seems to shake its mane and then close its eyes, perhaps taking a nap. With its mouth gently open in the final image, you can almost hear the whinny across the centuries. But while our cave-dwelling ancestors may have loved or even worshipped horses, those wild horses almost certainly did not love us back, at least not yet.

To get a sense of the kind of horses which were first tamed and domesticated by man, you can't get much closer than one of the last remaining populations of wild horses in the world, the takhi, or Przewalski's horse. After going extinct in the wild they were reintroduced to Mongolia and Kazakhstan from a captive population in the 1990s. They now number over a thousand. I was lucky enough to go and see a few of them while I was making a documentary. We arrived at the site by Russian helicopter and flew over a rocky stretch of Mongolian grassland. As the vast plain stretched out in all directions it felt like arriving on the

4

moon. The horses were tricky to see at first because they're so well camouflaged, but we soon caught a glimpse of a beautiful herd galloping below us free and wild. Flashing across the ground in unison they looked more like a herd of gazelles than horses. They're stockier and smaller than modern horses. Like those in many of the early cave paintings they have a more uniform sandy-yellow colour, with short black manes, rounded noses, donkey-like ears and occasional faint stripes or spots. They're a wonderful sight to see and the very fact they exist at all today is remarkable. It's tempting to want to see a line of descent from these beautiful takhi to our domestic horses but they only share about 3% of their DNA. They're most likely not the direct ancestors of *Equus caballus*, the modern horse. It's thought that most horses evolved from a different wild population around 3,500 BC between Eastern Europe and Central Asia. Equine teeth found in Kazakhstan show signs of domestication through marks made from rope or leather and pottery from the region has been found to contain traces of horse milk. As humans began to capture and tame horses for food and drink, they also started to breed some very specific traits into them, firstly compliance and docility, and secondly a stronger backbone. I guess it was only a matter of time before some joker, or some maverick, decided it would be a good idea to jump on one.

As human civilizations grew, horses would play a central role in who came out on top. In ancient Mesopotamia, horses, or 'equids of the mountain', were increasingly used for transporting people and goods. They were soon being harnessed to chariots and ridden into battle. The horse was at the centre of an arms race. Those who had them generally prevailed over those who did not. When both sides had horses, it was down to strategy and good horsemanship. In Japan the samurai had special status to ride horses and mediaeval European knights bedecked themselves in armour on huge steeds. I was once persuaded to try on a suit of armour and sit on a poor polo pony also wearing a full suit of armour to film a segment in a documentary. Polo ponies are not only incredibly tough but they can turn on a sixpence and they can stop on a sixpence too. I spent a large amount of that day halfway up the poor thing's neck and I should say before trying this at home, make sure the suit of armour has been made for you. I couldn't really see anything out of the helmet, but when asked to canter for the camera, I kicked him on and forward we went and I didn't even manage to fall off. I have no idea how anyone could have sat on a horse for long in all that clobber, let alone fight on the battlefield.

One of the most famous of all mediaeval horsemen was the Mongol emperor Genghis Khan. He was notorious for his horseback army who conquered vast areas of Asia. Horses also helped us open up trade and increased the movement of people and cultures along the Silk Road linking Asia, Europe and the Middle East.

Unsurprisingly, given their importance, horses have long been venerated and worshipped. There were horse cults and elaborate horse burials. Horses feature in many myths and legends from Pegasus to Poseidon. It's thought that when the ancient Greeks first saw the Scythians, a group of nomadic horseback warriors, the awesome sight inspired the legend of the Centaur. There are records of oracle horses, prophet horses and horses who were seen as guardians of divine secrets. There were elaborate pagan rituals involving the neighing and snorting of horses. Aside from the supernatural and the downright bizarre, horses opened up a new world for humans, not only of trade and war but of horse-manship and many of the equine skills we still see today. There were grooms, vets and horse trainers. Those who fed and cared for horses, those who shovelled their shit, those who tucked them in at night with a carrot and gained their trust. When we tamed the horse it not only changed history but forged a unique partnership.

The next horse to join our family was a grey Welsh section A pony called Tiny. She was the sweetest thing and blew my daughter's mind when she realized she had her own pony to pet, groom, ride and care for. At the time we didn't have a field, let alone a stable, so we kept her in livery in a field at the yard where Philippa kept Bee. It was lovely to see them go out together, truly joyful, and it never occurred to me to ride myself or even have my own horse. At that time I was just happy being part of the pony dad support team, hitching the trailer to the back of the car and making a fancy-dress cos-tume once when Emily wanted to be knighted. Tiny had a sheet over her with a random coat of arms that I had got off the internet and Emily had a cardboard shield and a card-board helmet over her hard hat.

As we spent more more time as a family at this yard, some-body suggested that there was a horse that would be right for me. His name was Chester and he was a Shire Hanoverian cross, who was kind of entering into semi-retirement and being used at the riding school at the yard. So in layman's terms, and I was every inch the layman, he was a strong draught horse, the kind they breed for heavy work like pull-ing barges, wagons and carts, crossed with the lighter, more athletic Hanoverian bred by King George II to be agile enough to perform on the battlefield but still strong enough to pull coaches and work on a farm. Anyway, he was massive.

I put my head over his door the first time I met him and he seemed to fill his stall right up to the roof. 'He'd be perfect for you,' somebody said. I didn't say it, but my feeling was thanks very much, but if I wanted a horse I'm sure I would have known. So that was that, or so I thought.

Chester

In 2006, I got a job doing a TV film in New Zealand and we took the opportunity to go out as a family. We went out a week or so before the filming started as there were various meetings and measurements and fittings, including . . . hold tight . . . a meet-the-horse day. There was a section in the film where I had to ride a horse bareback for a short distance and so they had arranged this meet-the-horse day for me. Obviously Philippa and Emily came with me and when I'd met the horse we all went out on a ride together. It was a revelation. I'd never before seen it as something that we could all do together and I'll never forget that feeling. Right there, in the saddle on Bethells Beach by where they shot *The Piano*, I asked Philippa to text the stables and tell them I'd buy Chester after all.

When I met him again and actually went in his stable with him, I realized just how big he was at 17.2 hands. That's just over five foot ten in his withers – the base of his neck. He wasn't the biggest horse in the world but he was definitely a big horse and, to be honest, I wouldn't have felt happy sitting on a tiny little skinny thing because I'm quite big myself.

At weekends we'd go to the stables and all three of us would go out for a ride, with me on Chester, Philippa with Bee, and Emily beside us on Tiny. Every now and again Emily would ride Chester. She was only tiny herself; we had to tie the stirrups up to the highest hole and then tie them in a knot as well to make them short enough for her little legs, just to clear the saddle on his back. Off they'd go with Emily beaming and Chester, whose trot at times could be quite bangy, carrying her like she was an egg as they glided off across the field.

As Chester was my first horse my main goal was to get my confidence up and build up the bond between us. When you start you have to learn all the practical stuff like how to tack the horse up, put the saddle on, how to tighten and untighten it, and how to put the bridle on and so on. It might not seem like much, but every step is about gaining the animal's trust. They're giant compared to us, but they're naturally extremely nervous and sensitive. Their first instinct as prey animals is that everything's going to kill them. So a horse will notice every little thing around it, every sudden movement and loud noise. When people think horses don't like them it's more of a case that if you're nervous, they feel nervous too, because they're picking up on what you're feeling, and if you're acting scared, they think there must be danger about. A horse will only really properly relax when it knows there is absolutely no threat. So from the off I was learning how to talk to and be around Chester with the kindness and empathy it took to gain his trust, and it all starts the minute you're in the stables. Of course for me it was also under the bossy guidance, or should I say strong leadership skills, of the women in my family. Once I had got to grips with the basics, and Chester was starting to trust me more and more, we'd go out riding together as a family near the stables. There were some fields and a lovely river there and we would plod a bit, then trot a bit, and then the part I always looked forward to, an open stretch where you could break into a canter and feel truly free.

At this point we had lived in Dorset for about nine years

in a really lovely Georgian vicarage with a lovely garden but no place for a pony. So for the previous five years we'd been looking for a field to either buy or rent. All we wanted was two or three acres, but nothing came up. In the way that these things so often happen, though, after a chance encounter followed by a coincidence we ended up finding the farm that we live in today. It's 100 acres with a farmhouse in the middle but it had no stables, so the first thing we did was to build some. So there we were, my family and our other animals, Chester, Bee and Tiny, plus our growing collection of dogs: Mary Elizabeth, a new spaniel called Tina Audrey and our first black Labrador Arthur. Some of my most precious memories from this time are of cantering together on the horses with the dogs running diagonally up the hill in front of us. There was one particular stretch where you had to take it slowly and care-fully to get up the hill before you could break into a canter. To make matters interesting there was a gate we had to get through, but because the horses knew what was coming they'd get all excited just at the exact moment you had to open a gate. So whoever was first had to lean over on horseback, open the gate and encourage their horse to walk on. Meanwhile the others were all behind going mental, and then whoever's job it was to shut the gate would have to give it a huge swing, and all the while all of us were trying to keep our horses from running off too soon. I enjoyed a fast ride like that because really I didn't have to do anything, just stand up and hold the reins while Chester took care of it.

When I got Chester I really was a beginner and was blagging and feeling my way. But I knew I had more to learn about how to bond with him at a deeper level. Although we were connecting I didn't feel like I had totally cracked being completely relaxed with him. So I was lucky when I got to film with the legendary American horse trainer Monty Roberts and he offered to give me and Chester a session together. Monty's known for his style of kind and natural horsemanship. Instead of using the millennia-old techniques of disciplining a horse with force or violence, he developed a quiet way of bonding with a horse which he calls 'Join-Up'. I didn't know what to expect before he came to do a session with us, but I was up for giving anything a go.

In the round pen at our farm Monty began by showing me a technique mother horses do in the wild themselves to discipline their foals. It sounds strange but you chase the horse away with your arms outstretched and then immediately turn your back on them and walk away. The horse, being an ambitious animal who wants to be part of the herd, will eventually follow you back. I can't claim to understand what was really going on when I did this with Chester, but when I turned my back and waited nervously to see what he could do, I was amazed that after a few moments he really did start to follow me. From that moment on he was at my side as we walked around the pen and it was truly remarkable. Monty explained that it's not really about gaining mastery over the horse but showing it that you are the protector and someone it can follow and trust. What I enjoyed most about Monty's technique was that it wasn't like 'look at you doing it all wrong', or 'watch me I'm doing it right'. He got you to do it yourself and to tap into what you've got to offer, and it made me really want a relationship with the horse. With Chester, I realized for the first time what it meant to bond with another animal that deeply, to begin to really gain the trust of such a huge creature who is genuinely terrified of everything until it knows it's safe with you.

Perhaps my fondest memories of Chester, aside from our family rides in the fields, are those evenings at the end of the day, when it was just the two of us in the stables. One of our dogs would usually join us hoping for a carrot or two. Then, just as the sun was setting and the swallows were settling in for the night, soon to be replaced by the bats, Chester would put his chin down my back and pull me in for a cuddle. He really was an affectionate horse and, dare I say it, my animal hero.

To say that horses have not always been treated well by humans must be the understatement of the century. Having seen how much time and energy it takes for this huge, nervous animal to allow you to nuzzle into its neck with no fear at all, and to look at you with its big eyes with a feeling of total trust, I find it heartbreaking to think about the horses who were for millennia whipped and beaten into submission. We've given horses medals for gallantry, put up statues in their honour and venerated them for their service to us as loyal and brave. But I feel sad when I think of all the horses who went into battle on our behalf with no idea of what awaited them. I wonder too, though, about all the quiet moments of connection, trust and companionship which must have developed between humans and horses through our time together, even in our darkest hours.

Theirs Not to Reason Why

On 25 October 1854 a dashing and accomplished horseman called Captain Louis Nolan galloped up to the man in charge of the British cavalry, Lord Lucan, to deliver a crucial message on behalf of the army's commander-in-chief:

> Lord Raglan wishes the cavalry to advance rapidly to the front –
> follow the enemy and try to prevent the enemy carrying away

the guns. Troop Horse Artillery may accompany. French cavalry is on your left. Immediate. R Airey.

It was a pivotal moment in the Crimean War, that power struggle between Russia and the Ottoman Empire, along with the usual suspects who liked to involve themselves in these sorts of imperial skirmishes. By this point in the war, British, French and Ottoman forces had laid siege to the Russian naval base at the Black Sea port of Sevastopol. After having fought a successful battle at Alma, the British had been gaining ground and feeling rather confident. But with a protracted siege at Sevastopol, Russia knew the British lines to the British-held port of Balaklava were now vulnerable along the surrounding valleys. Seeing an advantage, the Russians planned to break the British lines and take back control. When Russia claimed a major supply route, the conflict came to a head in late October with the Battle of Balaklava. Early that day the British had seen two knockout victories, the so-called Thin Red Line in which a Scottish regiment held off a Russian cavalry charge, and the Charge of the Heavy Brigade in which the British cavalry quickly forced the Russian cavalry into retreat. British horses had so far put on a jolly good show. But a number of British naval guns had been taken by Russia and commander-in-chief Lord Raglan thought this was a very rum move indeed and wanted them back. The only British troops available to help were the lighter horsemen cavalry, known as the Light Brigade. So Raglan instructed a senior officer, General Airey, to advance and stop the blasted Russians from getting away with those guns. With a pencil-scribbled note, Airey handed a message to his aide-de-camp Captain Nolan, and told him to convey the message to the man in charge of the cavalry, Lord Lucan. The trouble was, from his position on the valley floor, Lord Lucan couldn't see what his superiors Airey and Raglan could from their higher vantage point, that is which guns had been taken and where they were. While Lord Lucan tried to make sense of the order, there was a back and forth between him and Nolan. Lucan claimed that when he asked Nolan to clarify where exactly it was they were supposed to advance, Nolan waved in the direction of the Russian heavy guns in the valley. According to Lucan, the message he ultimately received was not to stop the Russian army from carrying away British guns but for the Light Brigade to attack. It's not clear whether Lucan's account is totally true or whether Nolan even understood the message himself, but when Lucan came to deliver the order to the officer in charge of the Light Brigade, another lord called Cardigan, neither of the lords seemed to really know what it meant. It didn't help that they were also brothers-in-law who apparently loathed each other and they weren't about to sit down and work it out logically between them. So, having apparently received the order to attack, Cardigan, astride his horse Ronald, proceeded to lead the Light Brigade straight towards the full force of the Russian army.

Poised and awaiting orders with his trusty horse Sir Briggs, was twenty-three-year-old cavalryman Captain Godfrey Morgan, who was in command of a squadron of Lancers. Morgan recalled seeing Nolan twenty yards ahead on his horse. The man had apparently charged ahead of Lord Cardigan and was waving his sabre in the air. Whether it was a moment of bravado or a signal from Nolan that they were going the wrong way we'll never know. A Russian heavy battery fired a shell and a splinter from the explosion went straight through Nolan's heart. Nolan's horse carried his limp body back to the men where it fell to the floor. Morgan had no choice but to grasp Sir Briggs by the head and lead his men and their horses straight into the enemy fire.

Morgan described the ensuing apocalyptic scene as shells and shot whistled and screeched around them, choking smoke, gravel and dust filling the air. Horses and men were dropping by the score as sabres and lances pierced and sliced in the most brutal way. Incredibly, after about three quarters of a mile of this hell on earth, many did actually make it through the artillery, only to find themselves head to head with the Russian light cavalry. After cutting down a fellow who had 'run through' one of his own fellows with a lance, Captain Morgan describes how he dug his spurs into Sir Briggs's side, and just as they had 'once approached a big fence at Monmouthshire', together he and Briggs went at it, narrowly missing being shot in the chest and making it through with only a few lance pokes from the Russians. For all their bravery, the Light Brigade were outnumbered eleven to one. The survivors had no choice but to retreat back through the valley still under fire. They lost around 120 men, about 130 were wounded, and roughly another 60 men had been taken prisoner. They also lost nearly 400 horses. Morgan summed up the futility of it all when he recalled: 'The worst of the whole thing was that the enemy still retained possession of the ground'.

Lord Cardigan made it out alive, but he did not apparently look back to see what had happened to his men or return to join the survivors. Instead it's said that he rode back down the valley to his yacht in Balaklava harbour and settled down for a champagne dinner. Things didn't go so well for poor Nolan. After his death many of those in charge dumped the blame on him, with more than a whiff of shoving the messenger firmly under the bus. It seems those at the top didn't much like the fact that Nolan was an accomplished horseman and, worst of all, he'd even had the temerity to once write a book about it.

We'll never know what really happened and it has been the debate of many a military historian, but the Charge of the Light Brigade has gone down in history as one of the biggest battlefield gaffes and the ultimate example of senior mismanagement. It has come to symbolize the folly of those who give the orders, in contrast with the bravery and heroism of those who are expected to blindly carry them out, most memorably in Tennyson's poem:

Someone had blundered.
Theirs not to make reply,
Theirs not to reason why,
Theirs but to do and die.
Into the valley of Death

That poem could be as much about the horses as the men, who have trusted and gone blindly, wherever we have taken them, even into death.

Many of the horses who made it through the fighting unfortunately went on to die of starvation and fatigue. Among those who made it out alive was Captain Morgan's horse Sir Briggs. Sir Briggs had during peacetime been a champion steeplechaser. There's a painting of Morgan and Sir Briggs in the heat of battle. It's dark and wild and full of heroism and action. Morgan has his sabre high in the air and Briggs is rearing up, his mane flying in the wind. Sadly there is another horse lying dead or injured at their feet. At least the army by this time had appointed veterinary officers to help sick and injured horses of the cavalry regiments.

Afterwards Morgan wrote to his father:

I am safe and well in my own person, having come out of that gallant, brilliant (but as all add, useless) charge under a tremendous fire of all arms from front and flanks, and a perfect forest of swords and lances, untouched, with only a sabre cut on poor old Sir Briggs' head just over the right eye.

There's another painting of Morgan and Briggs, probably painted from sketches made by the artist on location in the camp. It's an altogether quieter scene and feels like going backstage on the war in an almost pastoral setting. There are large tents and rolling fields in the background and absolutely none of the blood or gore in sight at all. Morgan is dressed down in a loose white shirt with his braces hanging down. He has an impressive handlebar moustache. In front of him is the athletic bay stallion Briggs, with his black-stockinged legs and impeccably shiny coat. Briggs is front and centre looking right back at us. Who knows what he's thinking there, but I'll hazard a guess that on that battlefield he was absolutely terrified. When the fighting was over, it wasn't quite finished for Sir Briggs. Before returning to Britain he was apparently entered in the Sevastopol Military Steeplechase, which of course he won. I'm also happy to report that when the pair returned to Wales, Sir Briggs went on to enjoy a long and happy retirement. He lived for another twenty years and eventually died at the age of twenty-eight. Morgan, by then also a lord and a popular local philanthropist, had his beloved horse buried in the grounds of Tredegar House where his memorial stone remains today.

Horses had played a pivotal role in the Crimean War, but the position they had held for millennia as heroic battle steeds was, perhaps with some relief on their part, coming to an end. By the beginning of the twentieth century there were around three million horses in Britain. They were used for everything from pulling carts on farms to hauling lumber. They kept our cities running by drawing trams, omnibuses and carriages. They entertained us at the races, thundered through our countryside with the hunt and, in the case of the poor little pit ponies, spent their lives down the coal mines, which helped fuel our lives. When war broke out in Europe in 1914 it's perhaps no surprise that horses, like people, were called upon to do their bit. During this time of national emergency if you couldn't prove your horses were needed for essential transport or farming duties you were made to surrender them to a purchasing officer who would make you an offer on the spot. It's sad to think of the many horses who were carted off to serve king and country. There are heartbreaking letters as people begged for their animals to be made an exception. I can't imagine how I would have felt if they had done that to my own dear old Chester. Since no horse under 15 hands high was allowed to be recruited, at least we know Emily's dear little grey Tiny would have been spared.

The army requisitioned around 120,000 horses in the UK and another 600,000 horses and mules were bought from North America. Several thousand died at sea through disease or shipwreck before they even made it to Europe. All kinds of horses were shipped out to the battlefront, from agile racehorses to rugged carthorses. At the beginning of the war the cavalry were still deployed for roles such as reconnaissance and defence. In the summer of 1914 a group of cavalrymen did charge across a field in Belgium. Devastatingly many of them were mown down by German rifles, machine guns and artillery. The age in which horses could face off man-made weapons was coming to an end. Mechanized and static trench warfare was the method of the moment and horses were no match for tanks, shells and heavy guns. The cavalry were still kept in reserve as mobile strike forces and took on other roles, but in the end most horses were used for heavy work behind the scenes like transportation. They would walk up to forty miles a day pulling supply wagons, heavy artillery and carrying packs of ammunition and supplies on their backs. Horses were useful to us because they could travel where motor vehicles often could not, whether through the mud baths of the front line, the desert sands of Egypt or the shell-damaged roads of the Western Front.

The horse's natural endurance and ability to cross rough terrain was utilized by us in every way imaginable. They hauled huge amounts of timber for trenches, railway lines and all the infrastructure of war. They pulled heavy guns on to the battlefield. In one photo a group of weary soldiers are sitting down in front of a horse-drawn ambulance loaded up with medical supplies. A speckled grey horse lies down in the dust beside the men. Tethered to the front of the cart the horse's eyes are half closed, head lowered to the ground. Alongside these poignant moments captured in time are the many images of the poor horses who didn't make it, and there were a lot of them. If horses didn't die by the guns, tanks and mines, they were at risk of disease, exhaustion or other injury. Barbed wire was a constant danger and many horses got tangled up and died; others were shot to spare them further suffering if they were injured or infected. There are sad images of horses with huge gas masks on their noses as they faced the same threat from deadly mustard gas in the trenches as the soldiers.

There are touching stories of men putting their horses' gas masks on first and saving their lives. Alongside all that horror they faced together I can only imagine the bonds of camaraderie which must have formed between the men and the horses they travelled with and fought alongside. I can imagine the gentle whispering of comfort into the ear of a horse would have been a moment of solace for both man and horse as the shells whistled around.

There was also a practical side to horsemanship in war; they had to be looked after and as far as possible kept healthy. This would have involved many now forgotten quiet moments between people and the horses they groomed, washed and inspected for injuries. There were farriers and shoe smiths who must have gained their trust as they kept them shod for the long journeys. There was an Army Veterinary Corps to treat sick and wounded horses on site and in specially made hospitals. While their job included the sometimes heartbreaking task of putting a sick or injured horse out of its pain, the rate of death for horses dropped from around 80% a year during the Crimean War to around 15% during the First World War. In many ways these men and horses were in the same spot, fighting a war over which they had no control and no say.

It's sad to find out that no more than one in ten horses which were sent from Britain made it back. Around 85,000 horses were sold for horse meat to feed prisoners of war. Half a million horses after the war were sold to French farmers.

One of those who did make it back was Warrior, the celebrated racehorse of Churchill's friend the MP General Jack Seely. Seely and his beloved charger, a thoroughbred bay racehorse, had survived some of the fiercest fighting on the Western Front at the Battle of the Somme and Ypres. Warrior survived machine-gun attacks, shellfire and was twice stuck in the mud at Passchendaele. The pair also took part in one of the biggest Canadian cavalry charges of the war, the Battles for Moreuil and Rifle Wood. Seely, who was commander of the Canadian Cavalry Brigade, managed to recapture a crucial area for the German offensive near Amiens, in what became a second battle for control of the Somme in the spring of 1918. The battle saw some of the fiercest hand-to-hand fighting in that crucial stage of the war and horses were right there in the thick of it. After the Armistice, Warrior lived out his days on the Isle of Wight and continued to race point to point. When he died at the age of thirty-three, Warrior's obituary in *The Times* was proud to declare him as 'the horse the Germans couldn't kill'.

Along with the horses of generals and Churchill's mates there are some lesser-known memorials to the horses who made it back. Tucked away in an obscure corner of Southampton is a memorial to another horse called Warrior. He was a white gelding who served with the 'Old Contemptibles', the British Expeditionary Force, in France for the duration of the war. He took part in the retreat from Mons and was wounded in the Advance to the Aisne. After having a piece of shrapnel removed, he continued to serve until the Armistice. On Warrior's return to Britain the horse was purchased by a local woman from Southampton called Miss Hilda Moore who, with the help of a local vet, presented him as a gift to the city. It's not clear who actually served alongside him during the war, but there's a wonderful black-and-white photo of Warrior, a pure white seventeen-hand charger with a neatly trimmed tail. There's a man in uniform sitting on his back and we know Warrior went on to become the chief stud in the local police force. He was a popular local character on the streets of Southampton until his death at the age of twenty-six. There's a touching marble head-stone to Warrior which, although rather sadly tucked away near the Southampton Golf Club, remains a fitting tribute:

LOVED BY ALL, NOT ONLY FOR HIS
FAMOUS WAR RECORD, BUT ALSO FOR
HIS EFFICIENCY, INTELLIGENCE,
GENTLENESS AND NOBLE CHARACTER

Many other horses have been recognized for their roles in battle and wartime. Notably in America Sergeant Reckless, a mare who was severely wounded several times in the Korean War where she was carrying ammunition on the battlefield. She was decorated with two Purple Hearts and has been named one of America's top-100 war heroes. In London, the Animals in War memorial was unveiled in 2004 to commemorate all the animals who took part in the major wars. It features a large bronze horse statue. There is also 'Poppy' the warhorse memorial near Ascot, which recognizes the part horses played in the First World War. I'm not sure whether the horses who died on our behalf really had much choice in all this bravery, but then again neither very often did their human counterparts.

Perhaps one of the best memorials to the horses of the First World War has been not a block of stone, marble or bronze, but the book *War Horse* by Michael Morpurgo, which went on to be a celebrated National Theatre play and Steven Spielberg film. It tells the story of a bay Irish hunter called Joey who is sold to the army in 1914. During a cavalry charge he is showered with machine-gun fire and then captured by the Germans where he is forced to do heavy labour and becomes trapped in barbed wire. I remember seeing the play version with those enormous puppets in the West End and being completely bowled over by the accuracy of the puppetry. It captured so perfectly the movement of real horses and so devastatingly portrayed their experience of that brutal war. After the show was over, like a giddy fan after a pop concert, I wanted to meet the main horse character Joey. They let me backstage and when he came over on his softly clacking hooves I couldn't believe how massive he was with his shining eyes looking right at me. As his huge head dipped down close to me and his tail gently swished, he looked and behaved so much like my own horse Chester that I took an absolute gut punch to the chest and began to cry.

By the 1940s, no longer a match for the weapons of industrialized war, the numbers of horses on the Allied side were very much reduced. Although they still played a vital role carrying messages, soldiers, ammunition and supplies, the days of cavalry chargers and war steeds were drawing to a close. During the Second World War horses were important as mounted patrols helping the police keep order and assisting civilians on the home front. During the 1944 London Blitz, one of those horses, Police Horse Olga, was on patrol with her rider near Tooting when a doodlebug, a V1 rocket, exploded 300 feet away. Four people were killed, several buildings were destroyed and a plate-glass window shattered right in front of Olga. She initially panicked and bolted – I mean, who wouldn't – but her rider, PC Thwaites, managed to bring her under control and they returned to the scene within minutes to help survivors, assist traffic and keep the anxious people of Tooting calm. Another horse, Upstart, was said to have 'epitomized coolness under pressure'. Having already faced the effects of enemy fire when his stable was damaged by an attack on a nearby anti-aircraft station, Upstart was relocated to Bethnal Green where a flying bomb exploded less than seventy-five yards away while he was on patrol. Despite having glass, debris and shrapnel blasted all over him, good old Upstart remained 'completely unperturbed' throughout and he and his rider continued to control traffic and keep the crowds calm. After the war had ended, in April 1947, these two Metropolitan Police horses took part in a ceremony in Hyde Park which recognized their part in the war. The final horse to be honoured that day was Regal, who was praised for 'remaining calm' during two incendiary fires at a stables in Muswell Hill. It seems like the ability to stay calm is prerequisite for being decorated as a gallant horse.

Recognizing animals in this way, for their gallantry and bravery, had all started a few years earlier, not with the horse but with the humble pigeon.

Simon the ship's cat, who was injured during an attack on his vessel during the Chinese civil war. The plucky rat-catcher won an award for helping protect his fellow crew's vital supplies.

2. What the Dickin

Pigeon Post

In 1917 a sign outside a Whitechapel cellar encouraged the people of east London to:

> Bring your sick animals.
> Do not let them suffer.
> All animals treated.
> All treatment free.

It was the radical idea of social welfare pioneer and animal lover Maria Dickin. A Hackney local, Dickin had made it her mission to save and better the lives of animals in the poorest communities. The day her doors opened, the dispensary treated a cat with mange, a limping donkey and a dog with a broken leg. The locals were amazed at this free service and there was an obvious and immediate demand. In the face of some disapproval from the general public about her plan to help animals in the midst of a world war, Dickin was quick to point out that they were often crucial to people's livelihoods in the poorest communities. Costermongers and hawkers depended on their donkeys and ponies to carry goods. Those who were living in the worst kinds of housing relied on cats to prevent their homes from being overrun by rats. As a young woman Dickin had already bucked society's expectation of her by having, heaven forbid, a job. For a while she ran a successful music recording studio in Wimpole Street. After she married it wasn't the thing for a wife to work, so she busied herself instead with social welfare. After founding the charity the People's Dispensary for Sick Animals, Dickin eventually moved to bigger premises. She set up horse-drawn medical units, animal clinics and dispensaries. At one point she apparently even took to hawking her husband's trousers to raise funds.

During the Second World War, when the Blitz brought destruction to the streets of London, Dickin and her plucky pet-rescue squads were on hand to care for over 250,000 animals who were injured or buried in the rubble. Her goal was to help animals and reduce their suffering. But Maria Dickin went a step further, celebrating and honouring animals for their own war efforts.

On 23 February 1942 a British torpedo bomber was returning from a mission in Norway. Its engine failed over the North Sea and the aircraft plummeted into the water. The four crewmen had managed to radio for help, but they had no time to relay their position before ditching the plane. As they struggled in the freezing-cold conditions they must have thought their lot was up. Then someone had a bright idea. Tucked away in her cage was a little bird who had survived the crash. Her official number was NEHU 40 NSL aka Winkie.

When radio signals were no longer an option, the air force back then relied not on GPS and satellites but pigeon power. One of the crew members scrambled over to Winkie's cage, released the catch and clasped the oil-covered bird in his hands. He lifted her up towards the sky and set her free. Now all the men could do was wait and hope the plucky pigeon would find her way home.

*

I had a pigeon when I was a nipper. I found a hatchling, a little squab, in our garden, which must have fallen out of its nest. I kept it in a shoebox for a while with some grass and fed it worms and bits of bread soaked in milk. It was a straggly bald little thing which looked like a tiny dinosaur. It had a crossed bill, which meant it couldn't really feed itself very successfully. Apparently this usually means there are likely to be other problems with their physiognomy, so it may well have been rejected. Sad to say, that little pigeon never made it to adulthood.

When you see pigeons waddling down Oxford Street or hanging around Hyde Park for scraps, you might not immediately think of them as the elite athletes of the animal kingdom. They have come to be seen as the scourge of many a town council, despised by many as 'rats with wings'. But as any pigeon fancier will tell you, these birds are capable of formidable endurance and speed. They can fly over a thousand miles and reach speeds of over 60 mph. While our hearts beat at around 150 times a minute during a workout, the heart of a flying pigeon beats around 600 times. They have huge flight muscles and really are the long-distance athletes of the bird world. What they're especially good at is finding their way home.

The feral street pigeon is the domesticated descendent of the wild and iridescent rock dove. They evolved over time to be able to navigate long distances back to their nests, originally on cliff faces and rocky crevices. It's not known exactly how the birds do it, but it's thought that they have developed a remarkably accurate internal compass. By using the earth's magnetic field they home in on the right direction and then, by observing and remembering features in the landscape, when they're close to home they have an almost magical-seeming pinpoint accuracy. When ancient humans saw what these birds could do, naturally we put them to work on our behalf. Long before WhatsApp there was the pigeon post.

The first-known references to pigeons carrying messages date from the time of the Egyptian pharaohs. They are said to have carried warnings of floods in the Nile Delta and news of royal coronations. Invaders and conquerors like Julius Caesar, Genghis Khan and Napoleon had carrier pigeons in their arsenals, to carry vital intel and news of their victories. In ancient Greece and Rome, pigeons with messages tied to their legs are believed to have conveyed sporting results to those who enjoyed a bit of a flutter at the Olympic Games or the chariot races. Initially, homing pigeons could only fly one way, back home. The sender would have to have the receiver's pigeon in order to send a message. They were eventually trained to send messages between two points if their home was in one place and their food was in another.

In the late 1800s, during the siege of Paris in the Franco-Prussian War, a pigeon postal service replaced normal lines of communication in and out of the city. Fleets of courier pigeons were escorted out by balloon to carry news back to the besieged city. Messages were written on paper, later on microfilm, and fixed to the tails of the pigeons. The messages were sometimes rolled up into the quill feathers of a quail or goose to protect them from the elements and then attached to the bird. It was a tough life being a courier pigeon. In Paris they faced the winter cold and frost and cannon smoke from the skirmishes below. There was also the ever-present threat of being taken down by falcons or hawks. The pigeon's natural enemy, these birds of prey were sometimes released into the air in a cunning Prussian countermove, to hunt and bring down the winged messengers.

Pigeons continued to be used by the military throughout the

nineteenth century. They even flew news of the stock markets between traders. But by the early 1900s the pigeon had been outmoded by the telegraph. Telephone and wireless communications were on the rise. Pigeons were now a bit of an old-blokes-in-flat-caps game, not an elite messenger service.

When the First World War broke out there was a sudden pigeon panic. It was feared that 'enemy aliens' might use racing pigeons to send messages back to the Germans. Keeping the birds was banned unless you had a police permit. All along the east coast flocks of pigeons were forcibly released from their lofts by the authorities lest they fell into the wrong hands. There was even a trend for shooting a pigeon down if it was caught flying in the direction of the sea. The Home Office finally came to its senses when a man called Alfred Osman, the editor of a prestigious publication *The Racing Pigeon*, calmly pointed out that these avian superstars, far from being a threat, could be a valuable weapon in the communications war. Weighing in at only about 350 grams, pigeons are easy to transport and cheap to feed. If telegraph cables are out of action and there's no wireless, it's not only quicker to send a bird than a human messenger, but it's also safer, for us at least.

In 1914 Alfred Osman called on the nation's pigeon fanciers to donate their birds for the war effort and the National Voluntary Pigeon War Committee was formed. He had mobile pigeon lofts built along the coast, and mobile bus-mounted lofts were created to move the birds wherever they were needed. Pigeons were bundled into cages or baskets and taken on to boats, aircraft and even into the trenches. They were then released back to their lofts with vital news from the front line. By January 1916 pigeons were appreciated once again and it was finally made an offence to shoot down one of our own.

Some pigeons showed an uncanny ability to make it back

even after being badly injured. In the autumn of 1918 around 200 men from the American Expeditionary Force in France found themselves surrounded by the Germans and trapped behind enemy lines. The officer in charge, Major Whittlesey, had already sent two messages by pigeon requesting help but both birds had been shot down. To make matters worse, the Allies, not realizing the men were there, had begun to attack their position. The so-called Lost Battalion found themselves surrounded on all sides. In a last-ditch attempt to get help, one of the men strapped a tube to what was said to be their final pigeon. The message from the major pleaded: *We are along the road parallel 276.4. Our artillery is dropping a barrage directly on us. For heaven's sake stop it.*

At first the pigeon was shot at by German troops, but amazingly the plucky bird managed to shake off its feathers and take flight again. After flying through heavy enemy shelling, he eventually made it back to his mobile loft in just over an hour. The tube was recovered hanging from the tendons of the messenger's badly damaged leg. Despite having severe wounds to his chest and an injured eye, the pigeon, who was named Cher Ami, was credited with saving nearly 200 lives. The poor thing had to have his leg amputated, but the men whose lives he saved are said to have carved him a little wooden leg.

Cher Ami was awarded the prestigious war medal the Croix de Guerre by the French government. He was then taken back to America where he received a hero's welcome. He eventually died from his chest injury and his body was stuffed and displayed in the Smithsonian Institution where he remains today, a memorial to the many pigeons who risked their lives in the First World War even if it was without their knowledge.

In the lead-up to the Second World War, it was anticipated in advance that pigeons might be called upon to do their duty.

The pigeon fanciers and breeders of Britain once again agreed to help supply the RAF with birds. At first, though, the National Pigeon Service was rather underfunded and not taken all that seriously by the powers that be. Wireless radio was more the thing and pigeon post was seen as old technology. They quickly began to prove their use again, though, especially by saving lives at sea sending emergency messages when wireless failed.

In 1940 the Army Pigeon Service was formed to extend pigeon power to the army and intelligence services. Civilian 'Pigeon Officers' and groups of breeders provided a steady supply of birds to keep communications moving. Thousands of pigeons sent messages of help and assisted with reconnaissance. There were even undercover pigeon agents, part of a secret pigeon service called MI14. They were secretly dropped by parachute into enemy territory in order to send back vital intelligence. At one point rubbish pigeons were dropped in the hope they would infiltrate the German pigeon ranks and be really bad at their job.

Those pigeons who were good at their jobs included Princess. This little bird was sent on a special mission to Crete and managed to fly back across the Mediterranean Sea some 500 miles to her loft in Egypt carrying valuable intel. Another, the wonderfully named Mary of Exeter, successfully carried numerous top-secret messages in spite of being injured multiple times and having twenty-two stitches. An American pigeon called G.I. Joe averted tragedy in an Italian village. The area had been taken by Allied troops sooner than expected, but wireless transmission had failed to alert anyone of their arrival. Not far away an Allied air raid was about to commence and G.I. Joe flew twenty miles in twenty minutes to deliver the message, arriving with just five minutes to spare before the bombers took off. He is said to have saved around a thousand inhabitants of the village and around a hundred British troops. It is slightly alarming, though, when you think that the Allies had been apparently perfectly happy to bomb those villagers before they received his message.

As for Winkie, that plucky pigeon who was released by the downed airmen in the North Sea in February 1942, she ended up making it back to her loft, flying 120 miles through the dark winter cold and arriving the following morning, exhausted and bedraggled. Although she was carrying no message, the RAF managed to track down the location of the survivors by calculating the time difference between when the plane ditched and when Winkie had arrived back. They took into account not only the wind speed and direction but the effect of the oil on her feathers. All four men were eventually rescued and later that evening they held a celebratory dinner in Winkie's honour.

Eight months later the crew of a Catalina flying boat ran out of fuel in a gale and were forced to ditch in the North Atlantic near the Hebrides. Two of the men had drifted off in a lifeboat so the rest of the crew elected to stay on the plane in the choppy waters. Unable to make radio contact, they attached the following message to their two messenger pigeons: *Aircraft ditched safely N.W. . . . Heavy swell, taxing S.E. No casualties.*

In terrible weather and a thick sea mist, pigeon number SURP.41.L.3089, also known as White Vision, flew 60 miles in nine hours and successfully delivered the message. Sadly the other pigeon never made it back. The crew had almost given up hope when forty hours later, help finally arrived. Immediately after the men made it to the safety of the RAF launch, the plane disappeared beneath the waves. The two men who had drifted off in the raft were also rescued. White Vision had saved eleven lives.

Winkie and White Vision were the first animals to be officially awarded the PDSA Dickin Medal by Maria Dickin. At a ceremony in December 1943 the award praised the animals for 'displaying conspicuous gallantry and devotion to duty'.

Thirty-two pigeons were eventually decorated with the award. There's a wonderful old Pathé film from 1944 of medals being hung round the necks of two D-Day messenger pigeons, Gustav and Paddy. There's much clapping all round for those plucky pigeons who had brought vital messages back across the sea in 'very British' weather. You can't help admiring the little birds, even if they do look a bit bewildered, and it was almost certainly instinct over any kind of devotion to duty towards us. I sometimes wonder, if we could find a use for the swallows who come back to our stables every year, would we celebrate them as much for their gallantry? As it is, they go about their own devoted duties unremarked and undisturbed.

Not all war pigeons lived to be decorated for their services. There's a poignant portrait in a book by Garry McCafferty about war pigeons *They Had No Choice*. He quotes the final thoughts from the diary of a First World War soldier called Tom Millar:

> Things don't look too good. I've been badly hurt, my left leg has been blown away from the knee. I don't think I will last much longer as I am losing too much blood. I'm in the South trench but everyone is dead; there is no movement, only the smoke and the smell. Please tell Mary and the children that I love them with all my heart, I hope they don't feel bad of me.

I can't write much more. I am weak. I know I will soon be with my Maker. I am not afraid. I thought I was on my own but a red pigeon has just fallen from the sky and is just a few inches from me. He must be on service too. We make a good pair, I have one leg left, and he is missing a wing. I will keep him warm, we will go on together, goodnight, God bless.

Tom

Perhaps that pigeon, and that man, deserves a medal too.

Decorated Dogs

In the summer of 1917 a stray brindle-and-white bull terrier of uncertain origin was found wandering around an army training camp near Yale University in Connecticut. The grounds were a temporary US Army training base for the 102nd Infantry Division who were preparing to leave for France now that America had joined the war. Although pets were officially banned from the site, the men took a liking to the friendly dog and he was given permission to stay. They named him Stubby because of his short stumpy tail, and the dog began to tag along with the men on their training drills. He was, it is said, even trained to pull off a kind of doggy salute with his paw raised to his right eyebrow. One of the men in particular, Corporal James Robert Conroy, became big pals with Stubby and adopted him. When it came time to leave, and the bugle call signalled their departure, Conroy couldn't bear to leave Stubby behind, so he smuggled him under his coat and on to the transport ship bound for Europe. Stubby hid in a coal bunker before being eventually brought out on deck where he apparently entertained the crew. On their arrival in Europe, Conroy smuggled

Stubby off the vessel and legend has it that when the command-
ing officer eventually discovered the little dog, he charmed the
officer by saluting him. After that, Stubby was allowed to stay
with the division as their official mascot.

On 5 February 1918 the 102nd Division, along with Stubby,
arrived on the front line in France. Officially the dog's role as
a mascot was to boost morale, but it soon became obvious
this dog had other talents. During a month of near constant
enemy fire, Stubby showed huge resilience. He was said to
bark and run with a 'mad canter' back and forth during attacks
but also to maintain a cheerful disposition. He survived a gas
attack and was fitted with his own gas mask. He proved adept
at detecting small amounts of gas and alerting the men,
running through the trenches tugging at the legs of sleeping
soldiers to warn them of an imminent attack. Stubby was also
a pretty good search-and-rescue dog. He was able to detect
the location of injured troops in dugouts or in no man's land
and rush through the barbed wire to their aid. He would either
bark for medical assistance or guide them back to safety.
Stubby once even helped catch an enemy spy who had infil-
trated the trenches. He apparently seized the man by the
breeches with his teeth until help arrived. As a result of all
this, Stubby was officially awarded the rank of sergeant. It
was the first time a dog was given a rank in the US Army. Not
long after that he was injured in an attack on a German-held
town and taken to a nearby hospital. The jolly dog was said to
have continued to boost the morale of injured servicemen,
even while he was himself recovering. Sergeant Stubby soon
returned to his division and got back to work. When they
recaptured the enemy-held town of Château-Thierry, some
of the townspeople were so grateful for his efforts that they
fitted Stubby with a regimental chamois coat as a thank-you.

I've never been one for decking my own dogs out in human clothing, but it must be said that he does rather look the part in that little jacket with all those military medals and stripes.

After the Armistice, Stubby was paraded through the streets of Paris. On Christmas Day 1918 President Woodrow Wilson came to meet the 102nd Division in France. The canine sergeant is said to have offered up his usual paw by way of a greeting to the big man. What a charmer.

There were thousands of dogs who, just like Stubby, acted as guards and sentries in the war, who helped save lives, sniffed out gas and carried vital supplies and messages. While most of those dogs are now long forgotten, Stubby became a kind of mascot for all of them. He clocked up quite the regimental CV, seventeen engagements and four military campaigns. On his return to America he was a massive celebrity, leading numerous military parades and visiting the White House twice. He even appeared on stage and was presented with a medal by General of the Armies John J. Pershing.

When his human pal, James Robert Conroy, went to study at Georgetown University Law School, Stubby stayed with him and became a mascot there too. The little dog died in 1926 in Conroy's arms. His body was stuffed for posterity and, perhaps a tiny bit ghoulishly, remains on display in the Smithsonian Institution, alongside that other animal veteran the pigeon Cher Ami.

Dogs like Stubby played a huge role in both world wars. In Britain, Army War Dog Training Schools were set up to train dogs to carry messages from the trenches back to army command centres. Dogs were donated by rescue centres such as Battersea or by the public. During war it was harder for people to feed their pets and dogs so giving them to the war effort seemed a better option than abandoning them or having them put down. During the Blitz of the Second World War dogs helped on the home front to find people buried in the rubble. They were also trained to undertake more daring feats on our behalf.

In 1944 a Leicestershire woman called Betty Fetch heard a callout on the wireless for dogs to be donated to the war effort. Lacking enough food for her pet Alsatian Brian, she decided to donate him in the hope she would get him back afterwards. It turned out he was required for a very specific task. Brian and his fellow canine students were initially trained to handle the loud noises of war. They were encouraged with rewards to sniff out explosives and detect mines. They also learned how to track human scent and to lay low under attack. Finally they were trained to leap from a plane.

Along with their handlers, these so-called para dogs were encouraged to jump from great heights with a parachute on a static line strapped to their backs. If they wouldn't leap of their own accord, they were lured out by the handlers with a piece of meat. I'm not sure any of my dogs would jump out of a plane, or that I would want them to. Although with a nice piece of sausage, who knows. The dogs were trained to land firmly on all four paws alongside their handlers. Brian the Alsatian successfully parachuted with the 13th Parachute Battalion into Normandy as part of the D-Day Operations.

At ten past one in the morning on 6 June 1944, in the midst of anti-aircraft fire, another para dog, an Alsatian-collie cross called Bing, was among the first dogs to parachute behind enemy lines. He jumped, or some reports say he was actually thrown, into the darkness, alongside his handler, the dog trainer Lance Corporal Ken Bailey. Bing made it down alive but found himself hanging from a tree with cuts to his face, most likely from enemy mortar fire. He was rescued a few hours later and was back in action in a couple of days.

Their mission was to clear bridges and roads of mines as part of Operation Overlord, which aimed to liberate German-occupied western Europe. Over the next two and a half months Bing and his fellow para dogs did vital work helping sniff out explosives and booby traps and alerting their handlers when enemy troops were present. By the end of August, although enemy forces had retreated, many lives had been lost and the war was not yet over.

The following year Bing was deployed again. It was March 1945, Operation Varsity. Sixteen thousand paratroopers and several thousand aircraft were on a mission to secure a foot-hold across the Rhine and push back German forces. This time when he jumped, Bing landed firmly on solid ground. Under fire and surrounded, he and Lance Corporal Bailey proceeded to undertake twenty-mile-a-day marches sniffing out explosives and tracking enemy positions.

The bond between the wartime para dogs and their handlers was strong. Bing slept alongside Bailey and they usually ate the same rations, probably a lot of tinned corned beef. It was tough-going for both man and dog, and I don't mean the corned beef. One paratrooper later recalled how, on a particularly exhausting night, clever old Bing managed to locate a barrel of wine in a barn and proceeded to lap up the contents of the drip tray.

On their return to Britain, Bing remained a war dog but it's not certain what happened to him after that or when he died. Eventually Lance Corporal Bailey's own ashes were scattered where the two of them had landed on D-Day.

It's sad to say but some of the dogs who had served our needs in the war were almost certainly humanely destroyed afterwards. There were not enough people willing, and there was not enough food, to take care of them all. Others were too traumatized to adapt to civilian life and their owners couldn't or wouldn't take them back. This is perhaps the inevitable and less glorious reality behind the celebrated bravery of all the animals who accompanied us into war with no choice in the matter.

Brian the parachuting Alsatian was eventually returned to his owner, Betty Fetch. He went on to be awarded with a PDSA Dickin Medal for gallantry. Betty had refused an offer from the War Office to buy him from her. She described the touching moment she was reunited with Brian at the railway station. At first he looked a little unsure of himself, she said, but as soon as the dog recognized her he rolled over on to his back for a good old belly rub.

Able Seacats

One of our cats, Max, lives most of his day in a bowl on the island in our kitchen and he would never dream of going to war, but he's almost fanatical about bringing us our mouse of the day. He didn't bat an eyelid when Penelope Jennifer, our Jackahuahua, would, in a slight trance, gingerly carry the mouse to the nearest basket and defend it fiercely like she was its weird mother until someone yelled at me to put it outside. I've seen this maternal instinct a lot less weirdly in many other species, but cats and predators are differently wired around the young of other species. When Emily was pretty tiny, we went on a visit to Shamwari in South Africa, which had been four giant sheep ranches but had been bought and rewilded into a magnificent wildlife park. A big cat sanctuary was built in the centre of it in memory of poor Julie Ward, the photographer, who so loved wildlife and was killed in Kenya in 1988. There were three young leopards who had been rescued from some nightclub nightmare somewhere, but they sat in a row as we watched them look back at us, and they didn't take their eyes off Emily; all three of their heads turned as if locked together as this young snack went toddling past. Later on that trip we were in the back of a Land Rover watching two prides of lions who had been dozing and lazing about, unfazed by us or the vehicle. Emily, as little people are prone to do, started crying, and instantly both prides in their entireties were heads up, ears pricked and taking a lot of notice. 'There you go,' they seemed to say, 'that's easy pickings right there.' After seeing so close up the instincts of those big cats, it came as no surprise to me when I discovered that the chief role of their domesticated descendants during wartime was to use their natural abilities to hunt and kill. Not children but mice and rats, and especially so at sea.

The ancient Egyptians and the Vikings are said to have taken cats with them on maritime journeys. Over hundreds of years explorers, cargo vessels and battleships welcomed cats aboard for good luck, to help with pest control and simply for company. I once saw a photo of a sailor from the 1940s who was showing off a little cat-sized ship's hammock complete with cat.

When, in May 1941, the German battleship the *Bismarck* was scuttled after a fierce battle in the Atlantic, a black-and-white cat was found floating among the wreckage. According to what has become something of a legendary tale, the cat was rescued by British sailors who called him Oscar, named after the International Code of Signals for the letter 'O' or

'Man Overboard'. The cat was promptly taken on board another ship, the destroyer HMS *Cossack*. Five months later the *Cossack*, on its way from Gibraltar to England escorting a convoy, was hit by a torpedo. The captain was killed along with 158 men. The surviving men and Oscar were rescued and taken back to Gibraltar. The ship itself later sank in bad weather on its way back to port. Oscar, who had now survived two maritime disasters, was naturally transferred to yet another vessel, the aircraft carrier HMS *Ark Royal*, to help with pest control. In a strange twist of fate the *Ark Royal* had carried some of the planes that had attacked the *Bismarck* from the air.

In November 1941 the aircraft carrier was herself torpedoed by a U-boat in the Mediterranean. Poor Oscar, who had been through quite enough, was apparently found floating on a plank, probably a bit pissed off but alive. He was safely taken to dry land in Gibraltar and it was decided to take him off maritime duties. Instead he took up a temporary position as mouser in chief at the offices of the governor of Gibraltar. Oscar, or as he has gone down in legendary retellings, Unsinkable Sam, was then shipped back to Britain to a home for sailors, The Sailor's Rest, in Londonderry, Northern Ireland. At least that voyage went unimpeded by torpedoes or sinkings of any sort.

After his arrival at his new home Oscar was said at first to howl when he heard the men's voices. He was also known to drink water from flower vases. We can forgive him a few eccentricities, though, after all he had been through. The manager of the home, a Miss Margaret Hill, became rather attached to Oscar and he became a bit of a local celebrity. He even at one point appeared on the radio. In a final twist in the tale worthy of any Hollywood movie, Miss Hill went on to meet an American GI from Pennsylvania called Paul. They fell in love, apparently having bonded over their mutual affection for the cat. The couple planned to marry and take Oscar with them to America, but it looks like he ended up staying in Northern Ireland until his death in 1955. Perhaps he thought another ocean crossing would be pushing his luck.

In 1948 another young black-and-white cat was found, this time scrounging for scraps in the Hong Kong docks. He was picked up by a young British sailor called George Hickinbottom who named him Simon and smuggled him aboard the navy frigate HMS *Amethyst*. It wasn't long before the crew and the captain of the ship found out about Simon, but they decided to keep him on board; it would be useful to have a good ratter about the place.

In April 1949 *Amethyst* was ordered to sail up the Yangtze River from Shanghai to Nanking to relieve another ship that was protecting the British Embassy there. China at this time was in the midst of a civil war between Mao Zedong's Communist forces and the ruling nationalist government. The two sides had declared a ceasefire and, as the British had not taken a side in the conflict, they believed they would be safe to make the trip. But the river was a key border between the two sides of the conflict and the *Amethyst* came under artillery fire. The ship was badly damaged and around twenty men were killed. Attempts from nearby vessels to rescue the ship and its remaining crew failed and the men were left stranded in the river under effective siege. After giving their ship mates burials at sea, over the next few months, in searing heat, the crew faced another battle, an increasingly bold and growing rat population. Their food and water supply was rapidly dwindling and the rats on board the ship also posed a threat of disease. Simon the cat had been badly injured in the attack. His face was burnt and he had been hit by shrapnel. After being patched up by the medical officer, his whiskers still singed from the attack, the cat eventually set about keeping the mouse and rat population under control. One day he managed to kill a particularly persistent rat, who had been named Mao Zedong by the crew, and was promoted by his shipmates to Able Seaman, or rather Able Seacat. As well as helping dispatch the growing rodent population, the amiable cat became a huge morale boost for the injured, exhausted and hungry sailors. After being trapped for over three months, the ship eventually made it out in July under cover of darkness.

When news travelled back to Britain of Simon the cat's remarkable feats it was immediately agreed by the PDSA that as soon as he got home he would be awarded the Dickin Medal. Simon became a celebrity and was sent gifts and fan letters, which dedicated officers were charged with dealing with on his behalf. As with all animals returning from overseas at the time, Simon was put in quarantine for six months. Rather sadly Simon died just before he came out. His crew mates were devastated and letters of condolence arrived by the sack-load from heartbroken fans. Simon was buried in a dark-wood coffin draped with a Union Jack in a pet cemetery in Essex. His obituary in *Time* magazine praised him as 'the most respected cat in all Britain' and for catching 'at least a mouse every day'. What a guy.

While Simon the cat was decorated for his rat-catching prowess, though, sometimes it's the rats themselves who deserve a medal.

A Gambian pouched rat. The clever rodent has been trained to find deadly landmines.

3. Hero Rats

A Rat Called Courage

It's dawn in Tanzania. The rising sun is a bright orange sphere above the misty foothills of the Uluguru Mountains. In the fields below, a rodent with brown mottled fur is moving through the dirt. His long white-tipped tail flicks along behind as he sniffs at the ground. In the wild this clever animal is very good at finding food, especially food which humans don't want him to find. He has been known to annoy many a local farmer by stealing his crops. But on this occasion this animal's enthusiasm for eating is actually helping us. He makes his way up and down the field a couple of times, then stops and sniffs the air. He moves his head left and right, his whiskers twitching, then he puts his nose back down to the ground and begins scratching at the soil. It's a sign he's found something. But it's not food. A few feet away a woman presses a metal clicker. *Click.* The animal immediately stops what he's doing and comes bounding over for a nice piece of banana. It's his reward for finding something underground, something so dangerous this animal has been named Courage by his human handlers, and along with many others like him, has earned the title 'HeroRAT'.

I'm not sure what I think about rats. I never had a pet one, but I know people who have and they've enjoyed their company. We keep hens and horses, so rats are a problem because they eat through feed bags and can spread disease. Jack Russell terriers are, as far as I know, the most efficient

way of dealing with a rat problem. I once saw a pack of terriers dispatching dozens of rats on a farm with such
enthusiasm and ferocity that I couldn't help giving a small
cheer for one that got away.

In Hinduism rats are considered by some to be the vehicle
of Lord Ganesha and it can be seen as auspicious to find a
rat in your house. As a natural lover of the underdog in all its
animal forms, I have always rather enjoyed knowing that
there's a temple in India where, rather than being loathed,
rats are actually worshipped. At Karni Mata Temple in
Rajasthan, rats are considered to be so sacred they are given
huge bowls of milk to sup on and encouraged to stay for as
long as they like. Known locally as *kābās*, they're believed by
some people to be the reincarnations of the goddess Karni
Mata and her devotees. But watch out, because if you accidentally step on one and kill it you may have to replace it
with a rat made of solid gold. The sight of over 25,000 rats
freely scurrying over the feet of visitors and along the walls
and floors of a temple may be lucky for some. It would probably send a shiver down the spines of others. Let's be honest,
rat worship aside, they're not everyone's favourite animal
acquaintance. Even lovable Ratty in *The Wind in the Willows*
isn't really a rat; he's a water vole. But whatever we think of
rats, they are here to stay. They thrive alongside us in our
towns and cities. Especially the brown rat, *Rattus norvegicus*,
and its smaller cousin, the excellently named *Rattus rattus*, the
black rat. Both animals originated in Asia and spread around
the world eating our food, hanging around our streets, sewers
and dockyards, and generally causing a bit of a nuisance. All
this success has ultimately led to their less than favourable
reception by many humans, especially when they damage our
property or carry diseases we might catch. It's not surprising

then that the concept of a hero rat might be hard for some people to swallow. But I'm willing to stick my neck out and say there is something worth celebrating about our tenacious furry friends.

Ironically the traits which have given rats a bad reputation are also those which have made them extremely valuable to us. They breed very quickly. They're clever and adaptable and they will eat almost anything. I might not necessarily want a rat hanging about my person, but I do acknowledge they've done a lot of good for humanity.

Despite our size difference, rats share many anatomical and physiological similarities with us. They're capable of many brainy things we have for a long time thought were uniquely human. Their talents include what scientists call counterfactual reasoning and what we would call having an imagination. It means they're believed to be able to reason about something that is not physically present, that they're not picking up with their sensory organs. Basically they can conceptualize something, taking its possible existence into consideration when they're making a decision, even if they're not experiencing it. Maybe this more human-like reasoning in rats isn't totally surprising. Scientists think we both evolved from the same rodent-like creature around sixty-five million years ago. The little animal managed to survive the asteroid strike which killed the dinosaurs, rather cleverly you might say, by hiding underground while most life on Earth was obliterated. Since then rats have helped us study everything from treatments for cardiovascular disease, diabetes and cancer, to HIV antiretrovirals, the flu vaccine and Alzheimer's research. While we have good reason to be exceptionally grateful to them for their contribution to medical science, we can't pretend that they were exactly willing participants. But that isn't true of one of their other great endeavours. No one could have predicted that the humble rat would go on to help to solve one of the most pressing humanitarian issues of our time.

In the 1980s and 1990s one of the most egregious weapons of war, the anti-personnel landmine, was increasingly hitting the headlines. These weapons of conflict, which often indiscriminately target civilians, had already been in use for decades. Their increasing deployment in modern conflicts during the second half of the twentieth century led to a massive crisis. More and more weapons were being left in the ground, across the Middle East, Asia, the former Yugoslavia and African countries including Mozambique and Angola among others. Thousands of deaths and casualties were being caused by landmines hidden underground. Leftover landmines were increasingly becoming a major barrier to economic and social development. Because they're activated by standing on or near them they can maim and kill indiscriminately in the most horrific ways. They kill without warning, often many years after the original conflict which led to their use is over. The risk of being killed or seriously injured by mines left around towns and villages eventually created a situation where people living in affected areas were unable to carry out everyday tasks like fetching water and firewood, using land to grow crops, even just going to the market, work or to school, without dicing with death.

Organizations have been trying to deal with the problem of landmines by clearing them for decades. It typically involves using metal detectors to safely find and detonate them. It's incredibly dangerous and painstaking work. If the deminers accidentally step on a mine they can get killed or seriously injured themselves. Another big challenge is that metal detectors tend to find any metal object they hit upon. This includes a lot of harmless scrap metal, which, although great from a litter-collecting point of view, makes the whole enterprise very time-consuming and expensive.

One of the biggest animal heroes of the global effort to clear landmines has to be the dog. As we know from our old friends the para dogs who sniffed out mines in Normandy, they have been used by the armed forces to find mines for decades. Canine units are still used now to sniff out leftover landmines. Dogs tend to be more accurate than metal detectors. They can be trained to find other materials such as plastic or batteries, as well as explosives. Dogs have been known to find mines which have been lurking underground for over fifty years. Canines can be anywhere from around twenty to thirty times faster than a human with a metal detector. The dogs employed are often Belgian Malinois, shepherd dogs or Labradors, all of whom have excellent noses. Mine-detection dogs are often trained when they detect the scent of a buried landmine to indicate to a handler where it is by stopping and sitting in front of it but not stepping on to it. They're then given a reward, a toy to play with or some food, after which the humans safely detonate the mine. These dogs have no idea how dangerous their job is – they just want their reward – but they have unwittingly saved thousands of lives. Between June 2020 to June 2021 the Iraqi dog team alone found and destroyed over 3,500 landmines and explosives left over from war. The mine-detection programme of the Marshall Legacy Institute has cleared around forty-nine million square metres of contaminated land since it began in the late 1990s.

Dogs have played a crucial part in the ongoing effort to

clear landmines but they do have some limitations. They're relatively heavy and while handlers and organizations do everything they can to keep them safe, the animals can set off the mines, especially if they accidentally sit back down on one. Dogs also generally like to build a relationship and a bond with a specific handler who they respond to and try to please. This can limit how easily they can be used over a very wide area globally.

Back in the 1990s, when the huge scale of the landmine problem was becoming apparent, a lot of people were looking for new and radical solutions. Among them was a product designer, then a master's student in engineering in Belgium, called Bart Weetjens. He had been assigned a project to 'solve a pressing world problem with an innovative solution'. Along with some of his fellow students Bart began to think about the growing landmine crisis. He wondered whether there might be other animals who could be trained to sniff them out. Bart came across a paper in which someone had trained gerbils to detect the scent of explosives. He thought, *If you can train a gerbil to do that, I'm sure you can train a rat.*

Most rodents are sociable creatures and, as we know from their use in scientific experiments, they can be trained to work with and for humans. The challenge with rats is that, compared to dogs, they don't live very long, on average about two or three years. It might take at least a year to train a rat to detect a mine. That's a lot of work for not much time working in the field. Your average brown rat might not have the stamina to work for hours at a time like a person or a dog would either. But Bart didn't give up. He took the idea to his professor, who told him about a colleague who was partnering with a university in Africa which was looking at animals native to the area. There were many different African rodents he could consider, they told him, but they had just the one. The rodent they had in mind had become a huge pest for the farmers. It was known to be very clever at figuring out how to break into barns to steal crops. 'It's giant,' said the colleague, 'but it has a long lifespan.' That animal was the African giant pouched rat. Something like this had never been done before, but Bart thought, *This might just be possible.*

The African giant pouched rat, *Cricetomys gambianus*, also known as the Gambian pouched rat, is so called because of its habit of storing food in its cheek pouches, rather like a hamster. It's a lot bigger than your average brown rat – about the size of a small domestic cat. In the wild they live in the wooded grasslands of sub-Saharan Africa eating mainly berries, nuts and insects. They can live for around eight years, sometimes longer. Until recently it was thought these animals were related to hamsters, mice and rats, hence why they became known as pouched rats. But it's now believed they're actually on a different branch of the rodent family tree called the Nesomyidae, along with the terrifying-sounding bastard big-footed mouse, the plucky, remarkable climbing mouse and a chap I think I would most like to meet, the dainty fat mouse.

They might only be distant cousins to brown rats, but African pouched rats do resemble them quite a bit in looks, although they're a lot bigger. They have long noses and whiskers and mottled rat-like fur, with a twitchy pink nose. They range in colour from fawn or light golden brown to a more greyish colour. They all have a light-coloured belly and a tail as long as their body. The top of the tail is a darker colour and the tip is bright white or pink. Like most rodents, they're born as bald, jelly bean-like pinkish creatures wriggling together in their nests. In the first days and weeks before their eyes open the pups are completely dependent on their mothers for comfort and food. Almost everything they experience comes from their sense of smell, which means they're primed to learn about the world using mainly their noses. Even when they can see things with their eyes, they continue to use their noses for most things. This great sense of smell is what gave Bart Weetjens the hope that he might be on to something. But he was up against a big challenge. The pouched rat had never been trained like this before. It was a shot in the dark, but it was worth a try. In Tanzania in 1995 the non-profit Anti-Persoonsmijnen Ontmijnende Product Ontwikkeling – Anti-Personnel Landmines Detection Product Development – or the slightly catchier APOPO, was born.

In the wild rats are naturally neophobic. This means they're afraid of new things. It's how they survive. If something startles them, they hide in a dark corner and freeze until danger has passed. In the wild African pouched rat pups stay with their mothers until they are a year old for safety. But they can also be very curious, which is how they have become so successful at stealing crops. APOPO took the idea that if you could release the rats from their natural fear and instead encourage them to express their natural curiosity, their ability to find things could be very useful to us. By teaching them that even when they hear a loud noise or encounter a massive human nothing bad will happen, and that they might even enjoy themselves, it could be possible to build a bond and work with the rats. APOPO began a breeding programme in the town of Morogoro and the whole thing grew from there.

The APOPO trainers begin handling the pups from when their eyes open at around four weeks old. It's the beginning of a process called habituation. The rats are slowly exposed to the world around them and they become more curious and sociable instead of fearful. The little rats gradually begin to meet people and take in the sights and sounds of their surroundings from their cages. Once they are weaned from their mothers at ten weeks old the rats are taken out and exposed to more and more of the things they might encounter in the real world. This might involve being taken into a garage filled with the smells and sounds of machinery, or being walked alongside a busy road. It may be as simple as sitting with a group of humans on the grass outside being held, petted and chatted to. On the APOPO website you can see lots of pictures of the trainers and handlers with their favourite pouched rat sitting on their shoulder. What you can't tell from these photos is that there are often conversations going on between the rats and the humans. The rodents naturally make a little sound when they're happy, a sort of clicking noise. So the staff who work with them have developed a habit of making this clicking sound back to the rats to make them feel secure. It makes the rats think they are surrounded by other happy rats. In the pictures it sometimes looks like the staff are kissing the rats, but actually they're just telling them that they're happy with a little clicking sound, and the rats are rather adorably telling them they're happy back.

Once the rats are no longer startled by the general hubbub of the world the real training begins. The first thing you notice when you see the pouched rats in action is that they are wearing a tiny harness. I love it that someone invented this tiny harness so meticulously. What happens next when they're wearing it is even more impressive. Before the harness is strapped on, the trainers begin by placing a small amount of TNT, the main explosive in most landmines, underneath a little hole near the rat in its cage. When it picks up the scent of TNT and holds its nose in the hole for three seconds the trainer clicks a metal clicker and rewards the rat with some food like some mashed-up banana or a peanut. It must be said that for a rat to hold its nose in the same spot for three seconds takes some training as they naturally want to keep moving. This process is repeated and repeated, until over time the rat learns to associate the smell of TNT with the subsequent click and treat, a process called conditioning. Once the rat has learned that the smell of TNT results in the reward he or she is taken out of the cage to a small training strip of soil and strapped into the aforementioned harness. The rat is secured to a leash attached to a long pole which is held by a handler. This is used to gently guide the rat to a particular area where patches of TNT are positioned at random intervals. The trainers walk the rat up and down the strips of earth bit by bit. The rat is only rewarded with a click and a tasty treat when it scratches where the TNT is located. The rat is now actively looking for the TNT because it has learned to associate its discovery with food.

One of the rats' favourite treats is what has been dubbed by the trainers a 'banana and avocado smoothie'. It's basically a shot into the mouth from a syringe full of mashed-up banana and avocado. Who could resist? After a lot of repetition the rat forms a kind of Pavlovian connection between the TNT, its own scratching response, the sound of the clicker and the food. It has been trained to clearly indicate where the TNT is located by scratching at the soil. It knows that the clicker sound means food, something it needs to survive, but it also knows it means enjoyment because the super-sweet and tasty banana-avocado smoothie is basically like giving the rat its favourite ice cream. Irresistible. All this becomes a kind of a language, a form of communication in which the rat can tell the handler that it wants that treat. After going through this whole process on a small strip of earth it's time for the rat to step up a gear. The handlers take the rat outside to large scrubby fields surrounding the centre, which look much more like the kinds of places they might be looking for real landmines. The site is again laid out in long strips and the process is much the same but on a larger scale. The rat works its way methodically up and down the field with the handlers guiding the rat attached to the harness. When the TNT is found and the rat scratches at the soil, it is once again rewarded with the treat. The trainers also gradually make it more difficult by giving the rat shiny metal balls to find but with no TNT. If they find that there is no click or reward, the rats can then learn that the only metal they are looking for is one which smells of TNT. Once the rat has cracked it, which takes about a year, and the handler is sure they can confidently identify a landmine with 100% success rate, only then are the rats ready to go out in the world.

To understand why what these rats are being trained to do is so important and so valuable, it's worth stepping back to remember the harm landmines can and still cause. Since 1997 more than 150 countries have joined a treaty which prohibits the use of anti-personnel landmines. This has led to a reduction of casualties. But many people are still dying or losing limbs from stepping on them. It's estimated they kill or injure around ten to fifteen people around the world every day. The majority of victims are civilians and more than half of those injured are children. Sixty countries are currently known to be contaminated by land-mines and massive areas of land are still simply too dangerous to use because of them. In spite of the treaty landmines are being deployed in more recent conflicts too. These include, among other places, Myanmar, Russia and Ukraine. The problem has far from been resolved, but these rats are becoming part of the solution.

The humans who are trained to find and deactivate land-mines know just how dangerous their work is. A pouched rat with its heart set on a banana-avocado smoothie, on the other hand, has no idea what it's really doing. This means it's up to us to keep them safe. Rats are too light to set off landmines themselves. They could jump up and down on one and not set it off. They would be perfectly safe working on their own in the minefield, but it's very unlikely they would be able to deactivate the mines on their own. If a human handler accidentally steps on a landmine, they may well detonate it. So to make it safe for everyone, before the work begins, human deminers have to meticulously clear what are called safety lanes inch by inch, using metal detec-tors. These are strips along the minefield which can be declared clear. Once there are two clear parallel one-metre lanes, a human handler will stand at one side of a safety lane and the other handler will stand in the other, side by side. The route is then systematically searched by the rat who goes back and forth between the humans on either side guiding them. Once the rat reaches one handler, both will take a half-a-metre step in one direction. The rat turns and walks the other way, searching the whole way as he goes, back towards the other trainer, all the while sniffing, sniffing, sniffing, sniffing, his nose to the ground. Then when the rat catches a scent of TNT you will suddenly see an immediate change in the animal's posture. He will begin to groom his whiskers, almost like he's thinking, *Where's the smell coming from?* His whiskers start moving as he sniffs the air. He'll then do a kind of circle round and then start to dig and dig and dig. Watching the rats do this, again and again, would give anyone goosebumps, especially when you think of the lives they are saving.

Once the rat has signalled it has found a mine by scratching at the soil, everybody can move safely away. The deminer will bring in a metal detector to confirm the find, and then either detonate it in situ, or a fuse can be run to explode it from a safe distance. It can also be removed and detonated some-where else. Repeated methodically in this way and by humans logging it all on a chart, the rat can literally search every square metre of the minefield. Because the rats ignore any harmless scrap metal it saves a lot of time. A rat can search an area in about twenty minutes and they can get through about 200 to 400 square metres every day. What would take a human about two weeks a rat can do in about a day.

Even though the rats don't bond with individual han-dlers like a dog would, they are still treated like trusted colleagues and seen as part of the team. Each of the rats has its own unique personality. Some are bold, some are a little bit shy, some are cheeky and others more serious. Most of them love to be stroked and cuddled. One of the biggest-ever rats at APOPO was a boy named Courage. He weighed almost two kilos. Courage particularly loved to have his back scratched. He had this habit of leaning back and almost balancing up on his toes. He loved having his back scratched so much, in fact, that he looked like he was about to fall over. He was also remarkably self sufficient. When Courage finished his day's training out in the field the handler would remove the harness and start to walk away. You might think Courage would seize the opportunity and make a bid for freedom. But no, instead he would just trot alongside his handler like a little puppy and then hop spontaneously into his open cage.

A fully trained rat like Courage has a potential six- or seven-year-career ahead of it. One of the places Courage worked was in the minefields in Cambodia. For the APOPO trainers who went with him it was incredible to see an animal they had known since he had first opened his eyes, a helpless wriggling pink thing, now out there in the real world going diligently about the business of saving lives. When Courage returned from Cambodia the staff back in Tanzania were happy to see his jolly face back at the centre and to see how healthy he looked after all that time in the field. When Courage came trotting back in, Dr Cindy Fast, who heads up training and innovation at APOPO, remembers running over to Courage. She could have sworn from the look on his face that he recognized her. He immediately leaned back and enjoyed that good old familiar back scratch.

The staff might bond with these characterful rats, but what do the locals who might be used to viewing them as the pests that steal their crops think of these animals now being trained to work in their communities? While they might still be seen as vermin by some, since seeing what they can do some people have been known to catch orphaned baby rats. Instead of killing them, though, they now take them to the APOPO centre and ask whether they can be trained to save lives. These rats have also been typically seen as a form of food, as bushmeat. Some people now say, knowing how smart they are and what they're capable of, that they would no longer eat one.

Getting people to fall in love with the rats is one thing. Convincing local communities that the land they have been terrified of for years is now safely cleared to farm or walk on is quite another. It doesn't help to clear a minefield if people are still too scared to go out there. One of the places APOPO has worked is Mozambique. After its fight for independence followed by a devastating civil war, in the early 1990s Mozambique was one the most mined countries in the world. APOPO, along with other agencies, have been part of the huge efforts to help clear mines. But they faced the problem that once a field was clear people were naturally still very afraid. After all, they couldn't see that the mines were gone. So once they had cleared an area, the staff at APOPO decided to host a community event. They organized a little carnival and a football game on the former minefield. It was a way of saying, 'We trust our rats. We believe all the mines are gone'. They asked locals to join them. At first nobody stepped up, but eventually a few people did and before long they were all enjoying a game of football together on the former minefield. Since then it has become sort of a tradition to have a football match in a mine-free area as a celebration and a show of trust. Thanks to APOPO and other mine-clearing and humanitarian agencies including the HALO Trust, in 2015 Mozambique was officially declared free of all known landmines.

Mine-detecting rats are now being deployed in Cambodia. Azerbaijan and Angola among other places and there is the prospect of sending rats to other countries including Ukraine and Colombia. As long as the climate and the terrain makes it possible for them to work somewhere, there's potential for the rats to help out.

So far the rats have cleared in the region of 160,000 landmines and unexploded ordinances. They've cleared over two million square metres of former minefields, which have been safely returned back to local communities. As if saving humanity from self-inflicted deadly weapons of war isn't enough, the hero rat's story doesn't end here because they have also been trained to help us in other ways.

Campbell

One of the biggest killers in Africa is TB, tuberculosis, and, guess what, pouched rats can smell that too. Rather than have a giant rat rock on up to a surgery full of sick people, though, these specially trained rats work in a laboratory setting. They're trained to distinguish TB from other pathogens and given samples which are coughed up by a patient to smell for TB. Like training them to detect TNT, the rats are given the target scent and rewarded for approaching it and investigating it. The trainer then clicks a clicker and gives the rat a treat. The trainers will also try to trick the rats with samples from patients without TB. The rat then learns these differences and that it will only be rewarded when it smells TB. One of the favourite rats of the staff at APOPO was a TB-detection rat called Campbell. She must have had the most incredible nose because, even when she was getting on a bit, she kept finding patients that none of the other rats were finding and that the clinics had missed. Campbell seemed to want to go on forever, but when she was nine years old the staff decided it was about time she got to enjoy retirement. Campbell was retired to a lovely spacious enclosure and ended up living two more years in the APOPO pouched rat retirement community.

The staff started having birthday celebrations for her when she turned ten and then again when she turned eleven. They even made her special rat cupcakes. Everyone was incredibly sad when Campbell eventually died at the age of eleven. Rats like Campbell are still screening for TB in partnership with local health clinics. They're helping out in Ethiopia, Mozambique and Tanzania, having so far helped find around 30,000 patients that clinics had initially missed. More lives saved by our hero rats.

It might seem like there is no end to what these rats can do when you discover they also help in other ways. Smuggling in the illegal wildlife trade, such as ivory or pangolins, remains a huge threat to biodiversity in Africa. Animals and animal parts are smuggled in vast quantities across the continent and overseas in shipping containers. While dogs are very good at being able to track poachers out in the fields, and they're great at carrying out vehicle checks at border crossings, the shipping container is sometimes a more challenging prospect for a dog. Especially when there are a lot of other smells inside, making it harder for them to distinguish animal contraband. X-ray scans can be used to screen visually for organic material, but smugglers can be really clever in how they hide things. They make it hard for us to see things and hard for dogs to smell them. It's also time-consuming and expensive to look in every container you might suspect. You would have to unpack a lot of it in order for a dog to sniff out all the material. What they sometimes do with dogs is drill a hole in the side of the container and suck up the air for them to smell. A rat is much lighter, though, and instead of drilling a hole a human handler can simply lift a rat up to the container's existing air vent. If the rat indicates that 'Hey, this smells suspicious to me', they can open the doors and send the rat inside to check further. They've even developed new technology for the rat to alert that he's found something. It's a smart little backpack that the rat can wear. It has a small camera on it and motion sensors. It even has a two-way microphone, with speakers connected to a micro switch. When the rat smells a wildlife product, he is trained to pull a little ball on his vest, which triggers the micro switch to tell the handlers that he's found something. The humans can then see on the visual interface of those motion sensors where the rat is inside the container. They send the rat a callback queue, a sound which he has learned means 'Good job, come back to us for your reward'. The human investigators will then come in and do the rest of the work. Because smuggling is often connected to other organized crime, including human trafficking, these detector rats are helping with what is now a massive threat to global security and national economies. When it comes to cracking down on smuggling it's also gratifying to know that the rats are helping not just us humans but fellow animals too.

The latest thing these remarkable rats are being trained to do is, like dogs, to help undertake search-and-rescue operations. When a large building collapses in an earth-quake or other disaster there are many layers, sometimes described as pancake layers. These can be difficult for dogs to penetrate. We have various technologies we can use to search, like radar, robots and video probes. But those can only go so far and they can also be fairly random as they probe about looking for any signs of life. When it comes to a rat, though, which is constantly being guided by its nose, the smaller animal can get into those areas that dogs can't always reach. Armed with their backpack, microphone and camera, if the rat ever found a trapped survivor it would pull on a small ball. The handler would then turn on the microphone and talk to the trapped person. They could find out whether they're injured and what kind of treatment they might need, not to mention if they are at all freaked out by what could be seen as a talking giant rat. This is all very cutting edge and still in development, but rats are currently training to be deployed for operational trials like this in Turkey.

All the incredible APOPO rats, no matter what their work is, end up retiring when they're ready. They tell their handlers, basically by kind of quitting work, saying 'I've had enough of this'. When they do retire they're all given the full hero treatment for as long as they live in those rat-retirement communities. There they have loads of attention and daily feasts, of the rat variety, of course, which is mostly fruit and vegetables and the odd smoothie. They can then live out the rest of their lives as super-happy, relaxed rats never knowing just what heroes they are.

These helpful, clever rats might be stealing the limelight a little bit. But don't worry – I haven't forgotten those remarkable, indomitable dogs who help us so much every day. There are some times when canines definitely do come out on top.

Jaina Mistry with her new guide dog Kath. We adopted Laura, Jaina's retired guide dog.

4. A Home for Laura

Meeting Jaina

Not long after I heard Jaina Mistry on the radio talking about how her guide dog Laura was looking for a retirement home, we got chatting. I told her about all our animals and how nice their lives are down on our Dorset farm, like Claridges for dogs. I had made up my mind already, after having been so moved by their story, that Laura would have a great time living with us. As we talked, Jaina told me more about how Laura had first come into her life, what their journey together had been like and she told me about her own story.

When Jaina was seventeen years old, studying for her A levels, she began to feel unwell. It was nothing really out of the ordinary. Her eyes were burning a bit and she felt under the weather. She went to the doctors and they gave her some antibiotics. Within a few hours her body was covered in chickenpox-like blisters. At first she didn't think too much of it but when it quickly spread she began to worry. She was sent straight to the hospital. The medical team managed to control the symptoms for a while. Then things got worse. The blisters were covering Jaina's throat and skin and they were affecting her lungs. The doctors had no idea what was happening and she was rushed into intensive care. It felt like she was burning from the inside out. They put her on intravenous morphine and she was bandaged up to protect the blisters which were becoming open wounds. It was so severe that Jaina was basically treated like a burns victim. After a while they discovered that she was having a huge allergic reaction to the penicillin. The medication had triggered a very rare skin condition called Toxic Epidermal Necrolysis, a severe form of Stevens-Johnson Syndrome. It only affects about one in every three million people but it can be life-threatening. Jaina was put on a feeding tube. The blisters had spread to about 60% of her body. She needed twenty-four-hour round-the-clock care and in an instant she had lost her health and independence. After twelve days in intensive care Jaina finally started to come round. Her skin was beginning to heal and they moved her to a ward to recover. She had been lucky to survive, but the impact of this traumatic experience would change her life completely.

The damage to Jaina's body had been severe. She had scarring on her corneas and damage to her tear ducts, which was affecting her eyesight. Part of one of her lungs had been removed. The whole thing had been incredibly tough and traumatic both mentally and physically. After three months in hospital Jaina was finally well enough to go home. But her muscles had become very weak from being in bed for so long. She needed physical rehabilitation with a walking frame to learn to walk properly again.

Sitting up in her hospital bed the day before she was discharged, Jaina made a decision. She was not going to let this awful thing beat her. It was as if she had somehow grown stronger, as though she had been reborn a different, more resilient person. She set her mind firmly on getting her life back on track and going back to college as soon as she could.

Jaina was relieved to finally be back in the family home in Leicester. She lived with her mum and dad, her sister and their pet cockatiels. She was having regular treatment to build up her strength and she had been given contact lenses to help with her sight. But over the next few months Jaina's vision rapidly got worse. A year after her illness had first struck she lost her eyesight completely. After seventeen years as a carefree child and teenager she was entering a new world of being a visually impaired person. Jaina also faced another tough realization. While she had been in hospital and recovering many of her friends had left college and gone to university. She had been left behind. Jaina was resolved on one thing, to focus on continuing with her education and eventually graduating from university. But she had no idea how she was going to do it.

Because she had lost her sight so suddenly, Jaina didn't feel equipped or prepared to deal with the world as a visually impaired person. She felt like she had lost her independence virtually overnight. She was now dependent on her friends and family to do some of the things many people take for granted, like going to the shops or out in the local area. She was afraid to use public transport. Then Jaina heard about a residential college near her home, Loughborough RNIB College, which helps young people with disabilities and other conditions to live independently.

Jaina immediately applied and got a place at the college. It meant she was now living away from her family, but she was excited about the possibility of being with other visually impaired people who would relate to her experience. Once she was enrolled, Jaina joined a reflexology course. She learned how to read Braille, use assistive technology and the long cane. This is using a long cane as a mobility aid to get information about your surroundings so you can avoid obstacles. It was quite a baptism of fire. Jaina felt quite vulnerable at first and found herself walking into things a lot. It's easy to misjudge where you're going and it takes a lot of skill and time before you're able to use the cane confidently. The other thing Jaina experienced for the first time at this college was being around guide dogs. When she had lost her sight she had ruled out the possibility of getting a guide dog herself. As a child she had been chased by a dog on holiday and developed a phobia. The family were unsure about having a dog. Jaina says at that time, being an Indian family meant there was a cultural stigma associated with having dogs in the house. So, all in all, getting a guide dog was not really on the cards for Jaina. Instead she focused on getting her education.

Jaina got through her courses successfully and she won a place at Derby University to study complementary therapies. It was a big step towards achieving her goal but it was very challenging. Having just left a college where there were lots of other visually impaired people, she was now the only one on her course. She had to rely on note takers in her lectures and, although she had learned to use a long cane, Jaina was hesitant to use it. She felt vulnerable and self-conscious standing out from the other students. The staff and her friends were considerate enough and helpful, but being the only visually impaired person was isolating. People all around her were living a typical student life, going to parties, socializing. Much of this now felt largely out of reach to Jaina. She continued to focus on her studies and in 2009 she became the first visually impaired person to graduate from the course. It was a moment of joy and celebration, a huge achievement after all she had been through. But there was still one thing holding Jaina back. She longed for the freedom to go where she wanted and to feel truly independent.

One day Jaina was chatting to a friend, who was also from an Asian background and who had a guide dog. The animal was calm and friendly and Jaina could tell their partnership was really special. Having a dog was helping her friend live independently. She began to wonder whether this might be an option for her. That is, if she could get over her fear of dogs.

A seed had been planted, but for now Jaina put all thoughts of guide dogs aside. After graduating she started working as a therapist. It was tough but she was making progress. Then came another blow. Jaina's lung had collapsed from the damage caused by her condition. She found herself back in and out of hospital again.

Her physiotherapist gave her a stark warning. She said, *If you don't want to be in here more often, you're going to need to take extra-good care of your physical health.* It was the wake-up call she needed. Jaina was more determined than ever to build up her fitness and independence, and that's when she made the decision to apply for a guide dog.

Jaina spoke to her family about it. They were happy and supportive but a little bit nervous too as they had never had a dog before. If it meant Jania getting her indepence back, they were right behind it. They had always had other pets like hamsters, rabbits, fish and their pair of cheeky cockatiels. In the end they all agreed to give it a go. Jaina filled out the application with the charity Guide Dogs. Now all she could do was wait.

Seeing-eye Dogs

The use of dogs to support and guide people goes back to ancient times. One of the oldest-known images of a guide dog is thought to be on a fresco in the Italian city of Pompeii. The man in the painting is holding a stick out in front of him and has a little terrier dog on a lead with its ears pricked up. There are also images in old European manuscripts which seem to show visually impaired people with canine companions. One medieval manuscript from France shows a man holding out a stick and being led by a dog. It has long pointy ears and a fluffy tail and looks a bit like a German shepherd. Another shows a blind man holding out a stick while a dog runs ahead on a lead with a bowl in his mouth. It wasn't until the eighteenth century that guide dog training began in any formal way. There were early experiments with guide dogs at a hospital in Paris. An Austrian man called Josef Reisinger trained his spitz and poodle dogs to guide him. They were so effective that apparently some people didn't believe he was actually blind. In 1804 the Institute for the Training of the Blind was founded in Vienna by Johann Wilhelm Klein, a pioneer of visually impaired assistance techniques. In one of the first manuals for coaching guide dogs, Klein describes the use of a harness paired with a long pole to help connect with your guide dog. It was during the First World War in Germany that the modern guide dog movement really took off. A doctor named Gerhard Stalling noticed that a German shepherd dog that was hanging out with a visually impaired veteran had begun to lead and protect the man. It got Stalling wondering. *Could he train dogs who had previously been used for tracking down wounded soldiers to guide some of the many soldiers who had lost their sight during the war?* Stalling set to work exploring methods to train the dogs and it worked. He went on to set up a guide dog school with branches across Germany. In the 1920s the German Shepherd Dog Association picked up on the idea and another large guide dogs school trained around 4,000 guide dogs to help both veterans and civilians. All this caught the attention of an American dog breeder and philanthropist called Dorothy Harrison Eustis. She was breeding and teaching police dogs in Switzerland at the time. Eustis was so impressed when she saw what the guide dogs could do that she wrote an article about them in the American magazine the *Saturday Evening Post*:

> No longer dependent on a member of the family, a friend or a paid attendant, the blind can once more take up their normal lives as nearly as possible where they left them off, and each can begin or go back to a wage-earning occupation, secure in the knowledge that he can get to and from his work safely and without cost; that crowds and traffic have no longer any terrors for him and that his evenings can be spent among friends without responsibility or burden to them ... Gentlemen ... without reservation, I give you the shepherd dog.

A nineteen-year-old blind man from Tennessee called Frank Morris heard of this. He immediately contacted Eustis, asking her where he could get one of these incredible dogs. Although Eustis hadn't actually trained a guide dog herself yet, she agreed to set about training a female German shepherd for Morris. He wrote back to her: *Thousands of blind like me abhor being dependent on others. Help me and I will help them ... I will bring back my dog and show people here how a blind man can be absolutely on his own.*

Morris travelled to Switzerland and spent several weeks

training with his new dog Buddy. The pair learned how to navigate crowded shops and busy streets together. When they returned to America, Morris and Buddy became huge advocates for the guide dog movement. At one point they demonstrated their abilities to the public by walking across a busy New York Street. Morris went on to campaign for equal rights for people with guide dogs. He met Presidents Herbert Hoover and Harry S. Truman. He paved the way for new laws and attitudes around guide dogs on public transport and in public spaces. True to his word, Morris eventually went on, along with Eustis, to found the Seeing Eye, the first American guide dog training school.

Back across the Atlantic, two British German shepherd breeders, Muriel Crooke and Rosamund Bond, were also inspired by what the German shepherd guide dogs could do. With backing from the Institute for the Blind, from a humble lock-up garage in Merseyside, they set about training twenty-eight female German shepherds. They then recruited four First World War veterans who had lost their sight to help train and work with the dogs. Tomos ap Rhys had lost his sight in a mustard gas attack due to a faulty gas mask. He, along with Musgrave Frankland, Allen Caldwell and G. W. Lamb, were successfully paired with the first guide dogs in the UK. Caldwell later wrote that his German shepherd, Flash, gave him *glorious freedom and independence, never known since pre-war days.* Frankland said of working with his dog Judith, *a guide dog is almost equal in many ways to giving a blind man sight itself . . . I would not be without her for a day.*

Guide dogs in the UK were initially met with some resistance and even hostility by the public. But once people saw what they could do and the extraordinary life-changing bond which could develop between dogs and humans, attitudes began to change. Muriel Crooke and Rosamund Bond went on to found the Guide Dogs for the Blind Association, now called Guide Dogs. Since then the organization has overseen around 36,000 guide dog partnerships and remain the world's largest breeder and trainer of working dogs.

Fast-forward to 2011. Jaina Mistry has just got confirmation she's on the waiting list to be matched with her own guide dog. They've tested her long cane skills, which fortunately she had learnt at college. During a home visit Jaina next had to chat to the Guide Dog trainer about her lifestyle. Every dog is different and it's important to find a pairing which fits when it comes to temperament, lifestyle and even walking pace. After chatting about what would work for her, and showing them how she walked with a harness, they set about finding a dog who would be the right fit. While she was waiting, Jaina was invited for an overnight stay to experience what it was like to be around guide dogs of all different sizes and temperaments. This was a bit daunting because she still had a fear of dogs. But once she started to meet the dogs, to walk with them and play with them, Jaina felt her nervousness beginning to subside. The true test came when she had one of the dogs stay in her hotel room overnight. She found herself huddled up in the middle of the bed anxiously while the dog sprawled out beside her. But the dog was so gentle she almost wanted to take it home in the end. It was progress. Now she had to wait for a dog of her own.

Over the next few months Jaina began to notice more and more just how much she had been affected physically by her condition. Since her lung had been badly damaged she was unable to walk upstairs without getting out of breath. She had achieved her academic goals, but her health was still a big problem. It was a tough realization but she simply didn't have the physical strength she used to. Jaina was determined not to let it beat her, though. She joined a local gym and took up regular fitness sessions with a personal trainer. She often had to take a taxi to the gym. She didn't feel safe on public transport and it was a long and difficult walk on her own. In the hope she would get a guide dog soon she set about learning her local walking routes using the long cane. When you hear the term guide dog you might think the dog does all the work literally guiding a person as they walk. In reality it's much more of a partnership. You can't just ask the dog to go and find the gym or the post office without first learning the route yourself. So over the next few months Jaina worked hard with her long cane to become familiar with all the streets, corners, crossings and obstacles in her area. Finally, in September 2012, roughly a year after she sent in her application, Jaina got the call from Guide Dogs. They had found her a possible match.

L is for Laura

When a litter of guide dogs is born they're usually all named with the same letter. Jaina's dog came from a litter with the letter 'L'. 'L' for Laura. This was the name of the black Labrador retriever cross girl they thought would be a suitable match and they were bringing the dog over to meet Jaina and her family. Jaina was feeling more confident with dogs by this time, but when it was time to meet Laura she was still a bit nervous. Laura had actually been partnered with someone else for about six months before this but that partnership hadn't worked out. As soon as Laura came trotting into the house, though, Jaina immediately relaxed. She could feel the dog's calm energy and presence in the room straight away. She could hear Laura's tail wagging against things as she came across the living room. When Jaina sat down Laura very gently placed her chin on her lap. Jaina could feel Laura's kind eyes looking up at her. Immediately she knew they had a very special connection.

After that first meeting the next thing to do was go on a walk together using the harness. Whenever you're walking with a guide dog you're holding the handle of the harness which is strapped to the animal. On this walk they were trying out one of the routes Jaina had been practising for months with her long cane. It was a short route along a few streets near her house. It was pretty safe, with no dangerous crossings, but with a long cane on her own it had been challenging for Jaina; she would snag her cane on obstacles along the way and it usually took her almost half an hour. She couldn't believe it when, as soon as they started on the route, Laura flew around the block with her in about five minutes. It was a total revelation.

After this Laura came to stay with Jaina and her family overnight. Jaina already felt completely relaxed with her but she had to make sure her family were OK with having a dog too. As soon as Laura was in the house it was as if she had always been there. It was immediately clear that Jaina's family absolutely loved having her around. She was friendly, calm and funny and she loved chasing her tail.

The next step was for Jaina and Laura to go on a training course together in Leamington with other people who had newly partnered with guide dogs. They would be learning daily tasks like how to groom and feed the dog, as well as something they rather delicately call 'spending the dog', which basically means taking it to the toilet and cleaning up its poo. They also went on walks together with a trainer around Leamington so they could start to learn all the commands it takes to work together as a guide dog partnership. These include a mix of hand signals and verbal signals for the many things you might want a guide dog to do. There are basic obedience commands such as 'sit and wait' or 'down'. There are signals for navigating together like the forward command, which is saying the word 'forward' with a swinging of the arm forward. As you learn more, the dog can do more complex things like finding specific targets, such as a road crossing, where the dog will learn how to 'find the box'. Or there are commands like 'find the kerb' or 'find a way' through a series of obstacles. Once the dog finds the target they are rewarded in some way, such as with a treat. Jaina found that often just a lot of praise and fuss would be enough for Laura to learn. She accepts flattery well. Learning all this new information about how to work, bond and care for a dog was intense; it was also mentally and physically draining simply being out every day walking in an environment that neither Jaina nor Laura were familiar with. They got through it together, though. They had already learned so much and this was only the beginning.

Over the next few weeks Jaina and Laura began to tackle the routes Jaina had been learning with her cane near her home. This is where the real work begins. Because you are a pair working together all the time, it's a real team effort to get to places, which means trust is really important. As well as verbal and physical commands, there are also more subtle signals you begin to learn through the handle itself. The verbal and physical commands then allow you to stay in charge, directing the dog, while the dog can in turn assist by indicating when there is an obstacle or road crossing ahead. With the help of a trainer, Jaina set about teaching Laura to find more targets in their local area, like houses or shops using the command 'find the door'. After they had been training for several weeks Jaina and Laura were getting really confident together. As soon as the harness went on each morning Laura was ready for her training, focused and looking straight ahead. She was remembering more and more of the targets and Jaina was beginning to be able to travel about with more and more confidence every day.

At the end of October Jaina and Laura had a training session booked in with a senior person from Guide Dogs as well as her usual trainer. They were asked to do a local route they were both familiar with and Jaina gave Laura the commands they had learned. Laura responded beautifully, manoeuvring round obstacles and stopping at all the kerbs and crossings. At the end they were asked to do it again and once again Laura smashed it. Afterwards the trainer turned to Jaina and said, 'I'm going to qualify you today.' Jaina was startled and over the moon. She had no idea they were being assessed. This had, it turned out, been their qualification walk. It was probably a blessing she didn't know, because Jaina wasn't nervous or self-conscious at all. What was even more special was that it was also her twenty-eighth birthday. This was the best birthday present she could have asked for. She and Laura were now fully qualified.

When I asked Jaina what it felt like to have Laura in her life the first word she said was 'empowered'. The next thing she said was that it made her feel safe. She had never put her trust so completely before in an animal and now she trusted this dog with her life. It was also an incredible feeling of liberation and freedom. After all Jaina had been through, with Laura at her side she now had a new sense of purpose, hope and confidence. This was something that in her darkest moments she had thought she would never be able to get back. All this is not to say it was easy. They certainly had their teething problems. For example, Laura had a penchant for wandering off up random people's driveways. There was no particular reason other than she was a bit nosy about what was up there. It would take a while before Jaina realized they had gone off route and that Laura was sniffing about at someone's bin, but they always got back on track. To Laura's credit, though, she never led Jaina into any obstacles, which could not be said for the cane. Jaina and Laura worked together to consolidate the main routes she needed, especially the route to the gym where Jaina was spending more and more time on her fitness. Previously she had taken a taxi because she did not feel safe on public transport, but now with Laura they could walk together, which was not only quicker and cheaper but healthier too. Eventually Laura knew they were going to the gym without Jaina saying anything, when she saw Jaina put her gym trainers on. Laura was starting to notice more and more of those little visual clues about where they were off to, even before Jaina gave her the commands. If they were going to the supermarket, for example, she knew because of the bag Jaina picked up. Now that Laura had proved herself to be so smart and they had built up more confidence on longer routes and at big road crossings, Jaina decided it was time to go on public transport with Laura. This was daunting because she hadn't used public transport since she was seventeen. She was now twenty-eight.

The route they were taking was the bus to the local coffee shop. A Guide Dogs trainer came along to help out the first few times. Jaina was relieved when Laura remembered the route to the bus stop and was immediately very confident when the bus arrived. She took Jaina straight on board.

Getting off was a little bit trickier. Jaina had to be in tune with where they were or ask the driver to let her know. But as soon as they were off again Laura helped her navigate all the obstacles to the coffee shop. When they arrived and Jaina sat down, having made it, she felt another sense of liberation. She had never pictured herself being able to get to a coffee shop on the bus again and now, with Laura at her side, she was finding the freedom to live independently again.

Another beautiful thing Jaina noticed, especially when they were at home, was that Laura would never take her eyes off her. Jaina could feel Laura was always watching her and she could feel her presence around her all the time. Even if she was upstairs she knew Laura would be waiting at the bottom for her to come down. If Jaina had been out of the house for a few minutes, when she returned Laura greeted her with such enthusiasm it was as if she hadn't seen her for months. Never having had a pet dog before, this kind of pure unconditional affection and love was a revelation to Jaina. To have this new adoring friend and companion who was completely non-judgemental, who was there for her every single day, literally watching out for her and being at her side whatever she went through, always lifted her spirits and was a great comfort.

Laura was also a natural icebreaker for Jaina when they were out in public. People were often more willing to help her out when they saw the dog than they had been when it was just Jaina with her assistance cane. When they got home at the end of the day and the harness came off, Laura was immediately off duty. Now it was time for play and fun either in the park or with toys around the house. It was time for Laura to relax and just be a normal pet dog.

Life with Laura had changed everything for Jaina but

nowhere more significantly than in her biggest life goal, to work on her fitness and her career. She was able to go to the gym more and walking with Laura meant Jaina's health improved with every day they were together. Not only was her own health and fitness improving, but she had also decided to pursue a career in the fitness industry and help other people. Jaina went back to college and did a gym instructor course. Laura became the teacher's pet on the course, managing to charm everyone. Jaina qualified as a nutrition and weight management consultant and started her own business, coaching and helping people manage their own health and fitness.

A year into her new regime, Jaina's personal trainer was so impressed with her progress that, in the winter of 2013, she was put forward for the National Fitness Awards. She was nominated in the Member Achievement category which celebrates people who are transforming their health through fitness. Jaina was over the moon when she discovered she had been shortlisted and been invited to attend a swanky ceremony in Manchester. All dressed up with Laura at her side, Jaina was up against five other people from across the country. When their category came around she couldn't believe it when the announcement echoed around the hall: 'The winner is . . . Jaina Mistry.' She and Laura got up from the table to huge applause and made their way up to the stage along with her personal trainer. It turns out that Laura is not at all averse to the limelight herself. While Jaina was accepting the award Laura was wagging her tail the whole time and soaking it up like a star. Jaina knew she couldn't have done it without her. It was only just over a year into their partnership and now they were on stage together receiving an award. As the crowd applauded and they walked back to the table it felt like a turning point. She felt like together they could do anything.

After having made so much progress with her health, Jaina was devastated when the following year she ended up in hospital again and was treated for a collapsed lung. While she was in hospital Laura stayed at home with Jaina's mum. The weekend before Jaina was due to have surgery she was allowed to go home for the night. As she walked through the door, feeling exhausted and nervous about her upcoming operation, Laura was right there, waiting to greet her. Jaina kneeled down to say hello and as soon as she put her hands on Laura's shoulders, Laura climbed up and placed a paw on the left side of Jaina's chest. Jaina couldn't believe it. The paw was right over her collapsed lung. It was as though Laura knew there was something wrong. As they sat there together Jaina felt surrounded by a beautiful healing energy and warmth from Laura. The next day Jaina went back to hospital for the procedure. She was under local anaesthetic so sedated but conscious throughout. As the doctors were working away on her lung, Jaina could still feel that powerful wave of energy she had felt with Laura at the house the day before. When the procedure was over her physiotherapist said to her, 'I've never seen a patient be as calm during this procedure as I've seen you today.' Whatever it was that Laura had given her in that moment had stayed with Jaina and helped her through it.

Laura became the first dog to be part of Jaina's family. She settled in really well and developed a special bond with everyone. Laura loved hanging out with her mum and getting lots of belly rubs, and whenever Jaina's dad went into the garden, Laura would follow him. She really enjoyed watching Jaina's sister bake cupcakes.

Laura helped Jaina with so much – not only to rebuild her health and fitness, and her career, but Jaina had also embarked on a new speaking career, talking about her journey with Laura and in health and fitness. Jaina had never done anything like that before but now she was doing public-speaking engagements. Laura had helped give her the confidence to talk about her story, to share it and inspire other people.

In 2019 Jaina was shortlisted for another award to win a support package to further develop her career. She, her mum and Laura went down for the ceremony. When Jaina won silver, once again Laura was with her on stage wagging her tail the whole time. The award helped Jaina to build up her business and together they appeared on more big stages at fitness events and speaking engagements. Jaina could feel Laura looking at her whenever they were on stage, her biggest cheerleader. It gave Jaina the confidence to believe *I can do this.*

Laura is a calm, confident and smart dog and she's great at problem-solving. If there was an obstacle in the way, she would always figure out the best and safest way for them to get round it. In all their years together she had never walked Jaina into anything. But nine years after she had come into Jaina's life, Laura was beginning to slow down. It was hard to admit it, but Jaina knew she was close to retirement. She was advised to put her name down for a new guide dog and picked up her assistance cane again to begin practicing getting around without a guide dog. While she waited to hear about a new guide dog, Jaina had a tough decision to make. Should she keep Laura alongside her new dog, or find a new home for her? It was painful to think about it, but she knew in her heart that she couldn't provide Laura with the retirement she deserved. Jaina did contemplate keeping her, but the thought of leaving Laura at home while she was out with her new guide dog was just too heart-wrenching.

Once Jaina had decided this was the right thing to do, in order to cope and pay tribute to Laura and the amazing work she and her fellow guide dogs had done, in 2021 Jaina did some fundraising for the charity Guide Dogs. She put together a series of memorable moments that she and Laura had together and shared it over social media. Their story really touched people's hearts and Jaina did press and radio interviews, talking about their journey together and how Laura had changed her life. They raised over £1,600. That November they were nominated for the Guide Dogs Awards and they won overall service user and partnership of the year. Jaina had to go up on stage to collect the award and Laura was right there beside her, tail wagging in approval. Another day, another award ceremony.

When Laura officially retired, overnight Jaina lost a lot of her hard-earned freedom. She could use her assistance cane but that feeling of independence Laura had brought her was now gone. It was tough, like taking a step back in some ways. But she had an even tougher moment to come. She was going to have to part with Laura.

Along Comes Kath

In the summer of 2022 Jaina and Laura came to meet us at our home in Dorset for a trial sleepover. Jaina, her mum and sister plus a whole load of home-cooked Indian foods came down from Leicester in a car with Laura happily squished in the back seat. When Laura came bounding in all our dogs loved her immediately. They thought she was quite remarkable and very clever. It was a lovely weekend and it didn't take long for all of us to decide this would be Laura's retirement home. After the meeting Jaina went home and began to prepare for when they would have to separate. The following January, while she was still waiting for her new guide dog, we started filming a TV programme named *A Dog Called Laura* about Jaina and Laura's journey. While we were filming Jaina was introduced to some new possible guide dogs and we were lucky to catch their first moments together on film. Jaina saw quite a few dogs, none of whom seemed quite the right fit. Then Jaina met Kath. She was a young and sprightly black Labrador retriever. It was very obvious that Jaina and Kath connected immediately. Kath was the right temperament and pace for Jaina. She was a bit faster than Laura, almost like her cheeky younger sister, but Jaina's fitness had improved and it just felt right. Before Laura was due to come and live with us Kath did an overnight stay at Jaina's house and she got to enjoy having them both together at home. Jaina didn't know it then but she has since discovered that Kath and Laura are actually related. Laura's granddad is Kath's great-grandad. It was another strange point of synchronicity in their journey together.

In April 2023 Jaina, her mum and Laura came to Dorset together. At the end of the stay the time came when they had to say their goodbyes to each other, when Jaina and her mum left Laura with us. They shared a moment and we all had a bit of a cry. Then Jaina said a final goodbye and headed home to forge her future with Kath.

While Laura is calm and sensible, Kath is quirky and

cheeky, almost like a naughty toddler. Whenever Kath and Laura meet now you can definitely tell that Laura is a wise, older sister. Kath turned out to be incredibly bright and a very quick learner. She was particularly fond of toys, which really helped with the training because she could be rewarded easily with some good old play time. It wasn't plain sailing with Kath at first. The first couple of months were a little bumpy. Because Kath is a bit more of a typical teenager and a lot cheekier than Laura it was much harder work. Kath is more excitable. But they got through it. Jaina and Kath have been together for over a year now and she's learned all Jaina's routes. She's a funny, cheeky little thing who Jaina loves very much and is always eager to learn. Jaina still really misses Laura. She misses the calm gentle nature, which helped her through her recovery and gave her new purpose in life, helping her become the strong, confident woman she is today.

As for Laura I am happy to report that she has taken to life in the country extremely well. We couldn't love her any more and she has fitted in to our family perfectly. She loves the space and even at fourteen she still runs for joy on a walk. She does like to keep her own counsel and will take herself off for some Laura time, especially in the evenings. She is completely unfazed by the horses and has discovered that they share a liking for carrots, which she now demands with barks. We love her bark and she knows it – she'll let out a woof with a look in her eyes like 'You like this, don't you?' There's an undeniable kindness in her eyes; she's very gregarious and loves meeting new people, but I guess she was always meeting new people, especially at all those award ceremonies. She's super bright. Jaina sends us these complex find-the-treat toys as presents for

Laura, which she studies and masters in moments, while our other dogs just look on in amazement.

There's one more remarkable thing Jaina remembers about her time with Laura. Jaina's mum is diabetic and she started to notice that at times Laura's behaviour would change when her mum's sugar levels began to drop. She'd hang around her mum more and try to get her attention as if she was trying to tell her something. Jaina wondered whether she somehow knew instinctively what was going on. Another time, when her sister came into the room one day, Laura touched her nose on her sister's tummy. Not long after that they found out Jaina's sister was pregnant. It was like Laura was somehow able to pick up on something we humans could not. I have since found out that it may not actually be that far-fetched to think that Laura really did know something we did not. A dog's natural ability to detect things which are beyond our own senses is now being taken to a whole new level. It's helping to change and even save some people's lives.

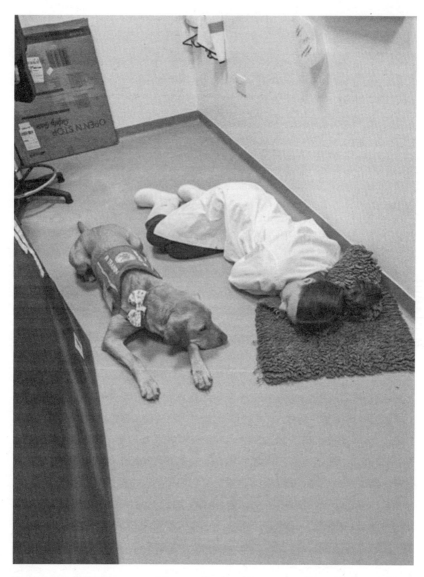

Trainee vet Jade Heaney and her medical assistance dog Jules. The fox-red Labrador was trained by the charity Medical Detection Dogs to alert whenever Jade has a PoTS episode.

5. Healing Paws

Best Mates and Lap Guests

It's no secret that our pets can make us feel good, especially dogs. Cuddling them releases a happy cocktail of serotonin, dopamine and endorphins, which can help lower blood pressure and reduce the risk of heart disease. Dogs lift our spirits when we're down. They help reduce loneliness, encourage us to exercise and make us laugh. Even when they're being a bit annoying, they can soon win us round by solemnly bringing over a ridiculous present. When a dog looks into your eyes, your body releases the natural love hormone called oxytocin. Like a mother with a newborn it can help build a bond of affection and trust. The fact that dogs can make our lives better is nothing new. For millennia they've guarded us, helped us hunt, herded our cattle and been our loyal and trusted companions.

Even the ancient Egyptians, who are much better known for their devotion to cats, really loved their dogs. While cats back then were usually called some variation of 'miu', meaning 'miaow', dogs were given individual names like Brave One, Reliable One and Good Herdsman, and in the case of at least one poor sod simply Useless One. When a pet dog in ancient Egypt died, sometimes whole families would show their grief by cutting their hair and shaving their bodies. Maybe not in the case of Useless One, though. I can't say I've ever felt compelled to shave my head after losing an animal, but I can relate to the long tradition of wanting to mark their passing and commemorate their lives in some way. There are ancient records of royal dogs being given grand burials in tombs and laid to rest in elaborate pet cemeteries. Dogs have been seen as sacred guardians, carefully buried alongside their masters to accompany them to the afterlife. The Egyptian god Anubis, protector of the dead, is often shown with the head of a canine. In this world, dogs have long been associated with healing. For centuries it was common lore that if a dog licked a wound it would heal quicker. Asklepios, the Greek god of medicine, is often shown hanging out with a dog. The ancient Mesopotamian deity or 'divine physician' Gula was called the goddess of dogs. Viewing our own dogs as quasi god-doctors or spirit guides might seem a bit far-fetched these days, but it turns out their power to help us heal can be very real and it goes way beyond them being our best mates and lap guests. Over the past few decades one pioneering woman, along with a group of other scientists, dog trainers and some very clever dogs, have set out to show the world of medical science just what they're capable of.

Jade's Dream

When Jade Heaney was growing up in the countryside in Northern Ireland, animals were a constant presence. Her family always had at least one dog, several cats and multiple fish. Her grandfather, who lived just down the road, also kept pigs, donkeys and horses; Jade loved to hang out with them whenever she got the chance. She also loved to go along to the vet whenever one of the animals had a check-up or vaccination. She was fascinated by the whole thing and would ask dozens of questions about what was going on and what it all meant. She was so chatty and curious that one kind vet gave her a giant model of a flea to take home with her. Jade thought it was simply the most marvellous thing she had ever seen in her life. By the time she was three years old she had it all planned out: she was going to be a vet.

When she was about seven, Jade began experiencing some strange symptoms. She felt a bit dizzy and breathless. She didn't tell anyone about it. She was too young to really understand. When she was about eleven things got worse. Then, just after her thirteenth birthday, Jade fainted and blacked out. Almost overnight her life changed completely. She began to fall over regularly, often injuring herself as a result. Her friends at school didn't know what to do. They became nervous to be around her in case she fell over. Even the teachers didn't really know how to handle it. They were always on edge, wondering if she was about to collapse.

Jade was eventually diagnosed with a condition called PoTS, postural tachycardia syndrome. I remember we once included this in an episode of *Doc Martin*. We were always on the lookout for new conditions for the Doc to diagnose. In real life when you have PoTS the supply of blood to your heart and brain can suddenly drop if you sit or stand up. Your heart beats faster than normal to try to get your blood moving. This causes the dizziness, fainting and blackouts Jade was experiencing. It's not totally understood why it happens but it's thought to be caused by a problem with the autonomic nervous system, the part of the body which regulates stuff like heart rate and breathing. While for some people it can be managed and be quite mild, for others it can be totally life-changing and there is no known cure.

For Jade the worst thing about having PoTS was that it was completely unpredictable. It could happen several times a day. One minute she would be standing with a friend or sitting in class. The next, completely without warning, she was on the floor, confused and with no memory of how she had got there. When she came round she was confused, her vision and hearing was affected, and, worst of all, she was often injured as a result of falling over. She would hit her limbs and her head on tables or sharp corners; she ended up with black eyes and was regularly in and out of A & E. Eventually things got so bad that she wasn't allowed to go on school trips any more unless a family member went with her. And no thirteen-year-old wants their mum or aunt following them around everywhere. Over the next few years Jade didn't go a single week without fainting at least a couple of times. She ended up missing a lot of school. She felt left out and isolated, like she was losing out on the life of a normal teenager.

Jade's biggest comfort during all this was the pack of animals in her life. Her grandmother had been really into horses and when she had died very young Jade's grandfather hadn't wanted to get rid of all her animals. So he had rented a stable and took care of all the donkeys and horses and a little rescue pony called Ryan. Jade would spend hours stroking and chatting to them and taking them round the fields. She took great comfort from just hanging out with them. Back at home with her mum and sister they also had several rescue cats, some rescue fish and a friendly old basset hound called Bailey. He was a very respectable eighteen years old, a lovely gentle thing. Then along came Oscar, a puppy they rescued from a puppy farm. He was young and lively and gave Jade a good dose of energy and companionship when she was feeling at her lowest.

Pretty soon it was time for her GCSEs and Jade had other things to think about. What was she going to do with her life? She had thought about being a doctor. But she had spent so much time in and out of hospital over the past couple of years that she didn't want to be anywhere near a hospital ever again. Then she remembered her childhood dream and all those visits to the vet. She also thought about how much animals had helped comfort her. She wanted to give something back to them. So she made up her mind. She would go back to her childhood dream and do everything she could to get into vet school.

Because Jade was missing so much school this was no easy challenge. She was given worksheets to do at home, then every couple of weeks she would go in and see her teachers. In the end she was basically teaching herself all the science, English and maths she needed. After a lot of hard work and persistence, Jade aced her GCSEs and got on to the right A level courses. She then took a punt and applied to the University of Surrey to study veterinary sciences. But though she was making progress in her studies, Jade's PoTS episodes had started to get worse. She had to miss school for three months and do her university interviews from home. She got through it, though. Conditional on getting the right A level grades, she had her place at vet school. This, along with all the animals in her life, was what kept her going. Then in early 2020 something happened that nobody was expecting.

No one could forget the shock of the Covid-19 pandemic. It seemed to come out of nowhere and changed all our lives completely. There was fear, panic and strange behaviour like washing all our shopping. There was confusion and sadness and weird restrictions about not sitting on benches, which none of us had ever experienced before. Not to mention all the tragic illness and loss of life. With schools across Britain suddenly shut many students also found themselves for the first time learning from home. For Jade this part wasn't all that strange; she had already been studying from home so much anyway. There was one positive thing for Jade which came out of the school being closed too. The teachers needed someone to take care of the school's bearded dragon. Of course Jade was the first to volunteer and that's when a cheeky little reptile called Norman moved in. Norman turned out to be remarkably cuddly and affectionate. For a couple of hours every night before they went to bed, he would curl up on Jade's shoulder with his spiny head resting against hers. Jade found hanging out with Norman a great comfort during this strange time.

Because she had already put so much work into her studies, despite students not being able to physically sit their exams, Jade had done enough to get the grades she needed. When her A level results came through it was official. She was going to vet school. Jade was ecstatic. This was her dream come true. But then another realization began to dawn on her. She would now have to leave the safe sanctuary of home and her animals. She would be moving on her own, to England. Jade thought about all the time and effort she had put into her schoolwork. She put aside the fear of her PoTS episodes and falling over in a strange place. It would be a challenge but she had to give it a go. Jade said goodbye to her grandma's horses, the donkeys and the little pony Ryan. She hugged her grandad. When all her bags were packed she snuggled up with old Bailey and gave the cats a cuddle. She said goodbye to Norman and gave one last hug to Oscar. Then she headed to the airport.

After having said a sad goodbye to her mum and sister, Jade was happy to discover that the university campus was nestled in the countryside. Although it was miles away from everything she knew, it did feel a little bit like home. Because of the Covid restrictions, though, it was an unusual start to the term. Apart from having some practical sessions once a week, most lessons were remote. This meant there wasn't much opportunity to meet people. Not long after she arrived Jade's PoTS episodes started. She fell over and hit her head and was completely on her own with no one around to help. As the episodes continued she found herself increasingly nervous about falling over with no one to help her. The university gave her something called a fall-detection bracelet. This meant whenever she fell an alert would ring through to security. They would then go to her and call an ambulance if she was hurt. This solved one problem. But now Jade's mum was getting phone calls at all hours of the night to say Jade was in hospital again. Being 500 miles away she could do nothing to help. This meant Jade was often on her own in A & E with head injuries and all sorts of bashes and bruises. She became more and more fearful of going out anywhere on her own. Because Jade regularly got black eyes from her falls, people around campus who didn't know her started wondering what was going on. They would often stop and ask if she was OK, or report it to university in case she was being abused. In the end all the attention was too much. It was easier not to leave her room at all if she could help it. If she needed supplies, she would get them delivered. Because so much of the course was remote during Covid, at first Jade wasn't missing out on too much of her education. But over the next few months things started to open up. Students were expected to attend more and more practical sessions.

When you're training to be a vet, it's inevitable that at some point you're going to need to get up close and personal with some animals. On campus they did a lot of husbandry, working with farm animals. They were lucky to have large animals like cows, horses, pigs and dogs on site. The students got to practise things in the clinical skills lab, like giving injections, surgical suturing or stitches and taking samples to test in the labs.

On the one hand, having access to all these incredible facilities and working with so many real animals was incredible; it was exactly what Jade had dreamed of doing. She was thrilled by all the sights, sounds and even the smells of real veterinary training. But instead of being able to focus on her practicals, she found herself increasingly preoccupied by worrying about whether she was about to collapse. At any moment she could black out and injure herself. Most scary of all was when she was holding a sharp instrument like a scalpel. If only she had some kind of warning to tell her when she was about to collapse she might be able to do something about it, to sit or lie down somewhere to recover, but it was always completely out of the blue. Then Jade heard about something which seemed almost like a miracle. Something which might be able to transform her life.

Daisy Knows

The something which Jade heard about was the bright idea of a scientist and animal lover called Dr Claire Guest. When

I met Claire she was surrounded by numerous dogs and had just come in from riding her horse. After the obligatory horse chat, which all horse lovers must have before they can talk about anything else, she began to tell me about her own story and the incredible research she and her team have been doing with dogs. It all began several decades ago. Claire was studying psychology at Swansea University and she and her pet dog Ruffles had, like many of us do with our first pets, formed a really strong bond. Claire loved Ruffles so much that when she graduated she decided she wanted to work with dogs as a career. So she got a job working for the charity Hearing Dogs for Deaf People. She became a dog trainer and eventually director of operations and research. The charity trains dogs to alert people to sounds like fire alarms, which if you're hearing-impaired or deaf you might otherwise miss. The dogs can also provide much needed comfort and emotional support for people. As well as harnessing their strong sense of hearing and their ability to keep people company, Claire also became fascinated by dogs' incredible sense of smell. We humans have around 5 million sense receptors in our noses. This might sound like a lot but dogs have a whopping 350 million or so. Any dog owner will know that our canine friends can sniff out the tiniest crumb of food at a thousand paces. Many a pet dog has been known to uncover that lost bit of sandwich which fell behind the radiator aeons ago.

Claire began to wonder whether dogs' marvellous noses might be put to something much more useful. She had heard stories about dogs having a kind of sixth sense, of them being able to somehow predict when their owners were ill. At that time in the early 1990s this kind of thinking was viewed very much as wild speculation. No one had ever been able to prove it and the medical profession didn't take it all that seriously. But Claire wasn't the only one wondering about this. During her work with dogs she met an orthopaedic surgeon called Dr John Church who had turned his attention to how animals could be used in human health care. He introduced a radical maggot treatment to the NHS, which is now used by hundreds of different hospitals. Who knew? Maggots being another remarkable animal, if not quite as cuddly as dogs. John was also exploring a growing body of anecdotal evidence that dogs could detect cancer long before any doctors knew about it. When he and Claire had crossed paths they realized they were wondering about the same thing. John told Claire he was looking for dog trainers to help him with a new study into whether dogs could detect bladder cancer. Claire had just the skills and just the dog, another pet cocker spaniel called Tangle. Combining Claire's knowledge of animal behaviour and her dog-training skills with John's medical experience, the duo started training Tangle to detect the smell of bladder cancer in urine samples. It was one of the first-ever research programmes in the world of its kind, looking into whether dogs might help us diagnose diseases. Using reward conditioning, Tangle was eventually able to successfully signal the right samples enough times for them to publish their results in 2004 in the *British Medical Journal*. They finally had the proof they had been looking for, that dogs could detect cancer.

They collected dozens more stories of dogs detecting breast cancer, melanoma and other cancers. But just as there had been scepticism when the first German shepherd dogs were trained to be guide dogs, for many people it still seemed like a wild and crazy idea to bring dogs into a health-care setting. How could they do something so technical and so scientific? How could they excel at something which we, with all our sophisticated technologies, are unable to do, picking out the smells of individual diseases with just a sniff and a treat? But John and Claire believed in their mission and they set out to prove to the world that this was not some kooky idea but real science with the potential to save lives.

By this time Claire's pack of dogs had grown. She had her cocker spaniel Tangle and another spaniel called Woody. She also had a gentle brown-eyed fox-red Labrador called Daisy. When Daisy was old enough they began to train her to detect some of the different cancers. One day, when Claire was out and about with the dogs, Daisy began behaving oddly. She was staring intently at Claire and sort of nuzzling at her chest and jumping at her face. Claire wondered why Daisy was being so strange and maybe even a bit naughty. It prompted her to check it out, though. Claire went to the doctors just in case. At first it seemed like nothing much to worry about. But then, on further checks, they found a deep tumour which needed immediate surgery. Daisy had been trying to tell her something all along. It had been so deep it would probably never have been found if it wasn't for the dog's persistence.

After having surgery and radiotherapy Claire's cancer went into remission. She is certain that Daisy's incredible sense of smell and the dog's cleverness helped save her life. As Claire began to tell people about what Daisy had done, you might think it would have helped persuade people they were really on to something. Daisy did help win some hearts and minds, but Claire and John still found themselves up against plenty of sceptics. Some people imagined scenes of chaos, with dogs running around hospitals sniffing people for cancers.

What they didn't realize was that all this work happens using samples in the lab and is totally safe and sanitary.

Undeterred, Claire and John felt more and more sure that dogs could be trained to distinguish not only cancers but the unique and subtle differences in scent between all kinds of human diseases. Determined to prove to the world that they were on to something big they set up the charity Medical Detection Dogs. They wanted to see just how far they could take it. Using breath, urine and sweat samples, they continued to train dogs to test for cancers. At one point they thought Tangle the cocker spaniel had wrongly diagnosed someone as having bladder cancer, but it turned out the dog was ahead of the game. He had, in fact, been the first dog to detect kidney cancer. Daisy the Labrador went on to become one of the first dogs to detect prostate cancer. She was awarded the Blue Cross Medal for animals who have changed or saved lives through their remarkable actions after having correctly sniffed out over 550 cases of cancer.

As well as these incredible successes in diagnosis, Claire and her team began to realize that dogs could also be trained to live and work alongside people more directly. Most people are now pretty familiar with medical-assistance dogs who live alongside visually or hearing-impaired people, and dogs as emotional-support animals. What Claire had worked out was that they could also be used to warn people of more immediate medical emergencies. As well as offering comfort and companionship, dogs could give life-saving alerts to people about their medical conditions in their own homes. She and the Medical Detection Dogs team had discovered that in the case of diabetes patients experiencing dangerously low or high levels of sugar in their blood, dogs could be trained to sniff out blood sugar levels and alert their owners to take insulin, extra sugar, get help or take other medical action. While many people can feel when this happens, some people have 'hypo unawareness', which means it can strike suddenly with no warning. Dogs can also sometimes detect faster and earlier than blood sugar monitors. Untreated low or high blood sugar can lead to seizures, comas and sometimes be life-threatening.

Claire went on to discover that dogs could also detect another condition called Addison's disease. This is when the body doesn't produce enough of the crucial hormone cortisol. It can be fatal if not rectified soon enough and it's very hard to predict. Having a dog who can alert when someone's hormone levels are dangerously low means they are able to take cortisol replacements before any life-threatening symptoms occur. Claire and her colleagues realized they were just scratching the surface of what dogs could do in medical science. Over the next few years they trained dozens of dogs, including some rescue dogs, to be not only pets but life-saving medical-alert companions. When in 2020 Jade Heaney discovered that one of the conditions these dogs had been trained to detect was her own condition PoTs, she wondered whether this might be the miracle she had been hoping for.

Finding Jules

At first Jade was a bit nervous about applying for one of these disease-sniffing dogs of her own. She had always been very private about her health and she was anxious that having an assistance dog with her all the time would, she thought, be quite literally a walking advert that there was something wrong with her. But the reality was that, with her condition being now serious and unpredictable, training to be a vet was fast becoming virtually impossible. Occupational health at the university had been getting more and more involved in her life. They were constantly monitoring her and assessing her fitness to practise. Sometimes they would completely write her off for all practicals telling her it was just too risky. Jade must have clocked up some kind of record for the number of occupational health reports of anyone at the university. Eventually they told her she would have to stop working with large animals altogether unless things changed. She realized she had been naive in a way. She had thought that somehow all her problems would just disappear once she got to vet school. She had never imagined it would be this hard. Now all she could think about was her condition and getting injured. Her last hope was to bite the bullet and apply for a medical-assistance dog.

After a quick application process in the spring of 2021, Jade was told she was definitely eligible for an alert dog. It was brilliant news. But it came with a note of caution. It would only be possible if Medical Detection Dogs could find and train a dog who was able to handle working alongside a trainee vet. It was not an easy task. The dog would have to be totally relaxed, obedient and calm alongside cattle, horses, pigs and other dogs. It would need to be well behaved and sensible in a laboratory setting, and not be phased by the bright lights and stark white walls, or disturb the microscopes and delicate medical slides. That's before you even get to the cadaver labs. Jade would be expected to practise on real animal carcasses, which would surely test even the most obedient of dogs. Jade just didn't know if they'd ever be able to find a dog that could handle all this. She kept everything crossed and somehow managed to get through her first year.

Back home for the summer holidays Jade's family noticed that she didn't seem very happy. She hadn't given up yet, though. She was holding on to that tiny ember of hope, the prospect of a medical-alert dog. But it was exhausting not knowing if she would be able to follow her dream. Soon it was time to say goodbye to her family and all her animals again and start her second year. This time the university gave her a bigger room with more floor space. It was supposed to stop her from hitting things. It didn't really work so they tried taping soft padding to the corners of tables to stop Jade hitting her head when she fell. None of it helped. She still found herself being rushed to A & E on a regular basis with bruises and black eyes.

With Covid restrictions being lifted Jade was now also expected to do a lot more on campus. There were more lectures, more practicals and more lab work. Being out and about so much increased her chances of passing out some-where unpredictable and scary. Not only that but her lessons were also becoming more and more dangerous, especially when she had to handle scalpels and work with large animals. In the end Jade decided she could no longer do large animal practicals at all. It was just too risky. The problem was that she needed to pass those practicals to pass the module and she needed to pass the module to pass the year. It was painful to accept but Jade knew it wasn't really safe for her to be there any more. One day she had a particularly bad fall during one of her sessions and right there and then she decided to put her studies on hold and go home. The university also gave her an ultimatum. They told her that unless she got a medical-alert dog she couldn't come back. It was a bitter blow. Her dreams seemingly in tatters, Jade wondered what she was going to do with her life.

Back at home Jade found herself on her own most of the day with just her animals for company. Her mum worked from seven a.m. to seven p.m. and her sister was out a lot of the time too. For months she was in limbo, constantly checking her emails for a message from Medical Detection Dogs. She also began to religiously follow their social media pages. They often posted photos of cute puppies staring up at the camera and stories about how they were getting on with their training. There were a few in particular who caught her eye, especially a little sandy-coloured Labrador pup called Jules. He had the cutest floppiest ears, fluffy big paws and adorable brown eyes. Over the following months Jade followed his progress. She discovered another photo of him excelling at his training, describing him as a 'clever, eager boy who loves to learn'. One day she noticed a post announcing that Jules had passed his assessment. He was on his way to becoming a medical-alert dog; she knew they usually got snapped up pretty quickly after that.

Over the next few months Jade continued with her quiet life, hanging out with her dog Oscar and the cats, horses and donkeys. Then, in the summer of 2023, two and a half years after she had first applied, a message finally came through. They had picked out some dogs for Jade to meet. She felt a buzz of excitement and hope. But she was so nervous. It was a bit like going on a blind date. What if she didn't click with any of them? What if none of them liked her?

She couldn't believe her eyes when the first dog to come bounding into the room that day was a young fox-red Labrador. It was Jules, the cute puppy she had first seen online, now all grown up. Jade could tell immediately what a bundle of energy he was, super friendly and eager to please. He immediately went round everyone in the room, wagging his tail and greeting them all, as if he didn't want to leave anybody out. Two of his trainers were there but, out of everyone in the room, Jules kept going back over to Jade for an extra snuggle and a sniff. She knew she wanted a dog with a lot of personality. It was obvious Jules had that by the bucketload.

After the initial meet-and-greet they kitted Jules out in all the medical-alert dog gear. They put a lead on him and gave him his special red assistance jacket. The minute the jacket went on it was just like switching on a light; he was so focused and serious. Jade walked up and down with him on the lead and it felt so natural. As soon as the jacket came off, Jules was back to being a playful dog again, pulling on a rope toy, happily going about the room and doing his own thing. Jade met a few other dogs that day. It was a bit like a kind of canine speed-dating session. But there was only one dog for Jade and that was Jules. She had never believed in love at first sight but she was smitten.

A few weeks later Jules came over to Northern Ireland to visit Jade at home with one of his trainers. It was important for him to meet her other animals to check they all got along. They all loved him, even the cats. What a charmer. During the visit Jade had a couple of PoTS episodes and the trainer took some sweat samples. This was how they would train Jules to detect the unique scent he needed to do his job. Eventually it was time for Jules to leave and Jade hugged him tightly. As he looked into her eyes, his tail wagging, his mouth seeming to open in a kind of smile, it was like he was looking into her soul, but Jade didn't know if she would ever see him again. The trainer took her aside and told her, off the record, that as long as the training went OK, Jules was her dog. It was the biggest news of her life. She couldn't quite believe it. Not long after that an email came through. She cried tears of joy and relief. It was really happening.

Over the next few weeks the trainer worked with Jules to condition him to alert whenever he detected Jade's PoTS sample. His alert was to put his paw up to her to get attention. The reports were that Jules was so enthusiastic about it all that while a lot of dogs need to be given something really tasty like cheese, salmon or sausages to reward them when they got it right, Jules seemed to love it all so much that a lot of the time he didn't even need a tasty treat. He found learning so exciting and rewarding that often just a bit of dry kibble as a treat was enough to keep him going. After only a couple of weeks of training Jade and Jules met up again. She couldn't believe it when he alerted for real by pawing at her. It was as if he just couldn't wait to get going. Pretty soon the trainer was confident Jules could be trusted to alert correctly whenever he detected the scent. It was time for him to get to work.

Almost as soon as he moved in with Jade, Jules started proving himself useful. Jade often had several episodes a day. This meant Jules had plenty of chances to show what he could do. Just as he had been trained to, he would put a paw up to Jade when she was about to collapse. She then knew to sit or lie down to avoid falling over or blacking out. For the first six months trainers from Medical Detection Dogs would come to check on how they were doing to help out with any training. Then, if it went well, Jules would be fully accredited. It quickly became apparent that Jules wasn't only doing what he had been taught during his training. He began to create his own set of more subtle alerts for different situations. Jade discovered that if they were out somewhere, such as walking down the street or in a shop, if she was distracted, he would start jumping on the spot. This was easier to notice quickly than just his paw. Sometimes she was able to tell when he was about to alert even before he did anything. He would all of a sudden get a really serious look. His eyebrows would freeze and he would develop a really intense kind of stare. Despite this incredibly serious face, though, he always had a really waggy tail. As with all Labradors, his bushy tail wagged from side to side like a mad thing whenever he was excited. But when he was alerting it went full steam ahead in huge circles like a great big furry windmill. The other thing which amazed Jade was that, even when he was in the middle of doing something really fun like playing with a toy or eating something tasty, the second he detected Jade was about to have an episode he would stop whatever he was doing instantly. He wouldn't even look at the toy any more, no matter how fun it was. Jade was always his priority. His eyes would remain fixed on her, tail wagging, face ultra serious until she did something about it. She then had a few minutes to find a safe place to sit or lie down. Once Jade had found a safe place, Jules would sit or lie calmly at her feet.

Another thing Jules became good at was knowing when her episode was going to be particularly bad. She realized he had developed another alert where he would puff out his cheeks and do a kind of silent bark. He made an urgent puffing noise, a bit like a horse. Jade began to realize this meant she had no time to mess about. She needed to lie down as soon as possible. If she just sat down, Jules would keep alerting with those horse puffs until she lay down. Then Jules would lie down beside her and cuddle right in, as though he also knew she needed extra comfort. When Jade comes round from her episodes she can be quite confused. Things are fuzzy and she sees double and sometimes she doesn't recognize people all that well. Her hearing can be affected and it can be quite scary and disorientating. Now when she came round the first thing she saw was Jules beside her; she instantly recognized him and felt safe. Sometimes he would gently lick her, which helped to bring her round a bit as well. As she recovered she would look at Jules and stroke his paws. He would stare back at her intently with his paws on her hands until she was feeling better. Then he would immediately snap back to whatever he was doing before. Job done. All this, the extra alerts, the comforting behaviour, was way beyond what Jules had been trained to do. It was as if he had his own instinct for what she needed, and they were fast becoming inseparable.

Having Jules in her life meant she was now able to go out and about in the world confidently. She still had PoTS, but she wasn't injuring herself or going to A & E all the time any more. She knew Jules would give her advance warning before she blacked out or collapsed. As the weeks went by Jade began to realize just how much she had been missing out on all these years. When they first went to the shops together, it had been so long since Jade had bought anything herself she didn't actually know how to use a contactless card. She had never been on a bus by herself. Now with Jules's help she got on the bus confidently without the fear of collapsing. She went to the cafe to meet her friends. She went to the cinema. These are things most people take for granted but which Jade had never had the chance to do. With Jules at her side her life had been completely transformed. And biggest of all, after two and a half years away, she was finally able to return to vet school.

Back on campus Jade was given her own flat with Jules. It had a bedroom, bathroom and even a little kitchen. In his downtime Jules relished the chance to run around outside in the fields and forests around the campus. The Medical Detection Dog trainers had been a bit worried because Jules was quite a goody two shoes. He was so well behaved when he was working, they wondered whether he might not alert during lectures for fear of being seen as a naughty dog. A medical-alert assistance dog needs to be quite a combination of obedience and professionalism but also know when it's OK to break the rules of polite society. They needn't have worried. Wherever they were, whether in the lecture room or out in public, Jules was always happy to jump up or paw at Jade whenever it was needed.

Another thing which had made Jade nervous was the thought of Jules in the laboratory setting, with all those microscopes and sharp instruments. The first time Jules alerted in a lab, a trainer from Medical Detection Dogs was there on a visit. Everyone was so excited, marvelling at how well he had done, that for a moment they all completely forgot what it actually meant, i.e. that Jade needed to find a place to sit or lie down pronto before she passed out. Jade quickly took off all her PPE so that she didn't contaminate Jules. She lay down in a side room with her head on a fluffy rug, still in her white lab boots and lab coat. Jules lay down calmly at her side, staring at her intently until she came round. After this the college set up a small room beside each of the labs. They put a mattress in each one which was supposed to be for Jade, although Jules was usually the first one on it. From then on, whenever Jules alerted she could slip out in her own time quietly. They didn't have to stop the practical or cause a big disruption. Then she could just slip back when it was over and finish the lesson.

Another of Jade's fears had been the cadaver lab. Would a dog ever be able to stay calm enough around an animal carcass and be able to detect the scent of her PoTS above the smell? Jules was put in a little office to the side of the lab so he wasn't in the main room but only six feet away from Jade. When it was time to alert Jade, as soon as he detected the right scent even above all the other smells, Jules dropped his favourite toy, trotted into the lab and went straight up to warn her. So it looked like cadaver labs were no longer a concern.

The other big challenge for Jade had been working with all the large live animals like pigs, horses and cattle. Doing clinical exams on these big beasts had become a huge no-go for Jade when she was collapsing all the time. If she was working there someone would have had to keep a close eye on her all the time. It wasn't much fun doing a practical with someone looking over your shoulder constantly. But it was immediately clear that Jules could be perfectly well behaved even with cattle and horses around. So Jade could now confidently do her practicals without being constantly monitored.

There had been such a big question mark over whether they would be able to find a dog who could behave well enough in these wildly challenging settings. A dog who could be around dead animals and live animals and sit through hours of lectures every day, all the while knowing exactly when and how to alert. Finally, after seeing just how reliable Jules was, her tutor told Jade that she didn't see any reason why alongside Jules she shouldn't be able to qualify and practise as a vet. This was huge. Having had people all around her for years doubting whether she could do it, to finally hear that she could fulfil her dream was the best news ever. She now felt like anything was possible. Best of all was that after six months Jules passed his accreditation. He was now an official medical-alert assistance dog.

It wasn't only Jade who was being helped by Jules. Having such a lively, friendly dog around campus was making other people more relaxed too. Jules became rather a celebrity. As soon as people saw him they were all oohs and ahhs. Even if they were having a stressful day or were feeling a bit grumpy, Jules could put a smile on people's faces. Jade had felt for so long like she was a source of fear and anxiety for people. Now everyone was now happy to see her – and Jules, of course.

You might be curious about how a dog like Jules would handle working in a real-life vet's surgery? Jules is brilliant at being with every other animal, but he might not like having other dogs barking at him day in and day out, or being confronted by sick cats. But being a vet can be much more than this. As a trainee vet you have a lot more choice about where you work than you do with human medicine. Jade is thinking about working with exotic animals or research. Or, given how well Jules behaves around cadavers, maybe even in pathology. At the moment, though, she's just going with the flow and keeping her options open.

Jade still has a few years to go before she qualifies. But her life has already opened up so much. The list of things she wants to do with Jules is growing every day. She's already ticked the *Titanic* museum in Belfast off her list and the West End musical *Frozen*. At some point she says she wants to go to Disneyland. For now she's content to go for long walks along the beach, just her and Jules, safe in the knowledge he's got her back. Jade used to be self-conscious talking about her condition. Now she's happy to chat away about Jules and the incredible things he does. Before she was shy and isolated. Now she gives talks about how Jules has helped her. She's been able to raise more awareness of PoTS and talk about the barriers and challenges you face as a person with a disability when becoming a vet. Jade's story and her resilience is giving other people real hope and she's an inspiration.

As for Medical Detection Dogs, when I spoke to Dr Claire Guest she was still bubbling with energy and enthusiasm about the latest mind-blowing things they're discovering about the power of dogs' noses. Thanks to Claire's persistence in the face of all that scepticism, she and her colleagues have now proven that dogs are up to 94% accurate in detecting Covid-19. Dogs have been able to detect the malaria parasite before symptoms appear. They're doing cutting-edge research around dogs detecting bowel cancer, UTIs in older people and Parkinson's disease. They've also trained and placed almost 200 assistance dogs to help with diabetes, Addison's, PoTS, allergies and more. In 2023 they got in the Guinness World Records book for the most medical conditions detected by dogs by a single organization: a whopping twenty-eight and counting. Every day these remarkable dogs are changing lives and, just like Claire's own dog Daisy, saving lives. Sadly Daisy passed away in 2018 at the age of thirteen. She had achieved so much and her legacy lives on. Claire's other fox-red Labrador Florin is actually Daisy's niece and has followed the trail Daisy blazed as a medical-detection dog.

Jade's condition hasn't gone away. But Jules has helped her feel better in so many ways. He's now her comfort and her best pal. Even though he sometimes has to alert up to seven or eight times a day, he hasn't missed a single episode yet. He never seems to get bored or sloppy and he puts as much effort into it as if it's his first. Jade has also found that since having Jules her episodes are becoming less severe. If she sits or lies down in time it helps her heart rate and blood pressure regulate, which helps to ease her symptoms. Best of all, those traumatic weekly trips to A & E are now a thing of the past. Jade finds it funny to think that after all the clever university lecturers, medical teams and health and safety experts she has come across over the years, it's a jolly three-year-old fox-red Labrador who now looks after her better than anyone.

Journalist Melody Horrill and a leaping bottlenose dolphin. Melody and lone dolphin Jock became friends when she was a research assistant studying the animals in Port Adelaide River [photo attr. Dr Mike Bossley].

6. Friends with Fins

Ocean Giants

When I was a child my dad gave me a book about the *Kon-Tiki* expedition by Norwegian explorer Thor Heyerdahl. It tells the story of a wild true-life adventure in which Thor and five crew mates drift over 4,000 miles across the Pacific Ocean in a handmade balsa-wood raft built to the spec that the ancient Polynesian sailors used. Along the way they encounter violent storms and enormous waves. At one point they see a huge sea monster with a wide gaping mouth, a broad flat head and two small eyes. I vividly remember the picture of the creature dwarfing the little boat in the book; it was a giant spotted thing the size of a whale. But it wasn't a whale. It was a fish. The world's biggest fish. The whale shark.

Given the choice I do generally prefer to snuggle up with something furry, like a dog or a cat. I've been known to nurture the odd colony of sea monkeys. I definitely have a soft spot for newts. But I've never been one for keeping a lot of the slimy, bald or scaly creatures of this world as pets. Ever since I read that book as a kid, though, I've been intrigued by the vast and mysterious whale shark and that image of it passing beneath the *Kon-Tiki*. A giant fish might not be as easy to cuddle up with as a puppy, but I've become more and more curious about the creatures we don't tend to bring into our homes. Those who lurk in the ocean.

I'm terribly lucky to get to travel and film around the world for the documentaries I've made and I'm often asked to do some quite random stuff. A high point was shooting a video for the West Australian tourist board. This was to include a new and exciting visitor attraction. Best of all, I would get to meet some wild dolphins face to face. On the morning of the shoot I set off in a boat with a diver who knew all about the dolphins and where to find them. It wasn't long before we found a pod hanging out where they liked to hang out, in the clear tropical waters of the Ningaloo Reef. My role as the punter in the video was to get into the water with the diver tour guide. He would be holding a handheld electric motor with a propeller. I would hang on to a loop on his belt and be dragged along behind as he whooshed through the water. I got kitted out in all the clobber, tipped myself off the boat and into the crisp, clear water. Almost as soon as we were down there, my diver went immediately steaming off towards the pod of dolphins with his handheld motor whirring away. I was flying along behind him having the time of my life. As we got closer to the dolphins they started to notice us. They quickly began to engage and interact with us, nosing about us with their shiny grey faces and curious eyes. It was all very thrilling and exciting. Although I did feel like a bit of a nit hanging on to this guy's belt while he did all the work. At one point a dolphin cut right in front of us and came really close. As I looked in awe at the creature, the dolphin responded by shooting a large cloudy deposit straight out of its rear. Oblivious to the events unfolding behind him, my electric diver friend proceeded to drag me face first into the resulting fish soup. This the only time I can ever say I was truly touched by a dolphin. Marine mammals like dolphins may be the stuff of many a motivational meme, but I like to remember the time a dolphin shat in my face to remind myself they are also real living creatures.

Their captivating nature hasn't stopped us telling mystical and spiritual stories about them, though. There are many myths and legends about our interactions with both dolphins and their larger cetacean cousins whales. In New Zealand's Māori culture water guardians and spirits, known as *taniwha*, were said to have taken the form of whales to help people navigate tricky passages by canoe across the Pacific. There are legends of whale messengers showing travelling tribes where to settle or whales carrying people on their backs across the water. The Māori tribal ancestor Paikea is said to have travelled from the Pacific Islands to New Zealand on the back of a whale. The legend inspired the film *Whale Rider* in which a young girl, also called Paikea, is trying to find her own way in a world where boys have all the fun. She eventually ends up having more fun than anyone as she rushes through the water on a whale's back.

Whales are so clever and mysterious it's perhaps not surprising they've acquired a reputation as kindly spiritual animals that want to help us. But they can also be quite scary. In Norse mythology a terrifying sea creature called the *hafgufa* was said to emit a 'perfume' to attract fish into its mouth. People now think it may have been inspired by the way real whales feed, with their huge mouths wide open. Whale-like creatures made their way into Greek mythology too. There was the *aspidochelone*, a vast sea monster known for its habit of tricking sailors into believing it was an island. The 'devil whale' also pops up in ancient myths as being so enormous it can swallow entire ships. These giant sea creatures may have struck fear into our ancestors, but whales are more similar to us than we might think. They're thought to be among the most intelligent animals on Earth. Whales are social creatures who love to play. They look after the young of other whales. They teach and learn new skills and they are sophisticated communicators. The main difference between us and them, apart from the obvious one of size, is that, rather than speech, writing and emojis, they tend to chat to their friends with their whistles, pulses and ghostly ocean songs. Whales are also known to cooperate with one another and occasionally with humans. There are records of whales and humans going out to capture orcas together in Australia. They have even been known to save humans. The marine biologist Nan Hauser described an encounter she had with a large whale in the waters around the Cook Islands. When she thought she was under threat from a possible tiger shark attack, a helpful humpback lifted her to safety. I can't say I've ever had such a dramatic encounter with a whale, but whenever I've been lucky enough to see them in the wild, I always wonder what they must be thinking. What lies behind those intelligent eyes and haunting long-distance calls? What do they think as they pop up out of the water and catch sight of a gaggle of humans in cagoules pointing and snapping photos? Maybe one day we might find out. There are serious ongoing attempts to communicate with them. A recording of a humpback whale contact call was recently broadcast by a marine researcher into the sea. One whale actually replied and the pair apparently had a twenty-minute chat. I'm not sure how much of it either party actually understood, but you've got to start somewhere, I suppose.

Encountering a whale in the flesh is always a joy. But never in my wildest dreams as I looked at that book did I ever imagine that I would get to swim in western Australia with another huge marine creature, the enigmatic and mysterious whale shark. So I was delighted when a marine biologist, Brad Norman, was asking members of the public to take photos of whale sharks so he could chart their movement. Brad and his team were using the unique marks, like fingerprints, on a whale shark's gill by their pectoral fin to identify individual animals. I volunteered to take some photos for the project underwater and we filmed it. A spotter plane showed us where the whale sharks were and into the water I went. They don't encourage scuba diving with whale sharks. They're relatively easy to keep up with if you're wearing fins. The sharks also dive very slowly and subtly, so you hardly notice you're going deeper. They're very mesmeric and you can find yourself in trouble quite quickly if you're not careful. Before you know it you can find you've followed them down to dangerous depths. Some divers have been known to go so far down with them that they run out of air and perish. Much as I admire whale sharks, I'll listen to experts, so I just had a mask and snorkel on. I hung in the water for a while and paddled about a bit. Then out of the depths emerged a huge stately creature with smooth scaleless skin. It was a twenty-six-foot-long female. Her back was covered in a beautiful pattern of luminescent white spots. She looked just like the picture in the book. It wasn't a bad day at the office as we pootled along together for a while. Her massive tail was slowly swinging from left to right, propelling her forward at a gentle pace alongside me. On her back she had a large fin which was shifting from side to side, a bit like a rudder to steer her. On her side there were large fins like small aeroplane wings and underneath her belly was all white. As I swam along with her I was able to see all the musculature of the cartilage under her skin. Watching it work through her body as she swam made me think of how a horse's muscles move as they walk or run around. Her large gills flapped slowly in and out, filtering oxygen from the water. Although they have about 3,000 tiny teeth, whale sharks are totally harmless to humans. They feed more like large whales by opening up their wide mouths to take in plankton and small marine animals. At one point during our swim her eye met mine and she seemed to look right at me. You mustn't touch whale sharks because it can interfere with a protective coating on their skin. I would have loved to have reached out and stroked her – instead I settled for gently drifting along beside her, awestruck by her beauty. I could have swum with her like this for ages. But after about twenty minutes our time was up. I took my photos and said my goodbyes. Then I watched as my new friend swam slowly off into the darkness below.

They may be enormous but whale sharks are real gentle giants. It was a truly memorable day learning about these huge cattle of the sea. They can swim at depths of up to nearly 5,000 feet. Their prehistoric ancestors date back around twenty-eight million years. It's sad to think of the pressures they're now under. Their spotty pattern acts as camouflage in the water, but these days, apart from attacks on their young by other sharks, their only real predator is man. There are estimated to be less than 200,000 whale sharks left in the wild. Their population has dropped by about 50% in the past ten years. While it's thought they can live up to a hundred or more years, they're still hunted for meat and oil and are vulnerable to being struck by vessels and the pressures of the fishing industry. Although whale sharks are known to travel thousands of miles across the ocean each year, exactly where they go and when is still a mystery. So part of this project was to monitor whale shark numbers and their movement around the world's oceans as part of ongoing efforts to help conserve them. When we got back on the boat Brad checked the gill pattern of my new friend against the others he had on file. The photos revealed that my whale shark was a newcomer to this area. She had been spotted elsewhere at least three times so they had her on record. To this day, whenever she's spotted around the world I get an email telling me where she is. Whale sharks, it turns out, are very good at keeping in touch.

In spite of their fearsome reputation, even the more aggressive sharks are worshipped in many cultures. They're seen as descendants of gods, representing power, guidance and wisdom. In Hawaii there are at least nine named shark gods. The Māori great white shark deity, Mangō-Taniwha, is thought to be a protector and guide for seafarers. There are also a few modern accounts of sharks helping humans. In 2012 off the island of Kiribati, 2,500 miles south-west of Hawaii, a policeman called Toakai Teitoi and his brother-in-law Ielu were out in a wooden boat fishing when they ran out of fuel and water. They became lost at sea for weeks. Sadly Ielu died of dehydration. After facing off a storm, the fierce sun and severe dehydration alone, Toakai saw a six-foot shark which proceeded to buffet the boat, guiding him to the safety of another fishing vessel. As for whether the shark intended to save him, the jury is still out. But lucky Toakai lived to tell the tale.

Aside from the random helpful shark, it's likely if you're out swimming you'd probably still prefer to encounter something a bit more benign. I always love it when I come across sea turtles in the water. They have such a wise and friendly look about them as they glide casually past. It's like being blessed when you see one. I was once lucky enough to help release some green turtle hatchlings into the sea and I named one of them. I like to think that Geoff and his fellow hatchlings who flopped their way across that Sri Lankan beach at sunset that evening are still out there somewhere.

Another animal I have been lucky enough to snorkel with are seals off the Isles of Scilly. It's a lot colder there than the Indian Ocean but the waters are gin clear. As the female seals swam among the kelp they sniffed at me and circled around me like weird little aquatic dogs. One even fetched a stick I threw into the kelp. Seals are predators and not to be messed with, but they reminded me so much of cocker spaniels, especially from behind. It's something about their tails.

One of the most enigmatic and exotic sea creatures you might encounter has to be the giant manta ray. They're sometimes called sea devils, but to me they look more like sea angels with their enormous stately wings. Manta rays are solitary creatures, but at certain times of the year they congregate in large numbers to feed on a rich plankton soup in part of the Indian Ocean known as Hanifaru Bay. After years of wanting to swim with these beauties, I eventually got to experience my own bit of manta heaven there.

Unlike stingrays, the tail of a manta ray has no deadly barb. Instead they use their size, speed and agility to escape from their few predators, the odd large shark or orca but mainly men. Some of them can grow up to thirty feet long, about the height of a three-storey building, and twenty-three feet across. They may be huge but they are so graceful and birdlike. When I got to snorkel with these gentle giants I watched in awe as they barrel-rolled over and over doing somersaults in the water. They also have the kindliest benign eyes. It seems as if you might actually be able to connect with them across the species divide.

Of all the marine animals you might encounter in the ocean, though, our old friends the dolphins must surely win the prize for giving the impression of being the friendliest and, along with whales, the most intelligent. Unfortunately for them their smiley faces may be what has made them so popular in marine parks. They always seem to look happy even while they might be having the most awful time in captivity. Like their larger cousins the orcas, dolphins can be aggressive, especially if they're defending their young, so it's best to leave them be if you see them in the water. But it's always a joy to encounter them from a respectful distance in their natural habitat. Even if you don't have an inspirational poster of a dolphin on your wall, I defy anyone not to be moved by seeing a pod of these sleek and shining creatures jumping about and racing with boats.

Dolphins have long been seen as our friends and helpers. The ancient Greek musician and poet Arion was said to have been rescued by a dolphin after being thrown into the sea by a bunch of robber sailors. The Greek god Poseidon is often shown surrounded by dolphins. He even has a kind of dolphin sidekick, Delphinus, who does important things for him like chasing down maidens. The goddess of love Aphrodite often has playful and affectionate dolphins at her feet. Like whales, dolphins have also long been viewed as guides and messengers for seafarers. Some of these stories may even have some truth to them.

In the mid-1700s a Māori woman named Hinepoupou was abandoned by her husband off the south-west coast of New Zealand. She set out to swim to her father's island across the treacherous Cook Strait, the Te Moana-o-Raukawa. Dividing the North and South Islands of New Zealand, it's one of the most dangerous seas in the world. Once she was in the choppy, unpredictable waters, Hinepoupou found herself in the company of a very helpful dolphin. The creature, thought to be a manifestation of a local deity, guided her safe passage across the almost fifty-mile stretch. Hinepoupou made the crossing safely in three days and completed New Zealand's earliest-known open-water swim.

Many years later another helpful dolphin found near the Cook Strait became a huge celebrity. In 1888 a Risso's dolphin was seen apparently escorting a ship from New Zealand's capital Wellington through a treacherous maze of rocky inlets called the Pelorus Sound. The animal became a regular sight swimming alongside and in front of ships, seemingly guiding them through this dangerous passage. Risso's dolphins are members of the dolphin family but they're closely related to pygmy killer whales and pilot whales. They tend to be lighter in colour than bottlenose dolphins and with a more robust body and a blunt, smiley face. This Risso's dolphin, nicknamed Pelorus Jack, was often seen surfing in the bow waves of the biggest and fastest ships. It's not certain whether Jack was actually helping the ships or just messing about. Either way, news of this remarkably useful dolphin spread around the world. Jack's photograph appeared on the cover of the *Illustrated London News*. American author Mark Twain made the journey to New Zealand to confirm that Jack really existed. There's even some grainy black-and-white film of Jack having what looks like a merry old time swimming along in the bow waves of a passenger ship. There are vivid descriptions of Jack's ghostly finned silhouette in the water at night, glowing green from the phosphorescent plankton. In 1904 a passenger aboard a ship called the *SS Penguin* tried to shoot Pelorus Jack. The gunman was disarmed and the dolphin survived. The *SS Penguin* later sank so maybe Jack put a curse on it. In any event, he was eventually seen as so valuable to safe shipping that the New Zealand government created a law specifically to protect Risso's dolphins. You could be fined for catching or killing one. It was the first time a marine animal was protected by law in New Zealand. The last-known sighting of Jack was in the spring of 1912, twenty-four years after he first appeared. There are various rumours about how Jack died. One man confessed on his deathbed to killing him. Some said Jack was harpooned by Norwegian whalers. Another person claimed to have seen his carcass washed up on the shore. Pelorus Jack may, in the end, have just died of old age and drifted off to sea. His memory lives on in the songs which were written about him. There was even a chocolate bar named in his honour. His biggest legacy was the many lives he probably saved by guiding those ships, even if, as is probably the case, he was just mucking about.

Saved by the Pod

The remarkable wildlife encounters in the waters around New Zealand are what, nearly a century after Pelorus Jack disappeared, led Rob Howe to up sticks from England and move here. But Rob experienced something else extraordinary in these waters which, if we didn't know it really happened, might seem more like the stuff of movie or legend.

The Howes, Rob, Sue and their four kids, chose to settle in a little coastal community near New Zealand's northernmost city Whangārei. In many ways this place is a subtropical paradise. It's surrounded by crystal-clear waters and beaches, lush forests, vast volcanic cliffs and tumbling waterfalls. The name 'Whangārei' is thought to come from the Māori word 'whanga', meaning harbour, and 'rei', which means to ambush. It was likely named after the local sentries who used to keep watch from the rocks over the bay. Whangārei also means a gathering place and might also refer to the local chiefs who came here to meet or to the enormous pods of whales known to gather here in the summer to feed.

It might look like paradise, but the waters in this part of

the world can also be treacherous. This didn't put Rob and his family off, though. As they got more into the beachside life, Rob got a job with the local lifesaving club. He was the one you called if a surfer or swimmer got into trouble in the water. With all the rip tides and unpredictable currents, Rob has lost count of how many tragic body recoveries he's overseen over the years. There are also success stories, though. He was once called to the aid of a surfer who was trapped by big rip currents and heading towards dangerous rocks. Rob and a colleague managed to get him into the boat just in time. But no sooner was this guy safely returned to shore, then they immediately had to do a U-turn to rescue someone else. Seeing someone right on the edge of life, looking up at you with wide eyes and about to go under, is for Rob a heart-stopping moment, especially when he knows they are only a matter of seconds away from drowning.

The waters may be dangerous here, but the marine wildlife can be truly spectacular. This is, after all, what keeps people coming back again and again. Rob remembers one time when, swimming a few hundred feet offshore, he caught sight of a dark shadow, a black dorsal fin. Out of the blue a huge spray of water shot into the air. Then a pair of creatures rose up. It was a female Bryde's whale, about forty feet long, with her calf, a perfect miniature of its mother. Bryde's whales, like humpbacks, feed by filtering water through their massive mouths and they're not aggressive to us. They're critically endangered and to see one this close to shore with her calf is a rarity and a privilege. A few minutes later, the black dorsal fin appeared again. Rob knew it was a killer whale, an orca, clearly stalking the young calf. Eventually the orca managed to separate the calf from its mother despite her attempts to save it, and the orca pulled the calf under the water. It can be hard to witness such visceral scenes play out in real life, but orcas hunt to survive too, and that's the truth of nature in the oceans – red in tooth and fin; the big fish generally eat the little fish.

This isn't the only hair-raising encounter Rob has experienced in these waters. Along with whales and orcas, you also get quite a few sharks along this coastline. One of the most feared is the great white. They're so infamous it can be hard to tell fact from sensationalized fiction. The Spielberg film *Jaws*, though a lot of fun, did little for the great white's reputation as wild, aggressive serial killers who are out to murder us at any opportunity. They are, of course, formidable hunters and will feed on dolphins, seals, turtles, large fish and even scavenge on whale carcasses. Apparently they don't like the taste of humans all that much. The chances of being attacked by a great white are low, which is to say relative to other dangers in life like crossing the road. They're still responsible by some margin for the largest number of unprovoked shark attacks on humans, though. So it's not without reason that lifeguards take it seriously when these animals come close to shore. Great white sharks are usually seen in the New Zealand summer between October and the end of January. That's when Rob and the other lifeguards gear up for action, warning swimmers and surfers if a shark is sighted. One way Rob can tell if there's a great white around is via intel from local fishermen. When the fishermen see huge semi-circlular bites out of their bait they know a shark is in the area.

The possibility of encountering sharks doesn't stop people swimming here, though. That's partly because of those other friendlier animals you might encounter if you're lucky. Dolphins. Sometimes the dolphins here come very close to shore. They can be seen riding the waves alongside the human surfers. You're not allowed to chase or pursue them – you have to let them come to you – but those who know the dolphins' natural habits can sense where to best position themselves in the surf to enjoy hanging out with them safely and respectfully. Rob is certainly no stranger to this kind of dolphin encounter. But even he could never have anticipated what they were really capable of.

In the summer of 2004 Rob, his daughter Niccy and two of her friends decided to go for a long swim along the coast-line. Kitted out in their fins, they got their heads down and, with their fins pushing behind them, began to make their way through the crystal-clear water. As they got into their stride they were soon a couple of hundred feet from the beach, heading south parallel to the coast. Some way along they saw a dark-coloured fin a few feet away sticking out of the water. Because it was face on, it was difficult to say what this fin belonged to. Side on, shark and dolphin fins are very different, but straight on it's almost impossible to tell whether it's friend or foe. Rob and the girls took a collective breath. They didn't panic but they stopped and hung back for a while, treading water and trying to work out what the animal was. After a tense few moments the creature's curved back appeared. It was a dolphin. Then this one dolphin turned out to be several dolphins. They had come across a whole pod playing together. This was really exciting. They had swum with large groups of dolphins before but it was always special.

All of a sudden the animals' behaviour started to change. They went from frolicking about to gathering together in a circle. They began to swim in tight loops round Rob and the girls, forcing them closer and closer. This was not something Rob had ever seen before, even after years of swimming in these waters. The circles got tighter, surrounding the group in a whirl of white froth. Rob, who was ultimately responsible for taking care of the girls, began to get very worried. He wasn't exactly panicking – the dolphins didn't seem threatening towards them – but he knew this was unusual and he was trying to work out what the hell was going on. Anxious curiosity soon turned to fright. The dolphins' behaviour had changed yet again. They were now hitting the water with their tails, splashing and slapping more and more urgently right in front of their faces. It was a constant frantic bombardment, with the dolphins bringing the group together tighter and tighter into a huddle, balling them up from below and all around. All the while Rob and the girls were drifting south with the current with absolutely no control over where they went; they were completely at the mercy of this circle of frantic dolphins.

By now the girls were panicking. Their tranquil swim had turned into a terrifying and confusing nightmare. Rob wondered whether the dolphins had young somewhere who they were trying to protect. Had they unwittingly done something to hurt or offend these animals in some way? Or had someone else hurt a dolphin and now they were taking their revenge? All these thoughts and questions ran through Rob's mind, but he also had another thought. What if there was something else in the water that these dolphins knew to be a threat? The circling continued. The dolphins were now no more than two feet away from them. There was a constant barrage of water and flipping tails all around and under them. From the beach people could see the action, but they just thought it was the lifeguard having a bit of fun as he often did with the dolphins.

Eventually Rob decided he had to do something. He lay on his back and gave a hard kick with his fins. After a few more sharp kicks he managed to break away from the group. He was on his back, still kicking really hard, and he managed to move a good distance from the circle to see what was happening. Then one of the bigger dolphins broke away from the group. It breached the water, slapping back down right in front of him. Rob turned in the water and looked down. There below, just a few feet away, was the unmistakable shape of a great white shark. Almost like a primal reflex, Rob brought his legs up and curled up into a ball. The shark, now only about five feet beneath him, arced round without breaking the surface, heading in the direction of Niccy and her friends. Rob didn't know whether the shark was moving beyond her towards a known local escape route in the rocks everyone called Shark Alley, in order to make its own getaway, or whether it was moving with intent towards his daughter.

For the next twenty seconds Rob was paralysed, watching the shark move closer and closer to the girls. Time seemed to slow down. He imagined the horrific scene which might be about to unfold in front of him but he had no idea how to stop it. Just at that moment a guy with a rescue boat appeared in the water nearby. The dolphins were still swirling around them and he had jumped in because he thought they were playing. As he surfaced, the guy went up to Rob and told him he could see a shark. He then got straight back in the boat while Rob managed to swim over to the girls. Rob was uncertain where the shark was or what its intentions were. Then all of a sudden the dolphins went quiet. They stopped splashing and began swimming normally again, this way and that, jumping playfully in the water. And, just as quickly as they had appeared, they disappeared. All around was totally calm and tranquil as if nothing had ever happened. The whole episode had lasted no more than fifteen minutes but it had felt like hours.

The girls clambered into the rescue boat exhausted and

confused. When they got back to the beach, the guy told Rob he knew he had seen a shark because its tail fin was straight-up, not horizontal like the tail fin of a dolphin. Rob then knew for sure that he had not imagined things; it had indeed been a great white shark. The girls still knew nothing about how close they had been to a very gruesome scene.

Once back at the surf club, they all got dry and changed, then Rob and Niccy made their way home. Rob told his wife that something really weird had just happened with the dolphins. He didn't yet mention the shark to anyone. First he wanted to make a few enquiries. He went to his computer and found the names of some marine experts who might be able to help him understand what had happened. He sent a few emails, telling his story, and then got on with other things.

The next day Rob wanted to make sure the girls got back into the water. It might seem a little foolhardy, but I suppose it's rather like when you get straight back on a bike or a horse after a fall; he didn't want them to become afraid of the water. So they got back to their normal swimming around the beach and had no more terrifying encounters. It wasn't until that afternoon that Rob finally told Niccy what he had seen in the water. She was shocked, of course. But like her dad she was undeterred and keen to continue surfing and swimming as she always had done. Not long after that Rob got an email from a scientist in Australia. The researcher explained that this kind of balling up and tail slapping is how dolphins defend their pods against large sharks and killer whales. So when the dolphins suddenly went ballistic in the water, it was very likely that they had identified the humans as being at risk from the shark and they were trying to defend them. Other emails came through with more theories along the same lines, that the dolphins were instinctively protecting them, possibly thinking they were part of the pod or just out of pure altruism.

Soon the tale of dolphins saving humans from a shark attack went global. TV cameras appeared and there was even a documentary where they re-enacted the scene with actors in the water. After they had finished shooting, one of the camera crew told Rob that one question had been bugging him. He said, 'You were in the water for nearly fifteen minutes and you didn't call for help? Why not?' Rob replied that it was because he had been so completely engrossed in what was going on around him that he could do nothing but focus on that. The guy behind the camera said that after seeing the re-enactment, he too now understood how dramatic and mesmerizing it must have been. Signalling for help didn't even come into it. Since this encounter, Rob says his perception of dolphins has changed. Before he had always loved being with them in the water, but there was always a kind of distance between them. Now he says the connection he feels to them has grown somehow. He compares it to how you might feel about someone who has had your back in the army; you have an unbreakable bond with that person which lasts a lifetime. Only this time it's not a person; it's a group of anonymous dolphins. Rob doesn't know whether he has ever come across any of the animals again. They can live for up to forty years. So, who knows, some of them might still be out there. Now, whenever he sees the dolphins playing in the water around Whangārei, he can't help but say a quiet thank you for saving their lives just in case.

Melody and Jock

Along with these stories of dolphins saving people from shark attacks, and guiding ships or swimmers to safety, there's another story of a lone dolphin who saved a life in a very different way.

Melody Horrill had learned from a young age to build a protective shell around her. She grew up in Cornwall with her parents, older sisters and brother. Ever since she could remember, their home had been a place where the kids held their collective breaths for the next outburst. Life was a regular warzone. Her parents frequently fought, sometimes physically, and at times the children bore the brunt of the violence. One day Melody's parents announced that her father had a new job and they were moving to the other side of the world, to Australia. Melody's sisters decided not to go. They were old enough to look after themselves and Melody didn't blame them. She would have stayed too if she could have, just for the peace. But Melody was only a child and she and her brother had no choice but to join their parents on this long journey to a strange new place.

Melody hoped moving to a new country would improve things at home. To her dismay things only got worse. The police became a regular presence at their house. Melody was bullied at her new school for having an accent. She felt on the edge of it all, like an outsider, clumsy and unable to make new friends.

For the next couple of years Melody found companionship mainly through animals. They had a pet dog and cat. Every other weekend she also took riding lessons at a nearby stables. She had got a job at a local amusement arcade spinning candyfloss to pay for them. One day she saw a notice up on the wall. Someone was looking for a home for an eleven-year-old bay gelding. He needed retraining, the notice said, but he had a good temperament. She just had to have that horse. Her mother agreed to help her out and Melody would cover most of the costs with her wages from the arcade. When she first saw Eddie standing in the paddock he was thin and looked a little bit sad. But he also had the most kindly gentle brown eyes with the longest lashes. Eddie looked like he was in serious need of some love and Melody was ready to give it to him. From then on, whenever she wasn't at work or school, Melody was with Eddie. She fed him up and started training him. She helped him get back his gloss and vigour. Melody chatted to him constantly. They went for long gallops on a patch of empty council land, around the paddock, and up and down the hills with the wind in their faces. During the summer holidays she rode him bareback on the beach. It all felt so free. Eddie would walk into the sea and afterwards he would roll in the sand like a huge dog with a look of utter joy. It seemed to Melody like she had found her paradise and her solace. Back at the stables Eddie loved a treat of carrot or a sugar cube. If she could have stayed there all night she would have done, curled up in the hay at his side, rather than going home. This gentle, non-judgemental creature became her comfort and her animal therapy through her most turbulent teenage years.

But just before she turned sixteen Melody's life took a dramatic turn. Eighteen months after she had got him, Melody was told by her parents that they had to sell Eddie. Although Melody was paying for him, they had decided they needed the money. They wanted $400 and had put an advert in the paper. Melody was distraught. It felt like part of her heart was about to be ripped out. An offer came in and when the day came Melody couldn't believe it. She said goodbye and in a matter of minutes her beloved horse was taken away. All she had in return was a cheque for $400. When she got home she gave the money to her mother. She had never felt so lonely in her life.

Not long after her sixteenth birthday things at home got worse. Her father was becoming more violent and angry, lashing out at her mother and her sisters and at her. They decided the only thing to do was to leave home or her mother feared someone might get killed. So they secretly found a small flat a few suburbs away. Before they could leave her father got angry and another vicious fight kicked off. The police were called and eventually Melody and her mother managed to get away. Once they had moved out her father tried to track them down. After a while her mother took out a restraining order against him, but it wasn't enough. He eventually found them and attacked her mother badly with a corkscrew, injuring her face. Melody testified in court and her father was sentenced to eighteen months in prison.

Melody worked hard to get her life back on track. She worked hard at her schooling and finished year twelve. A few months before her final exams, though, her father was released from prison. Not long after that Melody heard that he had taken his own life. At nineteen years old she was thrown into more emotional confusion and turmoil. She was full of self-doubt and guilt. She lacked confidence. She felt love and social connections to be fraught with danger. Melody worked her way through all this enough to get her life back on track and begin studying for a degree in communications in Adelaide, majoring in psychology. One of her tutors was a researcher called Dr Mike Bossley who taught psychology and environmental science. During their first lecture he told the class about a group of wild dolphins he was studying. Melody was intrigued. These dolphins had made their home in the large tidal estuary known as Port Adelaide, which flows through the outskirts of the city. In 1987 a photograph appeared in a local newspaper of a horse apparently swimming with a bottlenose dolphin in the area. The photo had attracted Dr Bossley's attention and ever since then he had been observing the behaviour of the dolphins in the area. The dolphin in the photo became known as Billie. It was thought she was an orphan, although it's not clear what happened to her mother. She became renowned for tail walking, something people thought she may have learned at some point in captivity. Remarkably other dolphins in the area seemed to have learned the behaviour from her. Mike Bossley was researching not only Billie but a whole group of dolphins who had made these waters their home. Melody had no experience with dolphins but she immediately asked Mike if he needed any help. He already had a few research assistants who were students but he told her they could always use another willing volunteer.

The first time Melody went on the water she had no idea what to expect. Port Adelaide River is in a fairly heavily industrialized area. It's set against a backdrop of factories and large infrastructure. As they motored along in an inflatable RIB they began to wind their way off the main river and through the backwaters. In amongst the industrial landscape were the remnants of mangroves tens of thousands of years old. Pockets of this rare rich habitat lined the water's edge alongside the factories and shipyards. Melody suddenly noticed a dorsal fin circling a nearby boat which was moored in the middle of a channel. She had to do a double take because it was such an odd-looking dorsal fin. Melody pointed it out to

Mike. He told her that they often saw this particular dolphin around here. Mike had first seen him a couple of years earlier and they had named him Jock. Melody could immediately see how badly mangled Jock's fin was. It was almost as if it had been randomly fashioned from playdough into an awkward shape. She couldn't believe he was really a dolphin, it was so disfigured. She also couldn't believe that he was here by himself. She knew from Mike's lectures that dolphins were social creatures. They generally like living in pods. Jock continued to circle the boat over and over again. Something out of nowhere struck deep inside Melody's heart. She felt she saw in him a deep sadness and solitude which she connected to completely. As he intently circled the boat she felt that he was disconnected from the world and everything around him, alone and adrift, just like her. Melody felt an unexpected surge of compassion for this solitary wild animal. She wondered whether Jock had been ostracized by other dolphins. Had he, because of some kind of trauma, chosen to remain alone? Or maybe he was an orphan who had lost his mum at a young age. Now he didn't know how to socialize because he'd never been taught. Perhaps his mother had died where he was swimming and he was waiting, searching for her. All these thoughts went through Melody's mind. Of course she had no way of knowing whether any of them were true.

Mike told her that they knew that at some point Jock had become entangled in fishing line and nets. He'd been saved a couple of times by local rangers. He'd also been injured with a spear and had that removed. So he had truly been through the wars at the hands of humans. They thought he was an adolescent because he was quite small for a bottlenose dolphin. Melody wanted to reach out and reassure him that he wasn't alone, to tell him that she understood, even though they were completely different species. Then Mike told her that he and the other research assistants had already started interacting with Jock. They were keeping it very much on the down-low – they were concerned about Jock being hurt again by people and didn't want to draw attention to him – but the tight-knit group knew Jock was very friendly. Mike demonstrated this by throwing a boat paddle into the water. Melody watched in amazement as Jock immediately stopped circling and swam towards it. He swam under the paddle and flicked it high into the air with his tail flukes. Jock started having more fun with the paddle, flicking it up over and over again as if he was playing a game. Once he'd had enough of that, he tossed it back in their direction. Game over. Mike picked it up off the water and Jock swam off while they went looking for other dolphins. As they pootled along in the boat, Mike continued to tell Melody all about what their work involved. He showed her how to drive the boat and how they took photos so they could identify the differ-ent dolphins and observe their behaviour. But all Melody could really think about was Jock. When the day ended she got home exhausted and exhilarated. She couldn't get the image of that lone dolphin out of her mind. She had never experienced this kind of instant, almost spiritual connection with another creature. She couldn't wait to get back out on the water again.

The next time they were back in the mangrove-lined back-waters of Port Adelaide, it wasn't long before they came across Jock again. This time he began to follow their boat. Mike asked Melody if she wanted to jump in and have a swim with him. Of course she did. So she sat on the edge of the boat, held her breath and jumped in. Don't picture a clear tropical paradise here. It's not the cleanest of waters. Run-off from the local industry regularly seeps into the water. Parts of Port Adelaide River are very warm. But not naturally. They're heated by a nearby power station. As the turbines suck in the water it helps to cool them. They spit the water back out and it has taken on the heat from the power plant, making it bathwater warm. As Melody became accustomed to the warm murky water, all of a sudden she saw the outline of a dolphin. Through the dull sounds of the water bubbling around her, she began to detect a light whistling and clicking sound, then she felt an otherworldly sensation in her body. She realized it was Jock. He was sending sonar signals at her and she could actually feel the echolocation vibrating through her. It seemed like Jock was checking her out, using all his senses to figure out the essence of her, working out whether she was friend or foe. Jock moved through the hazy water, getting closer, and then his face came into view. They made eye contact and Melody saw a look of such deep intelligence in his face. She also saw curiosity and maybe just a hint of mischievousness. She just couldn't believe she was in the water with a completely wild dolphin and that he was there willingly. There was no free fish on offer. He wasn't trained. Their interaction was wholly on his terms. Jock became more curious and more trusting. He was soon close enough for Melody to run her hands along his side. She couldn't believe how smooth his skin was, like cool silk. He swam underneath and around her. As Melody was hanging there in the water she steadied herself with one hand underwater on the ladder of the boat. She was moving her other hand back and forth to stay afloat. Jock swam away with a flick of his tail. Then he came back through the murk and swam right up to her, nuzzling his nose into her hand. The skin on his face was rough as if it had been damaged or scarred. Dolphins' snouts are not meant to be rough like sandpaper. Mike had told her Jock had to find food alone, scraping around on the bottom of the river looking for shellfish, which scratched his nose. He had also snagged it on fishing lines and hooks, leaving various scars. In spite of the damage caused to him by humans, Jock did not pull away from Melody. She had no choice but to trust him back. This feeling of mutual trust was not something she could ever remember having felt before, except maybe with Eddie the horse. All her life she had been forced to put barriers up and build a fortress around herself. Now a totally different species, who lived in a wild watery world so different from her own, had begun to crack at the shell around her heart. Melody felt like she might have a lot to learn from this dolphin. With so many emotional and profound feelings flooding in, her eyes filled with tears. When it was all over and they were back on the boat, Melody couldn't wait to get back in the water.

These days it's not considered a good idea to hang out too much with wild dolphins or to touch them. It can make them vulnerable if they learn to trust humans, because not all humans have good intentions. For this reason, even back then, Melody's tutor Mike was very strict about keeping Jock's friendliness a secret. As soon as Jock popped up out of the water, he seemed to welcome them with a raspberry and some watery bubbles. He would often tag along behind the boat until they were in among the back channels. Then he would either wait around for them or sometimes even tap on the ladder of the boat to get them to go in the water and play.

Before long Melody was back in the water. Because it was so murky she would feel Jock's presence before she saw him. She would hear his clicks and his raspberries, or feel the echolocation, then he would rock up into view. They began to play games together. One of his favourites was a form of hide-and-seek. Jock would swim off somewhere out of view and Melody would swim around looking for him in the hazy silence. Then all of a sudden he would pop up in the most unexpected of places and scare the hell out of her. She could swear she saw a grin on his face and that he knew exactly what was going on. He also loved that boat paddle. Melody and another research assistant called Steve would jump into the water and have the paddle between them. Jock would then try to work ways of getting it off them. It would often involve Jock jumping up to Steve and landing on him. Another game involved Jock pushing Melody on to her chest with his snout and then propelling her backwards through the water at breakneck speed. There would be the most enormous pressure wave behind her. It was almost like she became a sort of a giant human toy that Jock loved to play with. During these games she felt a sense of pure fun and joy that she had never experienced before. She had no choice; if she was going to play with Jock in this way, she had to let herself go and trust him completely.

As they motored away from Jock at the end of the day, sometimes he would follow them and leap up high in the frothy wake of the boat. When they upgraded from a rubber ducky RIB boat to a bigger boat with a half-cabin, Jock loved to leap higher than ever behind the more powerful boat. Mike would push down the throttle and Jock would jump up out of the bubbly water and then bellyflop back down. Sometimes he got so close to them that Melody would sit there thinking, *Oh my God, is he gonna land in the bloody boat?* Thankfully that never happened. Then when they got to a certain point, just before the river widened out, Jock would always break off.

He'd turn round and swim back to his own territory, his safe place. Although, as it turned out, it wasn't always that safe. Once they rocked up to find Jock had a massive fishing line wrapped round his dorsal fin. His dorsal fin was so badly mangled that fishing line would tend to get caught on it. Mike said they had to try to get it off, so they jumped into the water, but all they had on the boat was a rusty old pair of scissors. As they approached Jock he uncharacteristically became quite suspicious and didn't get very close. Steve ended up having to corral him into an area, while Melody wrapped her arms round him. Then, after a lot of wrangling and cutting, they managed to remove the fishing line, which was full of hooks.

During their more peaceful moments together, Jock would just hang around in the water with his snout in Melody's hand barely moving, bobbing along in the slight current, both of them completely relaxed. One of her favourite memories was when Jock turned over on to his back with his pectoral fins up in the air, showing her his tummy. Like when any animal rolls over to expose its tummy, you feel the irresistible urge to tickle it. So Melody did just that, she tickled Jock under his pectoral fins. His eyes were closed as she ran her hand over his tummy. She could see the blood in his blue veins pumping through his almost pinkish skin. It was so beautiful to see this living, breathing delicate creature trust her so completely. When they got back on the boat, Melody swore to God that if she could have grown a tail herself, she would have stayed there with him forever.

After all Melody had been through – the years of domestic violence, her dad going to jail and then taking his own life – she had had a lot of therapy. But now Jock, along with the other river dolphins, had become her natural therapy. He was teaching her the importance of living in the moment, not

Sir Briggs the war horse with Captain Morgan during the Charge of the Light Brigade.

The Panel of the Four Horses in Chauvet Cave, France, ca. 30,000 B.C.E., shows our human fascination with these animals goes back many thousands of years.

PALS!

A First World War postcard. Horses, like people, were called upon to do their bit, and strong bonds were forged between soldiers and the horses they served with.

My first horse, Chester, was a real gentleman and a great schoolmaster.

Maria Dickin, animal welfare pioneer and founder of the People's Dispensary for Sick Animals. The Dickin Medal (inset), awarded for animal gallantry in military service, was named for her.

Second World War pigeon Cher Ami, awarded the prestigious French Croix de Guerre for saving nearly two hundred lives.

Sergeant Stubby – the first dog to be given a rank in the US Army – in his regimental chamois coat gifted from the townspeople of Château-Thierry.

Hero rat Magawa receiving the PDSA gold medal for sniffing out landmines in Cambodia.

The UK's first guide dogs completed their training in Wallasey, Wirral, in 1931.

Jaina Mistry with Laura and her new guide dog, Kath.

Guide dog Kath. Jaina always dressed up Laura on her birthdays too.

Trainee vet Jade Heaney and Jules, her Medical Detection Dog.

Melody Horrill
with Jock the dolphin.

Melody and Jock hanging out in the Adelaide Port River.

Me and my whale shark. She still writes.

Canine movie star
Rin Tin Tin.

Strongheart, the first great
Hollywood film dog.

My mate Dodger.

A *Doc Martin* fan
knitted this for Dodger.

Michael Hingson and guide dog Roselle
at the World Trade Center before the 9/11
terrorist attacks.

John Gilkey and disaster
search-and-rescue dog Bear.

A canine search-and-rescue team search Ground Zero, or 'The Pile,'
as it became known among many first responders.

John Gilkey and Bear during the 9/11 search operation.

Police dog Obi on airport duty.

Emma and police dog Prince in action.

Phil Wells and police dog Obi, who received the PDSA Order of Merit.

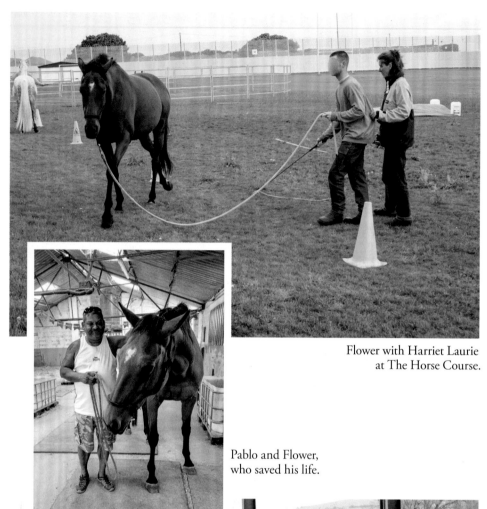

Flower with Harriet Laurie
at The Horse Course.

Pablo and Flower,
who saved his life.

Flower and a little superhero.

dwelling on the past or worrying about what was going to happen tomorrow. She realized she had stopped dwelling on all the crappy things that had happened to her. Her past didn't need to define who she was. Instead of focusing on the bitterness and sadness of her old life, she was focusing on now. She began to think more about her place within the natural world too, how we're all part of something bigger than ourselves. She began to embrace simply being alive and the natural connectedness of all things. Jock had also opened up her ability to trust again and to simply enjoy being in the company of another being, with no demands or expectations. One of the biggest things she learned from Jock was the power of forgiveness. Melody had never really forgiven herself for what happened with her dad and she had never forgiven him before he took his own life. But when she saw Jock's ability to seemingly forgive and trust other humans, after everything they had done to him, it made her realize she had to forgive herself and the other people in her life in order to move on.

Sadly what she had with Jock couldn't last forever. Dolphins need to be with other dolphins. So eventually she, Mike and the others decided that Jock needed to find a pod. They started to use his love of leaping behind the boat to try to lure him out of his safety zone. Little by little he started coming out into the wider river more. Then one day they came across a pod of dolphins when Jock was nearby. At first he stayed behind the boat like a shy kid. But over a period of time he ended up interacting with them. Then one day they went to where he usually hung out and he was gone. Melody started freaking out. She was so worried about him and wondering if he was hurt or worse. They looked in all his old spots. No Jock. They finally motored out into the broader river and there he was, swimming with a pod of other dolphins. As soon as he saw them Jock came up to the boat and seemed to acknowledge them, then he turned on to his side and swam away. It was a bittersweet moment. Melody knew that he needed to be with other dolphins, but it was like losing her best friend. She was happy for him, but it was incredibly painful. They drove back to shore and opened a bottle of port. Everyone had a tear in their eye that day. This was Jock's final lesson for Melody. She had seen that he had the courage to leave his comfort zone, to face his fears and go out to the broader river. He had opened himself up to the wider world. In that moment she realized that this was exactly what she needed to do herself. That day was like closing a chapter on her own old life. She now felt ready to go out into the world and start a new life. Melody saw Jock just one more time, swimming off in the distance. This time he didn't even come up to the boat. He ignored them completely. He had found his own pod.

In a sad twist to the tale, Jock's new life was short-lived. In 1993 he was found dead in the river. It's not certain exactly what killed him but he had high levels of toxic chemicals in his body. This was extra heartbreaking for Melody, but it spurred her on even more to bring the lives of these dolphins into the public consciousness. Together she and Mike started a not-for-profit, the Australian Dolphin Research Foundation, to raise awareness of the Port River dolphins and the importance of protecting them. Melody became an environmental reporter and in 2005 the Port River became home to Australia's first metropolitan dolphin sanctuary. Sadly their numbers have dropped by about half in the past ten years from around forty to around twenty. Recently there has also been an increase in dolphin calves dying young, possibly due to pollution levels in the water. Melody remains hopeful things can be turned round. She wants this work to help people appreciate these remarkable intelligent, sensitive individuals and look at ways to protect their homes and make them safe. She also wants young people in domestic violence situations to learn from Jock's story that you don't have to be defined by your past. If you can find that thing that makes your heart sing and the passion which allows you to change things up, then you can do anything.

One of Melody's fondest memories of Jock was when she was hanging out one day with her feet resting on the riverbed. Jock had disappeared and she didn't know where he was. Suddenly, out of nowhere, she felt his rough snout under her feet. It made her jump. She couldn't see him, only see some air bubbles popping up from below. She didn't know what he was up to. Mike was in the boat watching. He didn't seem all that worried. Melody asked what was going on and he told her, 'Jock's trying to lift you up. You know the way dead things sink to the ocean floor? Well, because you're on the bottom he's trying to save you.' Melody was so overcome with gratitude out of nowhere she burst into tears. Jock had wanted to save her and in the end he really did.

Two of the best actors I ever worked with: Dodger and Paddy.

7. Dog Martin

Dodger

One of the best actors I ever worked with was amazing: he knew what was required of him at every moment, he would always hit his mark, he could perform any stunt and one of his best tricks was to cock his leg on command; I know what you're thinking but it's not Neil Morrissey. It's my old mate Dodger, who played Buddy the dog in *Doc Martin*. The thing about being a dog in *Doc Martin* is that the Doc can't stand dogs but they are drawn to him. In the early days we would worry that we couldn't have the dog in a scene if he wasn't going to do anything, but then we realized that we definitely could. Just a look between the Doc and the dog was enough to score a point.

Before Dodger we had another dog in the first-ever series; his name was Gremlin and his audition piece had been to allow me to drag him along the floor while he lay still, which he did very well, though he didn't do much else to be honest, but it was early days for us all. In one episode the Doc tried to kill him by throwing a stick over a cliff and yelling 'Fetch'. We were all very sad when Gremlin retired from acting, but like all these things it opened the door of opportunity wide and in marched Dodger with all his tricks and skills. After that we decided to create more dog-centred storylines. In the opening episode of series four, the Doc, having split up with Louisa, is desperately looking for a way to escape Portwenn.

But the one thing stopping him from getting a new job in London is his debilitating blood phobia. The mere thought of it leaves him reeling and he's taking desperate measures to try to cure himself.

In the opening scene I'm walking purposefully down the main street of Portwenn, in real life the beautiful Cornish village of Port Isaac. I'm carrying a plastic bag at arm's length. It's all part of an elaborate plan to get over the Doc's blood phobia. It doesn't appear to be working yet, though, because the bag is absolutely dripping with blood and I look as if I'm about to throw up. I walk down the road carrying the bloody bag and soon begin to attract the attention of a couple of village dogs. The first one, a black-and-white spaniel called Tori (who played the queen's dog in *Young Victoria*), catches a whiff and starts following me. Then a little short-coated terrier pops up and gets interested too. A golden Labrador joins the gang, followed by another couple of terriers of varying sizes. They all begin to trot along behind. By the time I round the corner near the harbour, I'm surrounded by this pack of excited dogs. Long-haired, short-haired, big and small, they're all barking like mad and wagging their tails. It was one of my best days at work ever.

Martin walks down the street and is joined by a bunch of dogs sounds easy when you write it down, doesn't it, but in real life, in a real village with real animals, it's a whole different bag of kidneys. It was the director who came up with the bright idea for the dogs to appear one by one gradually over this long tracking shot. To get what we wanted they all had to be positioned strategically along the route in advance. We had various dog handlers, crew members and villagers, all holding the various dogs on their leads, waiting for the opportune moment. My daughter Emily was in charge of releasing Tori the famous Victorian spaniel. One by one they would release their dog just at the right time for it to join the pack. What could possibly go wrong?

We did a number of dummy runs to get the dogs used to playing along with us, then we began to shoot for real. It went remarkably smoothly. The first dog appeared as if it was coming out of an alleyway. Another one, which looked like it was sleeping in the doorway, got up and joined the pack. More and more dogs were released. We were close to getting to the grand finale by the harbour. As I turned the corner we really thought we had it in the can. What we hadn't taken into account, though, was that in a real village there are real village cats. The cat in this instance was asleep on a roof and minding its own business. It didn't look very happy when it opened its eyes and saw us lot hove into view. One of the dogs, a Staffy called Sykes (the one from *EastEnders*), caught sight of this cat and started barking. When the animal scrambled to its feet and legged it, Sykes shot off after it. All the other dogs were now wondering where the hell Sykes had gone in such a hurry and, instead of continuing to follow me, they unanimously decided to find out. The whole pack set off in hot pursuit of Sykes, who was now in hot pursuit of the cat. Meanwhile I was left standing on my own with a plastic bag of dripping blood and the director was left with an unfinished scene.

After much shouting, whistling, frantic chasing and rather a large quantity of sausages, the dogs were eventually all rounded up. Once everyone had calmed down, the trainers and villagers gathered the dogs back into position to shoot the scene once again. The camera rolled. I held aloft the bloody bag and began my descent again to the harbour. We got through the first section with no problem. All the dogs came out beautifully. When we got to that final corner Sykes suddenly stopped and barked. You could see him looking around wondering, *Is it here? Is it here?* He was looking for the bloody cat. All the other dogs began their own search and the whole thing collapsed once more into chaos. What the dogs didn't realize was that the cat had made its getaway the first time and was now safely ensconced in someone's house. But they really wanted to play. It took us another few goes before they finally realized they were looking for a long since departed cat. The dogs eventually turned their attention back to me and we managed to finish the scene. But it wasn't quite over yet. In the next bit they're supposed to follow me, or rather the now extremely pissed-off Doc, to the surgery. When we got there I then had to squeeze my way through the door and we ended the scene with a comedy kick at the dogs before I slammed the door shut in their faces. I must add, though, that no dogs were really kicked in the making of this scene. Once inside, I tip the contents of the bag into a bowl where it's revealed to be two enormous slippery livers. Repeated efforts to dissect them with a scalpel bring the blood-phobic Doc close to breaking point. At this point Auntie Joan, who is played by Stephanie Cole, comes in bearing two home-made pies and . . . you've guessed it, another dog. It turns out all those earlier dogs have been a bit of a red herring. This is Buddy, the Doc's real new canine nemesis. The cutest, most floppy-eared nemesis you've ever seen.

In the story, Buddy is a stray mongrel terrier who Joan has acquired from her recently deceased neighbour. When I first see Buddy I ask her blankly, 'What's that?' Stephanie Cole replies with an impeccably straight face, 'It's a dog.'

Meanwhile, Buddy wastes no time in locating the bowl of offal. He comes trotting proudly in with a mouthful of liver. I catch Buddy again later in the episode hanging around outside the pharmacy. He's apparently run all the way from Auntie Joan's farm to look for me. I try to shoo him away but he just carries on following me, wagging his tail and staring up at me the whole way home, as though he's found his absolute new best friend. And so begins the odd-couple relationship between the Doc and Buddy which would run for another six series and in all seriousness remains one of the happiest working relationships of my professional life.

As soon as we began shooting together I knew Dodger was a natural in front of the camera. From the minute he trotted on set to the moment the director shouted cut, he seemed to relish every second. He also loved all the fuss I gave him before and after we were filming. Our scenes together may only have been a couple of minutes long in the final cut but to get the shots you need takes a lot of time and skill and the help of someone who really knows what they're doing. The dog trainer behind all of the canine mayhem on *Doc Martin* was a woman named Sonia Turner who works for a company called Stunt Dogs. As well as being one of their trained screen dogs, Dodger was also one of Sonia's family pets. But he hadn't had the easiest start in life.

The little terrier pup was found wandering alone on the streets in Bradford, filthy and hungry. He was taken to an animal shelter and that's when Sonia first saw him: just a little scrap, only around nine or ten months old. Sonia couldn't resist adopting the scruffy terrier, who seemed to already be permanently smiling in spite of his rough start.

When Sonia got Dodger home his thick fur was still coated with dirt from the streets. She had to give him several baths just to get him clean. He was a mostly white mixed Jack Russell terrier, with brown ears and a black splodge on his back. His rough coat made him look quite scraggly and altogether very huggable. Sonia brought Dodger back to health and he grew into a happy little dog. She also saw he had a real talent for learning. From the vast array of rosettes on the wall at her home you can tell Sonia is no stranger to winning at dog shows. She was also by this point an accomplished film and TV dog trainer, so she decided to train Buddy in what's needed to be a dog on set. This takes a whole set of other skills in addition to the usual agility or obedience work you might do with your pet dog. For a start, no one wants to see the trainer trotting alongside the dog on camera. So handlers like Sonia have to get the dog to do what the directors and writers want while also staying completely out of shot. It takes a lot of practice and timing to be there but not be there. Obviously you can't speak over the actors to communicate with the dogs either, so very often the dogs will be working to hand signals while the handler stays at a distance. This presents its own challenges because the dog is then tempted to keep looking over at them, as if to ask, 'So what do you want me to do next?', instead of where it's supposed to be looking in the scene. Ever since working with dogs on *Doc Martin* I always notice when a dog on the TV is obviously looking at its handler off to the side. It's something with Sonia's help we always managed to avoid.

Film sets can be quite chaotic places at times, noisy, with a lot of bright lights, dangerous equipment and people. I've always been very conscious of not wanting to frighten or upset any of the dogs I work with. Dogs who work on screen need to be very calm and unflappable amid all this hustle and bustle, which Dodger definitely was. As the Doc tends to shout at Dodger quite a lot, I also wanted to find a way to not have to shout at him in real life. Even the most chilled-out dogs can be extremely sensitive to your tone of voice. They love to please us so much that if you sound cross or shouty, they think they've done something wrong and will look quite put out. Sonia gave us a funny demonstration of this once, to show just how much the way you speak to a dog matters. First in a gruff voice she said, 'Do you want a bit of sausage?' to a dog. Although she was offering the dog a treat you could tell it thought it had done something wrong. Then immediately in a really sing-song voice she said to the dog, 'I'm going to take you to the vets and have you put down today. Wouldn't that be lovely?' to which the dog immediately perked up and started wagging its tail ecstatically. It was a bit of a tease but she certainly made her point. From then on all the Doc's angry tirades at any dogs were filmed with me mouthing my lines. Then I recorded on the shouty bits afterwards. I never actually shouted at Dodger or any other dogs on the show.

There were quite a few scenes with the Doc and Dodger in which he runs up the hill towards the surgery, hanging on my metaphorical coat-tails. I then have to feign having no interest in him whatsoever, dart into the surgery and slam the door in his face. There are other scenes where I open the surgery door to see if anyone is coming up and Dodger manages to sneak in through the gap. Quite often Sonia would be inside hiding somewhere encouraging Dodger to come in with a piece of sausage, while a crew member released him for the shot. Other times they used the sausage to lure him after me so it looked like he was following me, but really he was following those sausages.

For Sonia, or any TV dog handler, sometimes the simplest-seeming requests are actually the most difficult. For example, wanting a dog on set to 'just be a normal dog'. Being normal for a dog is quite vague. It quite often involves just lying around on its back in various states of prostration, or randomly sniffing at stuff for a bit and then going back to sleep. But when you've got a trained dog on set like Dodger he's ready for action. He'll be looking at the trainer as if to say 'Now what shall I do?' He hasn't come all this way to lie about sleeping and randomly sniffing. It can be surprisingly difficult to get a dog to look normal. Unfortunately there's no direct command for 'just mooch about a bit'. Some dogs are very good at relaxing and interacting with the cast, though, which definitely helps with getting those more natural moments when they're needed. Dodger was one of those for sure. He was motivated but also quite happy to just sort of hang about in the background, not doing much in particular if that's what we needed.

Sometimes a scene might seem fairly simple on paper for the dog but it's actually pretty elaborate in practice. Even asking for a dog to do something like *come in, stop, look out of the window, see the postman, bark five times, then lie on the sofa* can take weeks of preparation before filming starts. This kind of set piece has to be broken into a series of choreographed moves which Sonia trains the dog to do in stages. She starts with the animal at home and begins at the end of the sequence with the dog on the sofa. To get that first move she has to basically pay the dog in sausages to lie down on the sofa on command. Once he's nailed that part, she tackles the next step back from the sofa, which is usually standing on a mark. This is a literal mark on the floor. Sonia then has the dog jump from the mark on to the sofa and then lie down. More sausages. Next it's another step back: bark five times. Sausages, sofa, lie down. Then another step back: look at the window. This is called 'take an eyeline', which means to have the dog look in a particular direction. So, from the mark on the floor, she would then entice the dog to look to the left say. This is done either with a bait stick, a long stick with a bit of sausage attached – it's basically all about sausages – or you can have someone strategically positioned to make a quick noise with a squeaker. When the squeaker goes, or the sausage bait comes out, the dog immediately looks to the left and then the whole thing begins again. Bark five times, get on the sofa, lie down. Working back another step, the dog begins at the doorway. The dog is enticed from the doorway to the mark with the command 'get on your mark'. Sausage. Squeak. Looks left. Barks five times. Jumps on the sofa. Lies down. Finally, to complete the scene, she takes the dog outside the door and entices it in through the doorway to the mark, squeak, sofa, etc. In this way the dog learns the entire series of actions one by one, like a dancer learning choreography. By the end it should be able to do the entire sequence in one and make it look like it's been doing it all its life. For Dodger he really did do it almost his whole life. He wasn't the first and he certainly won't be the last.

Rinty & Co.

From Lassie to Toto, Dodger came from a long line of canine screen stars going right back to the earliest days of film. Many of the very first dogs on screen in the late-Victorian era were there almost accidentally in the background, pretty much doing their own thing. There are dogs mooching about in some of the early Lumière brothers films and there's one early film in which a slightly bemused-looking dog watches on as a man very seriously exercises with a stick. I don't think that one was ever a box office hit. Among the first dogs to actually star in a moving picture was a collie named Blair. He was the family pet of one of cinema's earliest pioneers, the British filmmaker Cecil Hepworth. Known for his use of special effects, trick shots and clever editing, Hepworth often shot his silent films on location in his local area, Walton on Thames, using locals as extras. His films include such classics as *How It Feels to Be Run Over*, *Explosion of a Motor Car* and the first cinematic version of *Alice in Wonderland*, in which Hepworth appears himself as a frog. He also made full use of his family, including his pet collie. Blair's first starring role was in a 1905 short film called *Rescued by Rover*. In the film, a woman who is likely a family nanny, is seen out walking with a pram in a park. While she's flirting with some bloke, the baby is stolen from the pram by an old woman in a shawl. The nanny has no idea what's just happened and wanders off with the man, laughing. We next see her back at the family house frantically telling the mother of the child that the baby is missing. Enter Rover, aka Blair. Without hesitation the heroic dog jumps out of a window and legs it down the street to solve the crime. He fearlessly swims across a river, before appearing on a street, apparently going door to door, looking for the lost child. Rover eventually locates the child in an attic room with the old woman. He flees the house, swims back through that river and runs home to tell the father of the house, played by Hepworth himself. It's not an easy job as he tries to tell his master the news. Rover jumps up and down, pawing and licking at the man, trying everything to get him to follow. Eventually the dog gives up and opens the door himself, which prompts Hepworth's character to follow. The pair run down the street, Hepworth in a top hat and tails. They head back across the river and turn up at the attic room. The father grabs the baby and the little baby and her parents are joyfully reunited. Bravo, Rover!

This early cinematic enterprise was very much a family affair. Alongside Hepworth as director and cinematographer, Hepworth's wife, an actress and writer who called herself Mrs Hepworth, also stars in and wrote the film. The Hepworths' daughter Barbara plays the baby. Rover, who is really a kind of proto-Lassie, was so popular with audiences that the original negatives kept wearing out and the film had to be reshot twice to keep up with the demand. There was a sequel called *The Dog Outwits the Kidnapper*. This time Hepworth plays the kidnapper who steals a young girl, played by his daughter Elizabeth. He drives off with the child in his motor car and good old Rover runs off after them down the street. At one point the kidnapper goes inside his house, leaving the child behind in the car. Rover takes the opportunity to jump in the driver's seat. There then follows the most extraordinary few minutes of film in which the dog, somewhat convincingly it must be said, appears to drive the car home with Elizabeth in the passenger seat. The Hepworth family dog went on to star in a few other films including *The Dog's Devotion* (Blair saves a marriage), *The Dog Chaperone* (A man must win over the dog before the woman) and *Love Me, Love My Dog.* Quite right.

Blair may not be that well known today, but one dog's early cinematic prowess has definitely stood the test of time. In September 1918, in the Meuse Valley in eastern France, over a million members of the American Expeditionary Force were preparing to embark on one of the final major Allied offensives of the war. Their objective was to breach the Hindenburg Line, advance on Germany and force them to surrender. One of the men getting ready for battle that September was American gunnery corporal Lee Duncan of the 135th Aero Squadron. As a child Duncan had spent five years in an orphanage, before being taken back by his family to live on a remote farm with his grandparents. He now found himself thousands of miles from home at the centre of this devastating European conflict. Exactly what happened next has been subject to a lot of myth-making over the years, but it goes something like this. Sometime around 15 September Duncan was sent to check out a village which had been the site of a German encampment. Aerial bombing and shelling had hit the village, including a German military working dog kennel. When Duncan arrived, he discovered around a dozen dogs lying dead. Among the carnage he saw something moving. It was a female German shepherd lying on the floor surrounded by five wriggling puppies. The remarkable scene of new life amid the horror of war struck deeply at Duncan's heart and he took care of the mother and her pups. Once she was healthy and they were weaned Duncan gave three of the newborns and the mother away. He kept two for himself, a boy and a girl who he named Nanette and Rin Tin Tin. Rin

Tin Tin, known as Rinty, had long ears and strong white markings set against a full coat of dark fur. A striking German shepherd, he became a mascot for Duncan's squadron and helped keep up morale. After the Armistice, Duncan made the long journey home by ship. He sneaked his new friends on board with him. Sadly Nanette died of pneumonia before they could get home to California. Duncan was given another German shepherd puppy to keep Rin Tin Tin company. He named her Nanette II.

Like many veterans of that terrible war, when he got back to civilian life Duncan struggled with anxiety. The new Nanette and Rinty in particular became a comfort and a focus for him as he built his new life. Around this time Duncan may well have become aware of another German shepherd, one who had also been brought over from Germany. He was previously an attack dog called Eztel von Oeringen and he had been adopted by the American film director Laurence Trimble. He was now called Strongheart and he was about to embark on a new career as one of the first American canine movie stars.

In his first film, *The Silent Call*, Strongheart plays Flash, part wolf, part dog, who is accused of killing local sheep and sentenced to death by local ranchers. Flash eventually rescues his master's sweetheart from the real sheep killer and gets a hero's welcome. The film was a huge hit. It was rumoured to have cost $100,000 to produce and earned $1 million at the box office. One of Strongheart's most famous roles was playing the part of White Fang in the adaptation of Jack London's novel of the same name. In the end Strongheart became so famous he was treated like what he was, a movie star. He and a wife dog he had acquired, named Lady Jule, travelled in style in their own private train compartment.

They had their own hotel suite. He even had a dog food named after him. Eventually Strongheart set up home in a large bungalow somewhere in the Hollywood Hills. He was living the American dream. Although the legend goes that if he thought someone seemed a bit dodgy, his old Eztel von Oeringen attack-dog instincts would come out. He was even said to have gone after the odd embezzler or fraudster on the street if he came across one. One of his best reviews said of him *The greatest actor that the screen has produced is a dog, and he is the greatest actor because he acts just exactly as a dog would act . . .* Dogs make acting as dogs look so easy, but I know all too well what it takes to pull it off.

Although it can't be said that animals were by any means always treated well in cinema during this time, the playwright and screenwriter Jane Murfin, one of Strongheart's owners and trainers, cared enough about animal welfare to write a piece for the *Los Angeles Times* laying out how crucial it was to treat animals with kindness on set. While many animals, from horses and dogs to all kinds of tropical beasts, were treated very badly in film for decades, there was an awareness among some people, even then, that they deserved to be treated well and to enjoy their job.

As Strongheart made his name, former corporal Lee Duncan had begun to teach his own adopted German shepherd Rin Tin Tin, known as Rinty, a few tricks. At first, it must be said, Rinty was perhaps not the ideal dog to train. He was known to bark and growl and could be quite unpredictable, even a bit aggressive at times. The poor dog then suffered the misfortune of having a bunch of rolled-up newspapers, thrown from a passing car, accidentally break one of his legs. Duncan nursed him for several months until Rinty was back on all fours. He continued to train the dog, first to appear in regular show dog shows and in agility. While he was leaping over a high bar in the jumping category of one dog show, Rinty apparently managed to reach an extraordinary height of nearly twelve feet. The judges were very impressed and he won the round. As luck would have it, a mate of Duncan's who was experimenting with slow-motion film also managed to capture the award-winning leap for posterity. Seeing his dog perform on screen got Duncan thinking. Could Rinty, just like Strongheart, become a motion-picture star?

Duncan spent day after day, hour after hour, in pursuit of this ambition for Rinty, training him to do more and more tricks and follow his directions. When he wasn't doing that, Duncan was out touting for work, looking for a break by walking with Rinty down so-called 'poverty row' where a lot of the B-movie studios of Hollywood were located. Eventually all this persistence paid off. In the early 1920s Rinty was cast to replace a reluctant wolf in a silent western called *The Man from Hell's River*. After that came the dog's first big breakthrough; he got the starring role in a full-length silent movie *Where the North Begins*. It tells the story of a German shepherd foundling who is adopted as a puppy by a Canadian wolf pack. Rinty, or 'The Famous Police Dog Rin Tin Tin' as the opening credits declare, plays the role of 'Wolf-Dog'.

In the film the dog comes across a French fur trapper named Gabriel Dupre, who is in trouble, and he saves the man's life. There are many atmospheric shots of Rinty set against a dramatic landscape of 'endless snow and whispering pines – of trackless wastes and brooding silence'. It's ultimately a film about friendship, survival and a man's bond with a dog during hard times. So it's perhaps no surprise it was written specifically for Rinty by Duncan himself. As the pair build a friendship, the dog apparently decides that, instead of being allied to the wolves, man is 'his master and his friend'. But that trust in humans doesn't last long. Wolf-Dog is falsely accused of killing a baby and runs away. Meanwhile a nefarious trading manager is plotting against Dupre. Eventually the plucky dog manages to kill the dodgy trading manager, who also happens to be trying to steal Dupre's girlfriend. Wolf-Dog returns exonerated and is hailed as a hero. Then, as if it couldn't get any more heart-warming, in the final scene he's followed on screen by six very cute German shepherd puppies and his on-screen dog wife. The movie cost the equivalent of over a million dollars in today's money to produce but it made over four times that at the box office. Rin Tin Tin became so popular that thousands of fans wanted signed letters from him. He went on tours around the country and was even given the keys to the city of New York by the mayor. He went on to star in over twenty-four Warner Brothers movies and became the most well-known dog in Hollywood. There's even a rumour that Rinty was nominated as Best Actor in the 1929 Oscars. It's a classic bit of exaggerated Hollywood mythology, but it's fun to imagine that a dog could have been the best actor that year and, who knows, he may well have been.

Rin Tin Tin's bloodline continues today, along with the bloodline of another famous canine star I was lucky enough to meet on my own trip to the Hollywood Hills. The long-haired sheepdog in question was a ninth descendant of the original TV favourite Lassie. The handsome fellow who greeted me was accompanied by the dog trainer Bob Weatherwax. He's the son of Rudd Weatherwax, the man who bred the original Lassie. Bob told me that because the original trademark to the name had been sold, this dog was called not 'Lassie' but 'Laddie'. As I watched them film an advert it was obvious how having Laddie on set, just like all the dogs I've ever worked with, immediately lifted the spirits of everyone in the crew. It was fun to meet a member of canine Hollywood royalty.

As for Dodger, he was always happy mooching about on set and being fussed over and played with by me and all the cast and crew. The minute Sonia got out her little bag with all the sausages in it, though, you could tell he knew it meant we were back to work and back to business. One of Dodger's most dramatic moments on set was not while we were filming *Doc Martin* but when he got a part in one of the Pirates of the Caribbean movies. They were filming at the Old Royal Naval College in Greenwich and Dodger was playing one of the dogs in the background snuffling around in the gutter, as you often get in period films to make the scene look true to life. Although Dodger wasn't a key character, he found himself accidentally at the centre of the action when Johnny Depp's character, Jack Sparrow, was loaded on to the prison van to be carted off somewhere. The horse and carriage was about to make its way through one of the old archways of the college. It was quite tight so the carriage driver had to take it very slowly and carefully. Just as they were taking the horses through the narrow archway, a line of prisoners came out dragging shackles. The sound agitated one of the horses and then, just at the critical moment, a fire alarm went off somewhere. This was the final straw for the horses and they took off. Dodger, who had been nosing about in the gutter nearby, looked up. He thought this was all a fantastic game and proceeded to chase the carriage. Sonia saw a white flash disappear right next to one of the back wheels. She began to panic, thinking these were the last moments of Dodger. Over the sound of the fire alarm still going off, she started shouting for him to come out. Somehow, with huge skill, the guy driving the carriage managed to get the horses through the narrow archway with about a foot to spare on either side. He then steered the horses into a sharp turn and brought them under control again. Sonia was expecting to find Dodger somewhere flattened on the road where the carriage had been. The next moment the little dog appeared, walking nonchalantly back towards them with a look on his face as if to say, 'That was good fun, wasn't it? What's next?' Sonia was ready to cry with a mix of relief and anger. But you could never stay angry at Dodger for long.

One of his last acting jobs was when he was about fifteen years old. It was a short film in which he played the part of the oldest dog in the country. He actually had to roll over and die at the end of the film, which he did with characteristic aplomb. The next part of the story for any old dog never gets any easier. Sonia said goodbye to Dodger in the summer of 2023. Sadly he had developed canine dementia. It was heartbreaking, as it always is, when she had to let him go. But he had made it to the grand old age of nearly eighteen and he'd had quite the life after his humble beginnings as a straggly little stray on the streets of Bradford. Sonia now has two more screen dogs among her pack, Taffy and Paddy. I've had the pleasure of working with both of them. For me, though, no one has really ever beaten Dodger because we worked together for so long and had some real moments together.

Through all that time it was obvious that Dodger loved to work. He was always happy. He literally had a happy face. He loved being on set and he loved life and it remains one of the most rewarding acting partnerships of my career.

A group of canine search and rescue teams who went out on the rubble in New York after the 9/11 terror attacks.

8. Ground Zero

John Gilkey had never been to New York before but he hadn't expected his first visit to be quite like this. Walking with his eight-year-old chocolate Labrador retriever, Bear, he picked his way through vast steel girders, broken glass and concrete. John didn't know where exactly in Lower Manhattan they were or what this place usually looked like. He knew one thing, though: to anyone familiar with this part of New York City it was now completely unrecognizable. As they made their way carefully through the debris, dust clouds puffed up around them. Puff, puff, puff. John imagined this must be what it was like to walk on the moon. Suddenly he felt his leg giving way beneath him. He thought it was a hole in the road. John pulled his foot quickly back and steadied himself. Then he caught sight of something sticking up through the debris. It was the top of a ladder. A fire engine ladder. John realized it wasn't a hole he had nearly stepped into; it was a fire bucket. They were walking along the roof of a fire engine. The huge vehicle had been completely buried in the rubble and street level was now feet below.

Roselle

On the morning of 11 September 2001 Michael Hingson and his guide dog Roselle were going about their morning routine in New Jersey. The previous night there had been a bad storm. Roselle was afraid of thunder and Michael had spent most of the night comforting her. When the alarm went off at six a.m. they were both pretty tired. Michael had an important presentation at work, a seminar for a bunch of sales reps. He didn't want to be late. Roselle was his lovable golden-coloured Labrador retriever. Michael thought of her as kind of like a cute Labrador pixie. She sometimes had a penchant for stealing socks. That morning she was happily taking a nap while Michael got ready for work. After his usual cup of tea, Michael took Roselle outside along with his retired guide dog Jinnie. He ate his breakfast while Roselle played with her toy for a little while, then he got her kitted out in her harness. As soon as it was on she went from being a playful family pet to a totally focused guide dog, ready for whatever the day ahead had in store for them.

Michael and Roselle took a taxi to the railway station and then headed from New Jersey to Penn Station, Newark. There they got a PATH, Port Authority Trans-Hudson, rapid transit train to the subway station nearest to Michael's office at the World Trade Center. There were a couple of routes Michael could take to get from the station to his office. Sometimes they would cut through the car park and take a lift a few levels up before getting to the main lobby. At other times they would take an escalator up and go out into the busy central concourse between the towers and get to the lobby that way. The reason Michael did this was because he didn't want Roselle to get into the habit of memorizing the same route. Her job as his guide dog was to make sure he could walk safely and avoid any obstacles; it was not her job to navigate the route. So if she only learned one and that was blocked for whatever reason it would be a struggle for her to find an alternative route unless she had one already memorized. Each morning Michael would guide Roselle on which route to take with a combination of physical and verbal commands. That way he always kept Roselle on her toes in case of any obstacles. This morning Michael decided to take the route through the underground car park, which then took them to the main lobby of the North Tower. Once there, they got in the lift and made their way up to the seventy-eighth floor.

Roselle was Michael's fifth guide dog. He got his first when he was fourteen years old. He had from a very young age been encouraged by his parents to be independent and forge his own path in life. Michael was born in 1950; he was two months premature and weighed just two pounds and thirteen ounces. They didn't know it at the time, but the common practice back then of pumping oxygen into a sealed incubator was damaging the sight of many premature babies. The overexposure to oxygen led to constriction of the blood vessels at the back of the eye. When he was four months old Michael's parents realized that he was blind. The doctor recommended that they send him to a special home for blind people because 'no blind child could grow up to contribute to, or be a part of, society'. Michael's parents didn't react like many people would have at that time and regard this as a tragedy. Instead they stood firm and told the doctor that what he had said was absolute rubbish. They were going to give their child every chance. At times it would be tough, fighting against so much stigma, but they stuck fast to their philosophy. Michael was brought up believing that he could do whatever he wanted and that blind people could do whatever they chose to in life. In spite of the pressure to put him into a special school, Michael's parents encouraged and supported him to live a normal life. This meant he found his own way in a world of light-dependent people. Michael has a brilliant way of putting it, that much of the modern world is built for the light dependent. But when the lights go out he, and those who are not light dependent, have the advantage. Because of his parents' progressive can-do attitude, Michael was treated as far as possible just like any other kid.

When he was four years old he was given a pedal car to drive around their apartment. When he hit a coffee table and had to have stitches, instead of taking the car away from him, his mother told him to watch where he was going better. She really meant to listen better and so he did. Michael realized he could hear small changes in the environment which told him when he was approaching obstacles and he learned to avoid them. He trained himself to notice the different sounds of a room so he could tell when he had passed from one room to another. He learned to hear how it sounded to pass a doorway. Eventually Michael was able to race his car around the home with confidence, even in the dark. Later on he learned to ride a bike around the neighbourhood using the same methods. He could train himself to hear parked cars by listening for small changes in the sound of the tyres on the road. He figured out how to use a form of echolocation, clicking with his mouth and listening for the sound of the echo back, just like a bat would do. The neighbours were shocked to see this blind kid ride his bike around and would sometimes ask his parents why they allowed it. But Michael's parents knew what he was capable of and they trusted him. When he started kindergarten, his parents, along with a group of parents of some other blind prematurely born children, pushed for the school to bring in a Braille teacher. They agreed and from a young age Michael learned to read and write Braille. When the family moved from Chicago to California, though, his new school didn't have a Braille teacher; this meant he ended up doing a lot of his learning at home with his parents. He learned complex algebra from his dad and he got help with his schoolwork from his mum. Michael continued to explore the world outside, learning to hear and feel other small differences around the streets of their new home. He noticed differences in elevation along roads and driveways in order to help navigate and he taught himself to pay attention to small cracks and changes in road surfaces. Before long he was able to walk to school on his own and ride his bike around the new neighbourhood. The new school pressured his parents to send him to a special school and he also faced bullying from some of the other kids, but his parents continued to stand fast. Eventually the school hired a Braille teacher and he was able to pick it back up and gain a new love for books. Michael learned to adjust to a world built for the light dependent.

But when he went to high school there were new challenges. It was busier and louder and altogether harder to navigate using his ears. One day Michael's parents heard about a woman called Sharon Gold who worked as a teacher on the air force base where his dad was an electrical engineer. She was blind and had a guide dog, an energetic and playful German shepherd called Nola. Sharon and Nola came to visit and meet Michael and it turned out to be life-changing. It showed Michael not only that he wasn't alone but that as a blind person you could go out in the world doing a job like teaching and you could make a difference. What he didn't know yet was that his parents had applied for a guide dog for him too. He was younger than most people with guide dogs at the time, only fourteen years old, but he was thrilled and excited. Michael was dropped off at the campus of what was then called Guide Dogs for the Blind to begin his guide dog training. He learned all the footwork, commands and obedience, and three days later he met the guide dog they had selected for him, a dark red golden retriever called Squire. For the next four years Squire would be his best friend and teammate. After finishing school, with Squire at his side, Michael went to the University of California, Irvine.

Michael was able to build a mental map of the campus in his head to get around, along with the help of Squire and his white cane. During this time Michael and another blind student lobbied for new computer technologies to be made available and accessible for blind people. A researcher at UCI called Dick Rubinstein had created a Braille computer terminal. This helped start Michael's lifelong interest in helping to get the latest and best technologies into the lives of blind people. He had also fallen in love with physics. With a combination of Braille, audio recordings and the help of some student readers, plus a great deal of hard work and determination, Michael got his degree. He graduated with the highest honours and then got a master's and a teaching and some business qualifications. It wasn't all plain sailing, though. When Michael thought about studying for a doctorate, he discovered a note in his college file saying a blind person could not do the 'high-level work required for an advanced degree in physics'. As it happened, Michael had decided not to do a doctorate anyway and he went on to get a great job after college. From then on he took the philosophy that if someone told him he couldn't do something, he would ask why not? If he wanted to do it, he would do it. The job Michael went on to do after college was working with an inventor called Raymond Kurzweil. Kurzweil had created a machine which allowed blind people to understand written text through a computer which read it aloud. Michael was hired to work for the National Federation of the Blind to help test out the prototypes of the early reading machines. Over the next few years Michael helped gain feedback and refine the design. He eventually got a job in sales helping to sell the machines to the corporate world. These became revolutionary and a version continues to be used on computers today. By September 2001 Michael was working as a regional sales manager at a company called Quantum, selling big data storage systems. His offices were on the seventy-eighth floor of the North Tower of the World Trade Center.

On the morning of 11 September, when they arrived at the office, Michael's guide dog Roselle went straight to sleep under Michael's desk as usual. He was busy preparing his presentation and breakfast for a bunch of clients who were about to arrive. Whenever anyone arrived in the office Roselle would come out from under Michael's desk, her tail wagging, and she would go over to greet them. She had kind of become the official meeter and greeter of the department. Michael encouraged her to do this because he wanted a friendly dog who knew how to be relaxed in public as well as be on duty as a guide dog. A few people began to filter in, including David Frank, Michael's colleague from their offices in California. Once Roselle had made sure whoever came in felt very welcome she would go back under Michael's desk and snooze off again. Security at the World Trade Center then was pretty tight. A few years earlier, in 1993, a van bomb had detonated below the North Tower. The terrorist attack blew a huge crater in the ground below the tower. Six people were killed and over a thousand more were injured. The attack raised security to a whole new level. By 2001 you couldn't go up in the lifts without first being cleared by the Port Authority, who were responsible for the building. On 11 September, the final thing David and Michael had to do after preparing for the presentation was to fax a list of the names of everyone attending from outside to the security team downstairs. They could then all be cleared to come up to that floor without them having to call up separately each time.

They were just finishing the list when, at 8.46 a.m., they heard a muffled sound a bit like distant thunder; it wasn't that loud and it was very low. Immediately afterwards the whole building began to vibrate. Then it began to tip sideways. That isn't all that unusual with a very tall building. They're designed to act almost like springs, which can be buffeted by wind and storms and resist the force. Michael knew that Roselle was afraid of thunder and he was aware she would be frightened by this noise, but this was not a thunderstorm. It was a bright, sunny day. Michael wondered what could have caused such a dramatic shift in the building. A gas explosion maybe? He knew from living in California that it didn't feel like an earthquake. Whatever it was seemed to be on the other side of the building. Tiles began to fall from the ceiling. Things around the office were being dislodged. Some of the guests in the conference room began to scream. He and David began to say goodbye to each other. Michael prayed that this building wasn't about to fall over. At that point the tilting stopped and the building dropped about six or seven feet. This was the springiness of the building righting itself as the spring joints contracted and it went back to its normal configuration. Whatever it was seemed to be over. But what the hell had just happened?

Roselle, who had been asleep under Michael's desk, had by now come out to see what was going on. Michael took her leash and told her to heel. This meant to come round to his side and sit, which she dutifully did. Michael's colleague David looked out of the window. He said he could see some smoke and fire coming from the floors above. A few windows had been blown out and paper was drifting down through the air. It had now become very clear to everyone that they had to get out of the building immediately. Michael knew they should not rush or panic, though. Ever since the 1993 attack, everyone who worked at the World Trade Center had been doing regular drills to learn how to evacuate safely and many people had already been down the stairwells in simulated emergencies before. As the person in charge of his department, Michael had also spent a lot of time learning how to get around the World Trade Center safely. He had learned from the police, the Port Authority and all the security people exactly what to do in order to avoid a big panic. The reality was that many sighted people would focus on using signs to get around in an emergency, but because he was never going to get emergency access information by reading signs Michael had already learned where all the emergency exits were and visited them many times. He had learned where all the major offices were and had developed a complete understanding of all the emergency processes in the building. On their particular floor at this time there wasn't a lot of smoke. But if ever there was or there was a blackout, Michael would be at an advantage over people who relied on their sight. Because of all his preparation Michael had developed a calm mindset which seemed to click into place that day. Emergency procedures meant they were to take the stairs and not the lifts because it was safer, so Michael instructed David to start taking their seminar guests to the stairway. Meanwhile Michael called his wife Karen to tell her there must have been an explosion or something, but at this point there was nothing more he could tell her. They said goodbye and he said he'd call her back later. When David returned from the stairway, he and Michael did a final sweep of the office to check that everyone was out. Once they'd confirmed it was all clear they, along with Roselle, made their own way to one of the main stairwells. By this point there was some smoke in the lobby and people were starting to panic as they tried to get out. Michael remained calm. He trusted that together he and Roselle had each other's backs. When they got to the top of Stairwell B Michael held on to her harness and gave the command 'forward'. Then they began the long journey down the seventy-eight floors back to ground level.

As soon as they were in the stairwell Michael could smell a strange odour. He wasn't sure yet what it was. They continued their descent. Michael was conscious that with her fear of thunder, Roselle might still be frightened by the noise they had heard earlier, so as they walked down the stairs together he began talking to her gently, praising her, telling her she was doing a good job. In truth, she wasn't leading him as such; there wasn't really a lot to do as Michael was able to follow the stairs on his own by holding on to the rail, counting down ten steps, then turning 180 degrees and counting down nine steps. This way he knew when they were on the next floor. As Michael held on to the rail Roselle walked a little bit behind him and to the side. Although she wasn't leading him, the fact that they were together was comforting for both of them. They were supporting each other. Roselle was focused on the job in hand just like

everyone else around her: of getting to the bottom. At first
the atmosphere was relatively quiet. The stairway was filling
up with people from different floors. No one around them
was really panicking but there was an urgent energy. Michael's
heart was pumping.

About four floors down, Michael realized that he recognized the strange odour. He'd done a lot of travelling as a
sales rep. He knew this smell very well. It was burning jet
fuel. He had never imagined he would smell burning jet fuel
in the World Trade Center. As soon as he realized what it was
he told the people around him. They all began to smell it and
agreed this must be what it was. They knew this could really
only mean one thing. They had been hit by an aeroplane. But
that, and the fact that they had to get out of there as fast as
possible, was all they really knew.

As they continued their descent Roselle remained
focused. Michael's calm voice continued to direct her
onwards. 'Good girl, Roselle, you're doing a great job. Keep
going. What a good dog.' No one knew what was going on
because they had not heard any information from the PA
system in the building and mobile phones were not working, so this was also a comfort to other people around them.
They could hear that Michael was not sounding rattled, that
he was going down the stairs without any difficulty. At
around the fiftieth floor Michael's colleague David, who
was a floor ahead of them, called up. Some burn victims
from the floors above had begun to be helped down past
them and his voice suddenly sounded more panicked.
'Mike, we're going to die,' he said. 'We're not going to make
it out of here.'

Michael immediately snapped back down at him. He very
deliberately wanted to break David out of a possible

downward spiral. He said, 'Stop it, David. If Roselle and I can go down the stairs, so can you.'

This brought David right out of his funk. After that he began to shout words of support and encouragement back up to Michael and Roselle. 'I'm on the forty-eighth floor. Everything is good here,' he said. Then: 'Hey, Mike, I'm on the forty-sixth floor' and 'I'm now at the Port Authority cafeteria, not stopping, going on down'. Although Michael was already very used to making his way down these stairs during their drills, David's voice was a real comfort and a focal point for anyone who could hear him. Anyone within hearing distance knew there was somebody somewhere on the stairs who was OK. Michael feels sure that by constantly calling up to him, David Frank must have helped thousands of people that day to stay calm and comforted as they went down those stairs. At one point a woman began to panic. The people around her stopped to reassure her. Michael gave her a hug and Roselle nudged the woman with her nose. The woman patted her and it seemed to relax her a bit. They continued down. Michael could tell from her breathing that Roselle was becoming tired but still she continued on.

He wondered what would happen if the lights went out in the stairwell. It would not affect him since he was not dependent on the light to get down. But who knew what kind of panic it might cause? He prayed they would make it down before anything like that happened. Although nobody around them was outwardly panicking or screaming, there were a few moments when Michael noticed that people around him were starting to go very quiet. He became concerned that they might be going through the same panic that David had vocalized. So at one point he piped up and called out to the people on the stairs above and below him. 'Hey, not all of you can see me, but my name is Mike. I'm blind. I've got a guide dog with me called Roselle. And I don't want anybody to worry. Because if we lose power and lighting on the stairs,' he joked, 'Roselle and I are here to offer you a half-price special to get you out today only.' That got a laugh and definitely helped lighten the mood and boost morale back up. A couple of floors later, Michael felt that quiet panic start to descend again, so he called out a little more quietly, 'Hey, you know what, everybody? Let me just say that what happened happened. I suggest since we know there's a fire somewhere and they're not gonna let us back into the building for a while, let's all meet back at the seventy-eighth floor at eight forty-five in the morning and walk down the stairs together. What a great way to lose weight, huh?' Again this got a laugh, lightened the mood and got people chatting for a while.

The further they descended, the hotter it became. More people crowded into the stairwell. At one point some bottles of water appeared and began to be passed down the stairs. It was a relief to drink the cool water and to give some to Roselle. Around the thirtieth floor a murmur of excitement rippled through the stairwell. A group of firefighters were coming up. David could see they were wearing thick protective gear and carrying loads of equipment. He called up the stairs to ask people to make way for them. On the way past one of the firefighters stopped to ask Michael and Roselle if they were OK. Michael reassured him they were just fine. The firefighter petted Roselle and then continued upwards, not knowing what awaited him.

At 9.45 a.m. Michael and Roselle finally made it to the bottom. The sprinkler system had been activated and there was water everywhere. At one point they both got sprayed with water. It was refreshing and cool. Michael was so proud of Roselle. They had both made it back down. He stopped briefly to tell her she was a good girl and to give her a reassuring stroke, then they got out of there as quickly as they possibly could.

On the morning of 11 September John Gilkey was at work. He was an electrical engineer for an auto parts manufacturer. When he got to the office that morning he had found his colleagues huddled round a small TV set. On the screen they were showing news footage of one of the huge towers of the World Trade Center billowing with smoke against a clear blue sky. These were the live images of the iconic Twin Towers which were being broadcast across the world. They were intermittently interspersed with repeated clips of a passenger plane which had crashed into the North Tower a few minutes earlier. John couldn't believe what he was seeing. Like so many people around the world, people in the office began to speculate about what had happened. Then at 9.03 a.m., out of nowhere, a second plane appeared. At unbelievable speed it ploughed straight into the South Tower. What in the hell was going on? This was obviously not an accident. Could it really be a deliberate attack? John thought of the thousands of people working at the World Trade Center that day. Each tower had 110 floors. John turned to his boss and said, 'I'm outta here.' When his boss asked him why, John replied, 'I know what I have to do.' He and his dog Bear were needed.

Back at the World Trade Center, David, Michael and Roselle were outside the lobby. There were by this point many emergency first responders, police and FBI people clearing the area. Nobody was telling them what had happened, probably because they didn't want to cause a panic. As they began to cross the main plaza David said to Michael, 'Hey, there's a fire over in Tower Two.' Smoke billowing out of the windows. Apart from their own suspicions about the aeroplane fuel on the stairway, they still had no idea what was happening. One thing was clear, though. It was obviously not safe to be where they were.

They made their way as fast as possible out of the main complex and on to Broadway. They turned left and headed south. Michael was very familiar with these streets, having navigated them many times before with Roselle. As they walked up several blocks on to Fulton Street, David suddenly stopped. He said, 'I can see Tower Two. We're really close to it. I'm going to take some pictures of the fire.' Michael tried to call his wife Karen again. This time he couldn't get through. The signal was blocked.

As Michael put his phone away a police officer yelled over to them, telling them to 'Get out of here. It's coming down. Now!'

There followed the most enormous deep rumbling sound Michael had ever heard. It was like a combination of a freight train and a huge waterfall. He could hear glass breaking and metal clattering. Immediately everyone turned and ran. Michael realized he could no longer hear David nearby. So he turned round, holding on to Roselle's harness, and they started running back the way they had just come, away from the direction of the sound. Debris was falling all around. People were screaming. Pieces of concrete clipped Michael's ear. Eventually they made it unharmed to the next street and were back on Broadway.

Although he knew these streets well, being able to focus on giving Roselle commands to go from street to street helped them both not to panic. Even though they were running for their lives it was something familiar to hold on to. Michael heard David's voice again. He said, 'I was gonna come back and get you.'

Michael replied, 'Well, here I am. Let's go!'

They ran together, Michael holding tightly on to Roselle's harness. The South Tower began to pancake, collapsing down from top to bottom. Soon they were engulfed in a huge cloud. Michael didn't know whether Roselle could hear him or whether she could see his hand signals. He continued to give her hand signals anyway, telling her to go right, then go straight ahead. In the end the dust was so thick that David couldn't see his hand when it was just six inches in front of his face. Michael could feel the debris and dirt choking his lungs every time he took a breath. They kept running.

Michael was listening out for an opening in the streets, a doorway or some way they could get away from the growing dust cloud and the falling glass and concrete. Eventually Michael picked up on an opening between some buildings. He realized Roselle must have been able to hear him and see his hand signals because she turned on his command, just as he would expect her to do. She took one step and then all of a sudden she stopped. She stood stock-still. Her feet were firmly planted. Michael kept urging her to keep going, but she wouldn't move. Michael realized she must have stopped for a reason. He investigated and discovered they were at the top of a flight of stairs. Roselle had done exactly what she was supposed to do when she got to a flight of stairs. She had stopped and was now waiting for the command from Michael to go down. When he realized she had so dutifully stopped in the midst of all this chaos he was so overcome with pride that he bent down and gave her a huge hug. Then he told her forward, the command to start up again, and together they went down the stairs.

They entered a small arcade, which was the entrance to the Fulton Street subway station and joined a small group of people who had made it down there. After a short while an employee from the subway system came in and found eight or nine of them in the small arcade area. He took them to an employee locker room and they stayed there for about fifteen minutes, speculating about what was going on. Not long after that a police officer came and told them to leave. 'You can't stay here,' he said. 'The air's better up above.'

They followed him back up and back out into the open. The air turned out not to be that much better actually. But they had no choice now but to continue west on Fulton Street. In about ten minutes they were in a little plaza area when suddenly Michael heard that same freight train/waterfall sound again. He and David knew that this must be their own tower, the North Tower, collapsing. They ducked behind a small retaining wall and hid. Eventually the horrible sound died down and it was quiet again.

David stood up and looked around. He exclaimed to Michael, 'Oh my God, there's no World Trade Center any more!' All David could see was fire and flames hundreds of feet tall and pillars of smoke. The building they had only a couple of hours earlier been in, casually preparing for the day ahead, was now no more.

Michael called his wife Karen again. This time he managed to get through. Karen was the first person to tell them what by then was being shown all over the news. Two passenger jets had been hijacked and deliberately crashed into the towers. Another had also been flown into the Pentagon. At this time a fourth plane was still missing over Pennsylvania, flight 93. Even though they had literally lived through it, this was the first time they really understood the enormity of what had happened. Michael also discovered the awful truth, that the mobile phone circuits had been busy because so many people up in the towers had been calling to say goodbye to loved ones. Throughout it all Roselle had stayed totally focused. Michael realized just how fortunate they had been to be together.

Later that night Michael was reunited with his wife Karen. His entire body was aching from adrenaline and exertion. They had walked down seventy-eight flights of stairs and run for their lives through Manhattan. As soon as Michael took Roselle's harness off she jerked away and went straight to her toy box. She found her favourite toy and started playing tug of war with Michael's retired guide dog Linnie. The reality was that, apart from probably being quite tired, it was now all over for Roselle. As Michael wondered 'what if' and 'what might have been', Roselle, just like all dogs, was playing happily again as if nothing had ever happened. For those still in central Manhattan it was only the beginning. As darkness fell across the city, the loved ones of the missing began to mourn or hope and the search began for any survivors.

A Dog Called Bear

A week earlier, Cindy Otto, a clinical vet who works with disaster search and rescue teams, had been at a training session. One of the talks was on the theme of terrorism. At one point the lecturer had said to the attendees with a serious face, 'It's not a matter of if, it's a matter of when. There will be a major terrorist attack on US soil.' Cindy did not realize just how prescient this would turn out to be.

On 11 September, Cindy's husband called her at work and said, 'Have you seen the news?' Like many people that day, when she heard about a plane hitting the World Trade Center, she at first assumed it was a small plane and that it must have been some kind of accident. When the second passenger plane hit she realized, along with the rest of the world, that it was an attack. What that lecturer had told them was coming true. At one o'clock that afternoon a call came through. Cindy was needed in New York. She grabbed her kit and headed to Philadelphia fire station. There she was joined by emergency task forces from across Pennsylvania. They were packed into buses of firefighters, medics and other responders. Among them was also a group of dogs. These were specially trained disaster search canines. This would be the biggest disaster they had ever seen. Cindy's task was to take charge of health care for the animals during the search. Among the dogs she met up with that day was an eighty-five-pound eight-year-old chocolate Labrador called Bear.

That morning, electrical engineer John Gilkey had left his office at an electrical repair company in Pennsylvania and made his way swiftly home to collect Bear. A third plane had hit the Pentagon in Washington and John wasn't sure where he would be going. His pager went off and he got a message to say he was going to New York and when John discovered Cindy would be there to take care of the dogs he was relieved. They knew each other because John had worked with her at Pennsylvania University where she had been studying and training disaster search and rescue dogs. It was great to see a friendly face and to know there was a qualified vet on the team. As they made their way by bus into Manhattan they saw lines and lines of traffic coming the other way. The only vehicles now going into New York City were disaster response teams like them and line after line of ambulances.

They finally reached the financial district at around midnight and headed to a convention centre which would be their makeshift camp. Cindy noticed the remnants from an event the night before: champagne glasses, a coffee machine. The building looked like it had been abandoned in a hurry. Neither Cindy, John nor any of the other canine teams had any idea of the sheer scale of what they were about to find. Their first glimpse of what they would find at Ground Zero, or the Pile as it became known among many first responders, was when they picked their way through the Winter Garden Atrium. It was a ten-storey glass-vaulted pavilion which was filled with huge palm trees. It had been connected to the World Trade Center via a bridge and because of its close proximity to the towers it had been severely damaged when they collapsed. It was pitch dark as they made their way through the wreckage of the atrium. There was dust everywhere and, although severely crushed, the palm trees still stood among the wreckage of broken glass and steel. It made for the most surreal and shocking sight to see this icon of serenity and calm completely destroyed.

They made their way through what had once been the World Financial Center and set up their base of operations nearby. From there they would make their way out to the centre of the Pile and begin their search among the 1.8 million tons of wreckage now lying where the Twin Towers had been. When the actual search began, John and other canine handlers would be radioed with commands, telling them and their dogs where they were needed to look in the rubble for survivors. Thousands of people had begun to gather near the site to post missing-people notices, hoping and praying their family members or friends would be found.

As soon as John Gilkey got to the site he realized the magnitude of the task ahead of them. At first he thought they were at ground level, but then he saw the roof of that fire engine and he knew there were four storeys of rubble beneath them. Every time he took a step dust filled the air. There were fires still burning. The atmosphere was choking. John had been given the nickname Inspector Gadget by his buddies because he always had a lot of tools with him. If you needed a tool for a job, he was your guy. One of the useful tools he had in his bag that night, which not many other people did, was a respirator. Many people were still wearing paper masks at that point. As soon as he hit the Pile John put that respirator on. His habit of being well prepared for any eventuality may have helped him avoid some of the serious health issues that sadly many people later faced after breathing in the choking dust and fumes.

As they began to clamber over the wreckage John realized it was full of many void spaces. At any moment he or Bear could fall into a hole dozens of feet below. They could land on something sharp like broken steel or glass, or they could fall into one of the fires. As they picked their way through the wreckage, Bear ran ahead sniffing in and out of the rubble, clambering up and down over the steel and concrete. John kept his eye on Bear the whole time. He wanted to make sure he didn't get hurt. But the truth was, whatever he did, this was going to be the most dangerous mission they had ever been through together.

Today John Gilkey is a professional firefighter. He got into search and rescue dogs not through work but through leisure. He loved the wilderness and he had always been into hunting and fishing. Back in the days before GPS people often became lost and, as a practical kind of guy, John naturally found himself helping the volunteer search and rescue teams. One of the guides was a bloodhound handler and they always had dogs on the team. After a while John realized he loved working with the dogs and that he was pretty good at it. He decided he wanted to work with his own dog and one of the park rangers they worked with picked one out for him.

That's when John met Bear. Bear lived up to his name; he was a huge brown bear of a chocolate Labrador retriever. Bear was John's first dog and their bond became really tight. John's wife Joanne also loved animals. She kept horses and had her own lovable Rottweilers. Because Bear stayed at home while John was working as an electrical engineer, he was never one of those dogs who needed to follow him everywhere all the time. He was obedient but pretty self-sufficient and not very needy. When they were together, if John was up and about, Bear would position himself somewhere he could see John, lying down or hanging about, but he didn't need to be right next to him all the time. As Bear and John trained to be a search dog team, Bear got a bit of a reputation. Not only was he big and brown, just like his namesake, he was one of the most tenacious and persistent dogs anyone on the team had ever met. During search and rescue training people hide in all sorts of hard-to-reach places and the dog is sent off to find them. I hid myself once in Yellowstone Park in a kind of snow cave, while a search and rescue dog looked for me. To be honest, I had no doubt whatsoever that the clever dog would find me so I spent the time watching *Dad's Army* on my phone, but she didn't let me watch for long and I could only imagine what it would be like to be genuinely lost and then to hear a dog barking and the wonderful moment when the light comes flooding in and the dog's friendly face appears. During their training sessions John and Bear would work together on rubble piles. Instead of wilderness searches, these simulate the kinds of locations these dogs need to look through to find people after a disaster like an earthquake or when a building has collapsed. Bear's reward for finding someone who was hidden among the rubble would be a frisbee he got to play with. He loved frisbees so much that John reckons he was firmly convinced that everybody in this world had a frisbee about their person. If Bear found the 'victim', he knew at some point they had to, as John puts it, ''fess up that frisbee', and play with him. During one training session, John was working on getting Bear to alert closer to the victim, so they could pinpoint where they were more exactly. So he told the guy who was hiding in the rubble pile that, when Bear found him, he should not give him the frisbee until John got there. He wanted Bear to bark continuously until he arrived and only then should the guy give him the frisbee. That way it would be easier to hear exactly where the victim was because Bear would be barking until he got right up to them. So the guy went and hid and John waited a little while, then he cut Bear loose. Bear galloped off and on to the rubble. He was searching and searching all over the place, up and down and in and out of the concrete slabs. Then all of a sudden Bear disappeared. He had found a way to get inside the rubble pile and he was inside there tunnelling down. John heard him bark a couple of times but couldn't really pinpoint where he was. So, John thought, this is the perfect scenario. He's just gonna bark until I find the pair of them and then the training can really happen. Bear barked a couple of times, but then he went silent. John was trying to locate him, when, the next thing was he heard the guy screaming. Bear barked a couple more times. He really wanted his frisbee. The guy was doing what John had told him. He was not giving Bear the frisbee yet, but waiting for John to get to their location. Bear was having none of it. He reached down and grabbed the guy by the back of the jacket and began dragging him out of the rubble pile. He was literally moving a 165-pound guy with his teeth. The guy was screaming back at John, 'Can I give him the frisbee yet? Can I get the frisbee?' Bear knew what was supposed to happen at this point. He'd found the guy and he was like, 'Son of a bitch, you're gonna give me that frisbee.' When John finally got there he told Bear to drop the guy. Bear dropped the guy. He looked at John and barked a couple times. John said, 'OK, now give him the frisbee.' Bear got hold of that frisbee and he was ecstatic. The victim played with him, John played with him and Bear finally got his reward. That's what John means when he says Bear was tenacious. He knew that frisbee was his and he was having it.

John knew that if they came across anyone alive in the Pile in New York, Bear would find them. He was trained to search for and find live people and this was what they were looking for. They worked long days, Bear out ahead, walking around, sniffing and searching the rubble. Once they had cleared an area and it was declared free of live people, they would move on to the next area. At times John would need to lift Bear into a void so he could search deeper. He was a big, hefty boy so this wasn't easy hour after hour. One of the things which really struck John was how even though these two huge buildings had come down there was so little among the wreckage which looked like it came from an office. He never saw a computer, a copier or a filing cabinet. He never saw a chair or a desk or a telephone. Nothing was left from those offices, except for reams and reams of paper which were so light they floated down on to the Pile.

Amid the devastation, John soon realized that even though Bear was trained to find live people that was becoming increasingly unlikely. Even though he hadn't been trained to locate bodies, when John would cut him loose he would sometimes mark the site of a body. This was in the way only a dog knows how to make his mark. It may not seem like the most sensitive seeming thing, but the dog was just doing what it knew. Even though Bear wasn't trained to do this, instinctively he was able to give crucial information to the search teams about the locations of the people who had not survived. If they were recovered, they could be given a proper burial and it would help give their loved ones some kind of closure. Although everyone loves a story of a living person being found under the rubble, the awful truth is that when a building collapses, usually very few people survive.

Among the other dog handlers that day was another firefighter from Arizona called John Dean. He remembers clearly how struck he was by the monochrome landscape of the Pile. It was virtually void of colour because it was so full of dust. Whenever someone's remains were found the New York firefighters would come in. If they were able to recover the remains, they would bring out a wire stretcher called a Stokes basket. This way they were able to pull someone out from a remote location, strap them into the basket and extricate them from the scene. Whenever they were able to recover a body, if they could, they covered the Stokes basket with an American flag. John was vividly moved by the sight of the colours of red, white and blue among such a vast area of monochrome rubble, soot and devastation. As soon as they brought someone off the Pile, as the basket was lifted with the flag draped over it, everybody would stop and it would become completely silent. Spontaneously, without any kind of order or briefing, anyone who was there, all the construction workers, the recovery folk, the task force, the local firefighters and police officers would stop. Amid the pneumatic drills and saws and generators and cranes and trucks everything just stopped and everybody would take off their helmet and have a moment of silence. For John and everyone there it was such a solemn and respectful thing to see and be part of. John thought it was just tremendous in the midst of something so devastating to see all the respect which poured out.

At the end of a long emotional and exhausting day all the dog teams would return to their sleeping area at the convention centre. Cindy would be there to check the dogs over and give them any medical assistance needed. Then the dogs would in turn comfort everyone else, taking on their second job as companions and friends and quasi-psychologists. When they finally managed to get some rest, John Gilkey would cuddle up with Bear and they would try to get some rest for the next day.

By Thursday, two days after they had arrived, everyone was exhausted but continuing to search. John had become worried that Bear was getting no chance to do what he was trained to do and signal on a live person; he wondered whether he might be getting enough reward to keep him going. At one point John was working around a fire engine and he asked the lieutenant to clear some space for Bear to search by moving everyone out of the way just in case. And the next thing John knew he was barking his head off.

That was not the sign he gave for a body so everyone was very excited. When John got to Bear and the buried fire truck they discovered a very alive firefighter. But he was not a victim; he was a rescuer also looking for people – he just hadn't heard the call to clear everyone out. John tossed him Bear's toy and said, 'You've just bought five minutes to play with this dog.' Although this guy was not a buried victim it was comforting to know that Bear could still do his job. It was also a boost to morale for the team to know that even in the face of so much obvious sadness, they weren't just going through the motions here. If there was someone there still alive, Bear or one of the other dogs might just find them.

In total twenty survivors were eventually pulled out of the rubble in the days following the attack. They included six firefighters, three police officers and two Port Authority Police Department officers who were rescued by two former US Marines after spending nearly twenty-four hours under thirty feet of rubble. The final survivor to be found was a Port Authority secretary called Genelle. She was discovered twenty-seven hours after the collapse of the North Tower. She was discovered with the help of a German shepherd rescue dog called Trakr, one of over 300 dogs who helped with the search that day. Nearly 3,000 people died in the attack, including 334 New York City firefighters. John Dean, who took part in the search with his dog Reo, has a photo on his wall of each one of them. Since the attacks thousands of first responders have died from diseases related to the noxious dust and smoke.

John Gilkey had a few months in which to say goodbye to his beloved dog Bear before he died in 2003 aged ten years old. With vet Cindy Otto's help they discovered he had most likely been affected by his work on the Pile. Cindy continues to work on making search and rescue work as safe as possible for dogs at the Penn Vet Working Dog Center, which was set up after 9/11. She tries to make sure that the work of the next generation of search dogs is as humane for the dogs as possible.

John is now a professional firefighter and he has since had three more disaster search dogs. His second was Bailey who he trained from a pup. Together they helped with the response to Hurricane Katrina in 2005. After his third dog, Jester, his fourth and current search dog, Piper, now hangs out with him every day at the fire station. She also has another special role in John's life. Sadly his wife, Joanne, died in a road traffic accident just months before we spoke. When he gets home from work, Piper is always there for him. She watched him cry and talk to himself. She watched him stumbling around the house without judgement as he dealt with his huge loss, which helped him tremendously, along with Joanne's lovable Rottweiler Maggie.

After their ordeal in the North Tower, Michael Hingson and his guide dog Roselle appeared on *Larry King Live*. Michael went on to give talks around the world about how they had made it out of the tower together as a team and he is now a full-time keynote speaker. Unfortunately Michael's wife Karen has now passed away. He lives with his black Labrador guide dog Elmo, along with their fourteen-year-old black cat. Michael and Karen took the cat in when their neighbour died. When they found out this cat's name was Stitch, they knew it must be fate because Karen was a professional quilter. Roselle was awarded the Dickin Medal in 2002, along with another guide dog who has also been in the World Trade Center called Salty. Roselle died in 2011 aged thirteen. Michael will never forget her playful pixie-like and kind nature and everything they achieved and learned together. Most importantly, from all his guide dogs he has learned the power of teamwork and trust and what he calls 'how to live like a guide dog'. I'll leave you with Michael's own words on that: 'Don't worry about what you can't control. Focus on what you can and let the rest take care of itself. Because you're not going to be able to do anything about it anyway.'

German shepherd police dog Prince comes from a long line of canines who have helped solve crimes and keep our streets safe.

9. Sleuth Hounds

When I Grow Up

Most of us remember having a dream when we were children about what we wanted to be when we grew up. Maybe an astronaut, an explorer, a pop star, a vet . . . Not all our dreams come true. I wanted to be a milkman. But every now and then those dreams do come true. The moment Emma Dignam knew what she wanted to do, she was five years old. It was at a family day out with her mum and dad at a local police open day. There was a fun holiday atmosphere. Police cars were dotted around among stalls and displays. Kids were putting on helmets and playing with the police sirens. Emma's dad was in the river police so this was all pretty familiar territory. But there was one thing which caught her attention that day that she'd never seen before. A group of German shepherd police dogs were running round an agility course. Five-year-old Emma didn't really know what they were doing. To her they just looked like they were having a lot of fun. Knowing dogs they very likely were. As Emma watched them running through all the tunnels and over jumps and ramps she also noticed the way the dogs kept looking up at their handlers with such attentiveness and obedience. It seemed to her to be a look of complete and utter devotion. How wonderful it would be, she thought, to be loved so totally, utterly loved like that by a big, fluffy dog. Emma's family had never owned a dog, but from that moment on she knew that was what she wanted to do. In every school show and tell, every essay about her future and every conversation about her career Emma was set; she was going to be a police dog handler.

Dogs have been accompanying law enforcement in one way or another for centuries. In the Middle Ages they used to go out at night with parish constables, mainly to keep them company rather than to do any real policing. A type of blood-hound known as a slough dog or scent hound was used for centuries in Scotland to track down gangs of brigands and bandits in the wild borderlands. Also known as sleuth hounds, from the Old Norse 'sloth', meaning a track or trail, it's where we get the modern word 'sleuth'.

The use of police dogs in any official capacity really got going in the late 1800s. In their desperate bid to catch Jack the Ripper, the Metropolitan Police at one point brought in a couple of bloodhounds to try to sniff the killer out. It didn't go all that brilliantly. One of the dogs bit the police commissioner and the pair of dogs then ran off together. They had to be sleuth-hunted themselves by their own officers. Things were going a little better across the chan-nel. Inspired by the impressively large dog in Conan Doyle's *The Hound of the Baskervilles*, the Prussian police began using Great Danes as guard dogs and trackers. In Ghent in Belgium, when there was no money for extra police offi-cers, the commissioner asked the mayor if they could have a few dogs instead. The mayor agreed and the police started training Belgian shepherd dogs to help out the nightwatch-men. Over the next ten years, the Ghent police trained dozens of dogs to help with guard duties, especially around the docks. The idea of training dogs soon began to take root in other police forces around the world. The New

York police department visited Belgium to see what they were doing and took two dogs back with them. In Germany the police set up special schools, training German shepherds to track and help them seize suspected criminals. In England, inspired by those European successes, the North Eastern Railway Police acquired four Airedale terriers to help the police with security at Hull and other docks around the north-east. The method was crude in a way. They were basically conditioned with rewards to attack anyone who wasn't wearing a police uniform. Although they probably weren't far wrong in thinking that anyone lurking around the docks at night not in uniform most likely was up to something dodgy.

At the outbreak of the First World War, when some of the railway police were conscripted, a few of the Hull dock police dogs went along with them and eventually became sentry dogs in France. But while Germany had around 6,000 trained dogs in the army, Britain had just one official army dog. A canine enthusiast and officer, Lieutenant Colonel Edwin Richardson saw what dogs were doing for the police and thought the British needed more dogs in the army too. Richardson could see how a dog's affection for its handler and its natural love of a reward could be used to train the dog to do all kinds of useful things. In 1917 he set up the British War Dog School in Shoeburyness. His philosophy was that dogs work much better if you treat them with kindness and he avoided any kind of brutal training methods. Richardson worked with rescue dogs from Battersea and pets donated by the public and trained them not only as sentry dogs but also to carry messages on the front line. The heroic dogs on both sides had already proved just how useful they could be in peacetime.

After the war, in spite of their origins, German shepherds went on to become the favoured dog of the British police, but they called them Alsatians to avoid having to use the 'G' word. The focus of police dogs largely continued to be helping protect railways and docks, although some Labradors were also trained to patrol the streets. From the 1960s police dogs began to be used for security in the country's growing number of airports. More police dogs were officially trained at special police dog training schools and the police dogs we know today became an official part of modern British policing.

As well as their skills in guarding and tracking criminals, dogs came in handy in other ways for law enforcement. In the early 1970s a police dog in Southampton was trained to detect cannabis and alerted to a pile of cannabis in the back of a van by somersaulting backwards, not an alert which seems to have caught on widely as far as I can tell but it must have been good gear. While the use of police dogs to sniff out drugs is extremely useful for cracking down on organized crime, another threat in the 1970s was beginning to feel even more urgent. There was a spate of bombings at high-profile sites across London, including Westminster, the Tower of London and Oxford Street. The Provisional IRA had begun a wave of attacks on mainland Britain. On 20 July 1982 a remote-controlled car bomb exploded near Hyde Park, targeting soldiers of the Household Cavalry, the queen's bodyguards. Two hours later another bomb exploded underneath a bandstand in Regent's Park. Eleven people were killed that day and at least fifty-nine injured. Those who died included seven army bandsmen who had been playing on the bandstand, along with four members of the Household Cavalry and seven horses. The terror attacks continued, including a bomb outside the department store Harrods, which killed six people, and the Conservative Party conference in Brighton in 1984 in which five people died. In the wake of these and other attacks in the 1980s, explosive-detection dogs began to be used officially by the police. They were trained to sniff out explosives at the site of planned attacks, as well as to sniff out hidden devices at the location of ongoing emergencies. But there was another attack on the horizon which no one was expecting.

Just before Christmas in 1988 a Boeing 747 Pan Am flight bound from London to New York exploded over the Scottish town of Lockerbie. A timer-activated bomb had detonated on board. All 243 passengers, along with the sixteen flight crew, were killed. Eleven residents of Lockerbie who had been on the ground at the time were also killed. It was the deadliest terror attack in UK history. Two police dog handlers were among those who arrived quickly at the scene of the tragedy. For the next thirty-three hours they searched the area, this time not for explosives but for the bodies of those who had perished. Those dogs and their handlers recovered twenty-three people. But the wreckage had been scattered across an area covering nearly 850 square miles. More police dog handlers, along with search and rescue dog teams from across the country, continued to help for another four weeks. In a town which usually had four police officers, there were soon over a thousand police officers, along with hundreds of military, emergency workers and voluntary groups. In a moving gesture, if an item of clothing was found in the wreckage, local people in Lockerbie would wash, dry and iron the garments in order that they could be returned to the grieving relatives with a sense of dignity. The victims on this international flight were from over twenty countries including 190 Americans. They ranged from a two-month-old baby to an eighty-two-year-old and nearly half of those on board were under the age of twenty-five. It was eventually discovered that the explosives had been placed inside a cassette player in a suitcase and it led to an increase in the checking of luggage at airports. But it was another terrorist attack overseas, the Madrid bombings in 2004, which highlighted the need for even more security. In the aftermath of the terrible attack in the Spanish capital, which killed 193 people and injured over 2,000, British police added dozens more explosive-search dogs to their teams. It was only a matter of time before those dogs would be needed here.

On the morning of 7 July 2005 London woke up to the devastating news that four suicide bombers had attacked the public transport network, killing fifty-two people in addition to themselves, and injuring nearly 800 others. Among the many emergency workers hailed for their response to the attacks were three police sniffer dogs that had been brought in to check for more devices. They included two Labradors, Vinnie and Billie, and a spaniel called Jake, who risked their lives to assist the police in checking the sites of the attacks for more explosives. Black Labradors Vinnie and Billie both entered the choking smoke and heat of the London Underground tunnels with their police handlers. Black-and-white spaniel Jake accompanied his handler on board the wreckage of the bus which exploded outside Tavistock Square. The police feared there could be another device on the luggage rack. Thankfully there was not. It was dangerous work but this behind-the-scenes checking to ensure the areas were safe was needed before the rescue and recovery operations could begin. The dogs also helped check other locations throughout the day and afterwards all three were awarded the Dickin Medal for gallantry.

Along with the work of drug and explosive sniffer dogs many canines in law enforcement are what's called General Purpose Dogs. They're often German shepherd dogs that accompany police on their patrols. This was what Emma Dignam, twenty years after she had first seen the police dogs on the agility course at that open day, was hoping to do. She had passed her police training and become a regular PC, then she began to learn all she could from the officers she knew in the dog unit. On her days off she helped them out with their training, absorbing everything she could. Then one day a post came up. Emma knew she wasn't really qualified yet but she applied anyway. Unsurprisingly it was a hard no. A while later another post came up. Again the answer was: you're not ready. Then in 2010 ten jobs came up for dog handlers in her area. Emma applied again. The only snag was so did nearly 400 other people. But she was persistent. She went before a board to be assessed and she must have impressed them because she got through to the next stage. This was four days at the police dog training school in Keston, where you have what's called a suitability check. You have to show how you handle dogs in real life and demonstrate you'll be up to the role. The first thing Emma had to do was confidently get into the kennel with a load of huge shepherd dogs. As she climbed inside with the pack she kept her cool. In fact, she was so relaxed around the animals the trainers couldn't believe she had never even had a pet dog before. On the course Emma met a bloke, one of the other applicants, and they seemed to hit it off, but for now her focus was getting through to the next stage. The instructors told her to take one of the female dogs out and up to a nearby field. As they walked together Emma felt straight away that she had struck up a bond with this dog as it trotted along beside her, its ears up, tongue hanging out. By the end of her test Emma already felt like she was one of the pack, as if she had been born part dog. It felt like her destiny.

Prince

Emma's instincts were right. She was finally accepted as a police dog handler. It was a massive achievement. She was one of only ten people who got through. But this was only the beginning. She now had to start the long job of training her own dog. Eventually an email came through telling her she could go and collect a puppy. The police have their own litters, so officially it would actually belong to the constabulary, but for the next two years they would live together and train together and then hopefully fully qualify together. The other thing Emma had hanging over her, apart from the training, was that at any moment they could take the dog away if it didn't seem like the right fit or if it wasn't up to the job. It was Emma who was ultimately responsible for their success. When she arrived at the kennel, there was a litter of around twelve puppies, fluffy ginger-and-black beauties with long ears and huge paws. They all had different-coloured collars and each one also had a different bit of fur shaved off its tail. One had the tip off the end, another a ring around the base, to tell them apart.

It was a tradition to have a different letter for each group of new recruits. That year all the dogs were named with the letter 'R'. Emma's dog, with three rings shaved into its tail, had been named Regency George by the kennel staff. That would remain his permanent working name, but she could also give him a pet name. She chose to call him Prince. The bloke on the suitability course she had quite fancied had also got through the application. He also happened to be picking a dog out of the same litter as hers. When he told Emma that he was calling his dog Tanyon, she laughed. It would mean every time he wrote his name in a statement it would say 'Police Dog Tanyon'. So of course she married him.

Emma wasn't married at this point, though. But she was living with Prince. He wasn't just the first police dog Emma had brought into her home, but he was also the first dog of any kind she had ever cared for. There was an instruction manual and there were police trainers on hand to help, but when it came down to the hard graft and everyday work Emma and Prince were on their own. There were still no guarantees they would fully qualify.

Like an anxious new parent, Emma immediately began keeping a diary, logging everything Prince did. She wanted to make sure everything was happening at the right time. First they had to do the basic obedience training, the kind you might do with any dog: teaching him to sit, to heel and come when called and basically not be a total nuisance. The police element to the training began with scent detection, tracking of disturbed ground and then finding various objects. On the job the dog needs to be able to track a person who is hiding and find things they might have discarded, like a knife, a mobile phone, drugs or other potentially nefarious items. We've taken every dog we've ever had to puppy class; it's essential to get them socialized. But working at this level is something I, and probably most pet owners, are not so familiar with. For Emma it all started in a two-foot-by-two-foot patch of ground outside. She had to stamp it down with her feet then lead Prince into the square and introduce him to the scent left by her feet. She would then reinforce this scent with a food reward. That way Prince learned to associate her scent with something good. After they had done this for ages repeatedly, Prince eventually came to know that he only found the food in the areas of that two-foot square where the ground had been disturbed. When Prince fully associated this scent with his reward, Emma was then able to progress to training Prince along a whole trail of footsteps. They gradually worked further across the field, two fields and beyond, until Emma was laying a track of human scent all the way along a route. She would then leave the route for an hour before taking Prince over. She would release him and then see if he could follow the route the whole way. The biggest challenge was that it's not easy to find a piece of ground in an urban area which is free of other human scent. Eventually Emma had to get up at four in the morning to lay a scent track in her local park, just to make sure no one else had recently walked there. If she waited until everyone else was up it would be so full of the smell of other humans it would be impossible to train Prince at all. Prince turned out to be a pretty good learner and excellent at sniffing out a track.

Next up was something called 'ground service'. This means locating and indicating a piece of property which has recently been handled by a human. It isn't just a case of locating a discarded knife or a bag of drugs. Prince also had to learn to be incredibly careful not to disturb it. It's not only about finding the object but also about keeping it intact enough to preserve any forensic, DNA or other evidence. In policing terms this could mean the difference between having enough evidence to prosecute someone or not. Teaching

Prince, an excitable young German shepherd, that when he found something at the end of a long trail he wasn't allowed to pick it up and play around with it was not the easiest job in the world. In the end, though, after many weeks of practice, Prince was being a star and was able to restrain himself enough to leave the object alone.

There was one thing he couldn't quite get right, though. Another reward Prince liked when he did something well, in addition to food, was a toy to play with. The problem was, once he had hold of that toy he would run off with it and not come back for ages. He was thinking to himself, *Job done, great. I can go off and do my own thing now.* He'd be having the time of his life, frolicking about in the park with his toy and he had no idea he was supposed to be doing anything else. If she was going to get him to come back to her, Emma now had the challenge of becoming more fun than that toy. She tried everything, running backwards the length of three fields, jumping, dancing, shouting and hollering all at once to try to get his attention. Then one day – maybe Prince just decided to appease her – it suddenly clicked. She couldn't believe it. He had that toy – he was so happy – but she called him and he came back straight away. From that day onwards, even with his favourite toy, Prince's recall was perfect.

There was one more thing he still had to crack, though. During training they use a lot of cut-up hot dogs and chicken sausage to reward the dogs. Emma found that when they were doing group training with other dog handlers, Prince quickly learned that if he just kept his nose on the ground behind the others he'd find all the bits of sausage everyone had dropped. Smart dog. Because he was always sniffing for sausages he never wanted to put his head up, which was where it was meant to be to pass the training, so Emma was then never in a position to reward him for being in the right place because he was basically just rewarding himself. In the end Emma worked out that if she was able to reward Prince with something even tastier than sausage, which didn't need to be dropped, he would keep his head up. The answer: squeezy cheese. Emma carried a tube of squeezy cheese with her everywhere they went, and Prince, who loved a bit of cheese, eventually learned to take his reward from her with his head up. As Prince kept his eyes on her more and more as they worked together, she was also now realizing that the adoring look she had seen in those police dogs when she was five may have looked like love – it probably was love – but there was also a good dose of 'If I look at you long enough and adoringly enough, you're going to give me something nice, aren't you?'

After two years of training together, in addition to her job as a general purpose PC, Emma and Prince finally qualified as a dog team. Now the real fun and the real challenges would begin.

With general purpose policing, the day shifts start early, at six a.m. As you take over from the night shift you might get things like early burglaries coming in. Or you might have time for a cup of tea first. When the day starts, if there are no emergencies to deal with, it's a case of driving around, patrolling and waiting for a call. Emma worked in south-east London so her area included Bexley, Bromley and Lewisham. On any given day or night they might be responding to multiple calls and assisting their fellow PCs when needed. If a call came in, she and Prince would respond to that. There might be a robbery in Bromley, a missing person in Croydon, and a dog team needed to help with somebody who has run from the police, dropping a load of drugs. They might not be things which hit the headlines but as Prince began to go out in the real world Emma kept a log, like a proud parent, of all the positive things he did. Like the time a bloke was acting suspiciously and ran away from the police. Emma and Prince caught up with him three streets later. He had nothing on him so the question was, why did he run? Emma was able to retrace his steps with Prince and find a bag of drugs, a knife and some car keys. When they hit the car keys it pinged in the next road. Job done. This could be the proof they need in court to convict the guy. Because Prince had indicated that these objects all had the scent of the man who ran, it could be the extra layer of evidence that made all the difference in court.

One of the proudest moments for Emma was when she was asked to help find a missing person who was a suicide risk. The family were beside themselves with worry. Prince managed to track the route the missing person had taken from the back door of their house. It was the middle of the night and Emma and Prince ended up being led by the scent over numerous fences through the neighbourhood. Time was critical. Eventually Prince found the missing person in a patch of woodland three quarters of a mile away and got them back to their family. It was a good night's work.

One of the biggest tests for Prince was whether he was going to be able to stop someone running away, not on a training course but in the real world. While you have more control of what you can see in a park, in a street environment it's not always possible for the dog to keep the person in sight given all the obstacles around them. In one particular incident some schoolkids had had their mobile phones and pagers stolen. Emma was driving around with one of her dog handler colleagues, when they saw someone who fitted the description of the suspect in a nearby golf course. It was still early days for Prince. Emma was nervous about using him and not her colleague's dog for this one. In the end they decided to risk it and give Prince a chance to prove himself. So Emma got him out of the vehicle, released him on to the golf course and told him to 'Go, go.' Prince immediately chased after the suspect. The suspect started running past a lot of bewildered golfers. Prince was hot on the guy's heels and gaining on him. Eventually the dog managed to get hold of the man's coat and held on to him until Emma arrived. The problem was, because Prince only had hold of his coat, the man was able to simply shrug it off and keep running. When Emma, who had not caught up with them yet, saw this she wondered what Prince would do next. Would he think he'd done his job now that he had the coat? Prince dropped the coat and kept running. He got hold of the bloke again, this time on his arm. Emma arrived and put the handcuffs on. The suspect had all the stuff from the robbery still on him so it was a slam dunk.

Working with Prince was a 24/7 partnership. Not only was he a police dog but he was also Emma's friend and companion. After a long day's work they would curl up on the sofa together. He was with her every day and their bond grew immensely. During this time Emma got together with that bloke from the suitability course. He was also a dog handler and in the end they had a house full. When Emma eventually had her first child and went on maternity leave, Prince was also off and kept her company. He was so gentle and caring and he didn't complain one bit about becoming a house dog for a while, even as his police dog mates were still getting all the action on the streets. When the time came, Emma was nervous about them going back to work. She had already faced some not so harmless banter about being one of the few women in the dog section. She knew she was seen by some as a 'girl doing a bloke's job'. She had always felt she had to prove that she was up to the task and just as capable of being part of a working dog team as the men. She had proved it and she and Prince were respected by their colleagues 100%, but now they had been away for a while and some of them wondered whether she would be able to do it now she had a child. Prince has had his feet up, they would joke. He's gone soft. No sooner was Prince back on the streets, though, than he and Emma were proving them all wrong. One of Prince's first jobs was to track down a guy who had run away. He got straight to it and rumbled him hidden in a wheelie bin. Prince was back in the game.

When Emma became pregnant with her second child she wasn't as keen to get back to work as she had been the first time. She had been fortunate that her mother-in-law had been willing to help with looking after her first baby, but it felt like too much to expect that of her again. Also, if Emma didn't go back within the time limit she would have to give Prince back. She didn't think she could bear that. Prince was at an age where he was eligible to retire, so Emma decided to retire him so that she could spend more time with her baby and keep her beloved dog. Just as before, Prince was a perfect gent about being a house dog. Emma did everything to keep him motivated and stimulated at home. Both her kids fell in love with him. Then the worst thing happened. After he retired, Prince was diagnosed with something called idiopathic vestibular disease, which can cause a loss of balance. Emma took him to the vets to try and get him well again. Just after Christmas 2018, Prince went in for an operation they thought he would come back from. Sadly, they discovered he also had liver sarcoma and Prince died unexpectedly on the operating table. They had been together every day for eight and a half years. Now with no warning at all he was no longer there. The only way Emma can describe it is that it was as if she had lost her shadow. Prince was so closely bonded to her that he would be at her side all the time, even if she just got up to make a cup of tea. The grief was strong and deep. She could hardly speak to anyone for ages.

When her partner's police dog, Tanyon, died they both knew what it was like to lose your shadow. When they decided to get married, she had both Prince and Tanyon's paw prints printed out and made into a bracelet. She wore it as she walked down the aisle and felt in some way as though both dogs were with her. After losing Prince, Emma also got her first tattoo. It was not something she had ever thought about doing before, but now, in her forties, she took the plunge. She wanted some way for Prince to remain with her. She got a tattoo of his paw print and now, if she's ever feeling down, she can reach out and it helps her to say to herself it's OK. Her friend isn't here any more. But it's OK.

Losing your friend and your workmate isn't the only thing Emma and other police dog handlers have to face. When Prince and Tanyon retired, Emma realized that another huge challenge for police dog handlers can be the vet bills. These can sometimes very quickly become unmanageable, especially if the dog gets ill or has had any injuries, something which police dogs, due to the risky nature of their jobs, are more likely to suffer than the average pet dog. Emma ended up having to remortgage her house after paying £11,000 worth of vet bills and she discovered she wasn't alone. She and another dog handler, Phil Wells, realized that many police dog handlers end up in the same position and they decided to do something about it.

Obi

Phil Wells's first police dog was an eight-week-old German shepherd dog called Obi. Phil and Obi went through all the same training as Emma and Prince. Then Phil and Obi joined the support team for firearms officers. Being a police dog can be pretty dangerous, chasing people with knives who might have something to hide, but the stakes could be a lot higher supporting the firearms team. Dogs who work with firearms officers have to be ultra reliable. The work often involves sending a dog into a building first. Firearms officers will then go in after them to search for anyone with a lethal weapon. Sometimes a suspect is hidden, under a bed or in a wardrobe, say, so the dog has really got to use its nose to find them. Wherever they are, the dogs are trained to go in and bark at the suspects. It's their handler's legal obligation to make sure that people are challenged to come and show themselves. If someone is not compliant, the dog is trained to grab hold of them with their teeth. In one incident a firearm was seen inside a building through a window. When Obi went in ahead of the team he found the suspect hiding under a bed. He grabbed hold of him until the team arrived and were able to detain him. At any point the man could have used that gun against Obi. But Obi didn't know this. For him it was just one big game. Getting to be out and about, having fun, barking at people and getting his rewards. While a pet dog might walk around the same park every day, or if they're lucky dash about in fields like our lot, the things Obi did from day to day, finding blood-soaked knives and bags of drugs, and sniffing out people hiding under beds, would make that seem like, well, a walk in the park.

What neither Phil nor Obi knew was just how real that game can sometimes get.

In August 2011 Phil and Obi had not long been qualified together. They were working a shift patrolling Heathrow Airport. They would arrive in a dog van and then walk through the terminals checking for any issues. It was all so new it was exciting for Phil, being in a dog van then going out with Obi and doing some real policing at one of the biggest airports in the world. They spent their shift checking the terminals for any suspicious activity. Every now and then an excited holidaymaker would come over and give Obi a stroke or a pat. It was also a form of community engagement to be out and about with the dog. At around about eight o'clock at night a call came over the radio. They wanted all the units in London, all available dog vans, to head to Tottenham High Road on what they call 'the hurry up', which means with their blue lights and sirens. Phil was wondering whether he was allowed to leave the airport. He wondered if he might get in trouble for leaving his official post. Then the call came out again. Every dog van down to Tottenham High Road. It was obviously something big.

They jumped in the van and on the way over they heard over the radio how events were unfolding. It had begun as a peaceful protest march to demand a dialogue with police over the shooting of a local black man, Mark Duggan. But that night the protest had turned into something else altogether. Phil had done a lot of public order training but he had not expected to have to use it that night. By the time they arrived things had started to kick off. Some of the local police officers, although they weren't actually in riot gear, had round shields. Missiles were being thrown. Phil located

his supervisor, who briefed him. He said they would probably want the dogs to be deployed. At first Phil thought
things might calm down, like they sometimes do at football
matches. You get a small crowd who seem to be a bit hyped
up and violent, but then it all just sort of peters out. But
this time things kept building. A huge industrial wheelie bin
was set on fire. A couple of people pushed it into the police
lines. More officers joined. They made the decision to send
all six dogs in and begin public order tactics. Phil put his
flameproof overalls on along with protective guards and a
helmet. Then, with Obi on a nylon harness, they made their
way closer to the front. They were behind the shield officers who were moving forward slowly towards the crowd.
Windows were being broken, missiles were being thrown
and fireworks were being let off. There were burning cars.
A bus was ablaze and a police van was set on fire. Phil
couldn't believe he was in the middle of London. It was so
surreal. It was like watching an episode of *The Bill* or a TV
series he might have watched as a kid. But it was real. At
one point Phil looked up to see objects coming through the
air. All of a sudden he saw something coming close. It hit
Obi straight on the head. It looked like a piece of masonry
or brick. He heard Obi yelp. By this point it was around
eleven o'clock. It was pitch black, other than a bit of street
lighting and the light from a car burning nearby. Phil didn't
really have time to assess what had happened. Going
backwards at this point wasn't really an option. So he got
down on his hands and knees to check Obi and give him a
once-over as much as he could. Obi had no visible injuries.
The dog was by now pretty revved up and excited too, along
with the other five dogs. It was a kind of wolf pack

mentality, a 'we're gonna take on the world' sort of thing, although Obi was more barking at the other dogs than the crowd. He and Phil along with the other officers continued trying to hold back the crowd. After a while they got to a shop where there was more lighting. It was one of those shops where the fruit and vegetables are out the front. The shopkeepers came out with huge bottles of water. The officers turned what they call short shields, smaller round shields, upside down and poured the water into them like big bowls so the dogs could have a drink. The shopkeepers also brought apples for the police horses who had been called in. Many people from the community not involved in the disturbances were supportive of the police. After all, they didn't want their shops being looted, smashed up or set on fire.

All of a sudden Phil saw an old art deco building on the corner had been set alight. Flames were billowing out of all the floors. The night sky was lit up orange. Phil thought he saw snow falling. But in August it obviously wasn't snowing. It was ash from the fire. The whole place was awash with embers falling down. While the initial protest may have begun as a genuine grievance, people wanting to find out what had happened in the shooting and to discuss long-standing issues in the community around the policing of young black men, it had turned into something else altogether. Partly fuelled by opportunism and overexcitement, it had clearly gone way beyond the original protest. But because it had been spontaneous there had been no real plan for the police to follow as they might have had for an organized demonstration.

By around five o'clock in the morning things were beginning to die down. Phil was dazed and exhausted. He and Obi made their way back to the van. They took a breather with their colleagues for a while, trying to take on board what had just happened, then they drove back to their base in west London. When they got there, Phil noticed a trickle of blood coming out of one of Obi's nostrils. Phil knew the dog was tired but he seemed unusually lethargic. Phil and a friend drove Obi to the local vets who straight away told them Obi had suffered quite a severe impact to his head but they didn't have the equipment to scan him. After fifteen months of training and one of the most ridiculously bizarre evenings anyone could expect to have in their career or lifetime, Phil was devastated, as he realized that his dog might have an injury which could impact Obi's working ability or even his life. Phil got Obi booked in for a CT scan as soon as possible. This revealed that Obi had a major trauma to the skull just above the eye socket. The force of the object that had hit him had also caused multiple fractures in a kind of rippling effect. Phil feared the worst. But he was reassured that Obi didn't need any major operations. After some rest and recuperation and a few months off Obi was able to go back to work.

What Phil had not anticipated was that, basically overnight, Obi would become a dog celebrity. Dozens of police officers had been injured that night and two or three other dogs had suffered more minor injuries, but the story of this injured service dog really captured the public imagination. They found themselves sitting on the BBC's red sofa doing live interviews. Sky News turned up at their base, then ITV News. Phil went from being a Joe Bloggs police officer slash dog handler to now being asked for interviews and photographs. It was quite a whirlwind. Obi, after some training to make sure that he was still able to do the job and that he was comfortable doing it, was eventually signed back to work. He was awarded the PDSA Order of Merit on behalf of all the police dogs deployed during the disturbances.

The London terror attacks weren't to be the last dramatic moment in Phil's dog-handling career. When Obi retired, Phil got another police dog, another shepherd dog called Quinn. They were deployed together during the 2017 London Bridge terror attacks. When a van was driven into ten pedestrians, three attackers came out armed with knives and what looked like suicide vests and ran through Borough Market attacking members of the public. Phil and Quinn assisted firearms officers as they carried out searches for any outstanding suspects who may have been involved. Eight people were killed in total during the attack, with forty-eight people injured. Many police dog teams were rewarded for their actions that day. Obi retired after doing his full eight and a half years of service. He lived with Phil until he sadly died in 2019 aged eleven. After Prince died, Emma Dignam decided to go back to general purpose policing and leave the dog unit. She didn't handle another dog, but she still has a houseful as her husband is still in the dog section. She will never forget how she and Prince lived the dream together.

Phil has since worked with another police dog, Parker, an English springer spaniel who was trained to locate firearms, cash and narcotics. Both Parker and Quinn are now retired. Phil's newest recruit is Dora, who passed out of doggy training school last year.

In 2019, Phil and Emma set up the London Retired Police Dogs Trust. So far, they have paid out over £160,000 to provide support for officers in London to care for their retired police dogs.

Working dogs don't always find it easy to retire. They can get bored, stuck at home. Like my retired guide dog Laura, who spent so many years being clever and attentive, all working dogs love to have something for their brains to do. So every once in a while the charity also arranges to take some of the retired dogs to London City Airport. It helps keep them ticking over, even if it's just meeting people and getting a good old pet and a stroke. All the working dogs we live with also have another purpose in our lives. Some of Phil's fondest memories of Obi are of when they would go for walks together, just the two of them, after their shift. Even if it was in the middle of the night, in the pitch dark after a long day, even when he couldn't even see Obi, it was a chance for Phil to take stock and get his breath back after whatever the shift had thrown at them. He knew Obi was there trotting along right by his side, a most wonderful therapy and friend.

Flower the horse and Harriet Laurie, who founded TheHorseCourse to transform lives through natural horsemanship.

10. Horse Therapy

Flower Power

For almost as long as she can remember, Harriet Laurie has wanted to be around horses. She was born, as she puts it, with a mane and tail. As a child she had a dream of being in an open field. She would whistle and a beautiful horse would come galloping over. In the dream Harriet would jump on its back with no saddle and off they would go. Or sometimes in the dream she wouldn't even ride the horse; they would just play games or walk alongside one another and the horse would be a willing partner, enjoying it as much as she did. Harriet did eventually get to be around horses. She even got a job as a helper at a yard where they worked with Olympic dressage horses. It was, in a way, a dream come true. She got a really high level of education in horsemanship and saw and experienced some wonderful things. But she also saw some miserable things going on with the way the horses were treated and it made her really sad. It was far from the vision she had of playing freely in harmony with a horse with no ropes or equipment.

When Harriet grew up and had children her horse obsession wasn't supported by her partner, so she had to take a break from them for a while. But when her children were a bit older, and she had ditched the partner, she eventually found her way back to horses. This time her experience was very different. She discovered a way of working with horses that's called 'natural horsemanship'. A bit like what I experienced with Monty Roberts and my horse Chester, it's based on being kind, loving and playful. It takes its inspiration from how in the Wild West, cowboys went in two directions. There were the ones who were really good at tying horses down and essentially breaking their spirit. Then there were those who didn't like getting injured so they took a more subtle, nuanced approach. This more natural style was picked up and per-fected by a number of people over the years, including Monty and a man called Pat Parelli, whose teaching is called the Parelli method.

When Harriet found out about the Parelli method she became obsessed. It seemed to fulfil everything she had dreamed about of connecting with horses completely natur-ally. Harriet got her own pony, a sweet Connemara gelding called Stormy. She kept him and another horse in a ten-acre field on a farm. As she got more and more into it, she got pretty good at working with horses in this way, even to the point where people were asking her for advice about their own horses. The more Harriet learned about connecting with horses without dominating them, with no ropes or harsh words, the more she wanted to see how far she could take it. When it was time to get another horse for the herd she decided she wanted a young one she could start with from scratch. She also had another requirement. It had to be a really difficult horse that everyone else had given up on. Harriet began ringing around local stud farms asking if they had any horses they thought were beyond training, basically looking for their rejects.

Of course when the stud farms found out Harriet wanted their worst horses they said, 'Fantastic, come right on over.' On one of the huge farms where they bred racehorses,

Harriet was taken into a field which was mostly full of old mares. Among them was a young filly, a three-year-old called Flower. She was, as they put it, 'a nightmare and totally unmanageable.' When Harriet swung a rope around to see how the horses responded, they all set off together. But this young filly set off at the highest speed of all. She was also the first one to screech to a halt, turn round and come prancing back to see what they were going to do next.

Harriet was impressed. She really wanted a playful horse. It seemed like as soon as Flower saw Harriet swinging the rope, she thought, *This is fun. This is interesting. I'm really bored out here with all these old mares. What are we gonna do next?* Flower was bred to be a racehorse and she was absolutely, stunningly beautiful. She was a big classic bay thoroughbred with a white triangle in the middle of her huge head. She was very shiny, sleek and dainty on her toes too. She had the most glorious elevation of movement. She seemed to sort of float across the field. Flower was bred to be quick. Her father was a really famous stallion. She could have been worth a fortune, but she refused to be controlled in the way they controlled the horses on this big stud farm, running them in huge herds and halter breaking them en masse. When they tried to halter break Flower she wasn't having any of it. Her mother, rather tellingly, was called No Bid. By the time Harriet saw Flower the stud farm had completely given up on her. So of course Harriet said straight away, 'I'll take her,' and they said, 'Great!'

The next day they put Flower in the lorry and took her over to the field where Harriet kept her Connemara pony Stormy and another horse. She left them to it, hoping they would form a herd of three. When Harriet came back up to the field later that evening she was shocked to see that Stormy had banished Flower to the side of the field. It's unusual for a gelding not to accept a new mare into his group so she wondered what was wrong. In her imagination she thought that when Flower had discovered her new herd consisted of this fluffy little pony and another random horse, she had been a bit fussy and gone, 'But where are all the big stallions?' She had, after all, come from a huge stud farm with hundreds of enormous thoroughbreds. Stormy stood on his dignity and had seemingly responded with something to the effect of 'Well, if you don't like it, you can get out of my herd of two.'

So poor Flower was left standing in the field alone. Horses get really anxious if they're alone and Flower did look sad and anxious; she was clearly pining for company. After a while Harriet became more worried because Flower wasn't eating either. Then one day Harriet came into the field to see that Flower had obviously decided, 'I've had enough of this. I'll make a herd of my own.' She was standing at the far end of the field casually grazing with Thelma and Louise, the farm's resident giant pigs. With her own herd of two pigs Flower now had company and was eating happily, but she was still reluctant to be touched. Harriet began gradually building things up to normalize her presence. She reached out gently with a stroking stick, but she always backed off as soon as Flower seemed to have had enough. She would try to pique Flower's curiosity and encourage her to come over and see for herself. Harriet encouraged the horse's playfulness and bit by bit Flower did begin to allow a small amount of contact.

One day Flower got into a fight with a gate and cut herself badly. Harriet had to go in and treat the wound. The horse was in the pigs' barn and she just about accepted Harriet touching her, but she couldn't be restrained or held at all.

This would be the ultimate test of whether Flower trusted her. So Harriet sat with her for hours until she finally let Harriet check and clean the wound and then treat it. Almost like a light switch turning on there was a moment when Flower suddenly seemed to understand that Harriet was purely trying to help her. She seemed to say, 'OK, I get it now. I know your sort all try to tie me down and force me to do things, but this is OK.' It was a turning point. Flower went from being tense around Harriet – tight-lipped and unnaturally still, she would hold her breath and had a kind of staring look in her eyes – but after that day she was relaxed. Her breathing became normal. Her head was down and calm and every now and then she would give it a relaxed little shake. The more time she spent with her, Harriet realized that Flower was the most emotionally connected horse she had ever known. If she was ever feeling sad, Flower would come and stand by her. She would put her head round Harriet so she was in the curve of Flower's huge neck. Then she would just stand over her, as if she was protecting her. Being around Flower was its own kind of therapy. If Harriet was stressed, Flower would immediately pick up on it. That's how horses survive in the wild, by being able to tell when something's not right. So Harriet began to search for what she calls 'true neutral', being totally calm in the mind and in your emotions, and being really still and quiet in your body. When Harriet was completely calm, Flower was completely calm and she knew that everything was OK.

As things were going so well with Flower, Harriet started teaching other women in her area how to be around their own horses in the same way. She would do a series of exercises with the horses, like going from running to stopping and going backwards, all without any ropes or sometimes without even a halter. It was about doing it all through body language. The trick was that while the women thought they were learning horsemanship, under the radar they were really learning about themselves. There were loads of things Harriet knew the horse could teach you. How to be calm. How to be a better leader. She soon found that although the women came to her to learn about their horses, after spending a few days learning about natural horsemanship they discovered they were also able to get on better with their kids and their partners at home. They found it altogether easier to manage their lives. They were more focused, confident, assertive. They had a plan and were able to confidently lead. All the skills which Harriet was teaching with horses, it turns out, work just as well in your own life and relationships.

When people found out about her transformative work with these women and their horses several people made the same bizarre suggestion to Harriet. 'You should do this work in prisons.' At first she wondered why people kept trying to send her to prison. 'Don't be ridiculous,' she'd say. 'You can't take horses into prison.' Somehow, though, Harriet was cajoled into meeting with the head of reoffending at Portland Prison in Dorset, a young offenders institution. Around that time an ex-death row inmate from America called John Thomspon was visiting. He had been exonerated for a murder he didn't commit and was over from America to talk about prison reform in the area. John had spent fourteen years on death row in solitary confinement. He had only ever known horses used for crowd control and he was afraid of them. So naturally they asked Harriet if she would give him a horse session.

That's how one midwinter day on a hilltop in Dorset,

Harriet found herself introducing ex-death row inmate John Thompson to Flower. Knowing that John was afraid of horses, she was a little apprehensive. But when she saw them together it was one of the most beautiful things Harriet had ever seen. It was clear that John immediately understood Flower in a way that she never would. He spoke to her so gently and so calmly. In his New Orleans drawl he whispered, 'It's all right, darling. I get it. You're scared. You're safe with me. It's OK.' Somehow John was able to totally empty himself of any predatory or worrisome behaviour and Flower immediately fell in love with him. Harriet was a little upset by this, since she had by this point been wooing Flower for about five years. Flower couldn't get enough of John. She was wrapping herself round him. Somehow she seemed to almost mind-meld with him as if she knew exactly what he was thinking. If he wanted her to put her foot in a tyre, which is quite a challenging task because for a horse this feels very dangerous, John seemingly only had to think about that tyre in a way that said 'Shall we?' and Flower would look at him and look at the tyre and go, 'Yeah, I'll do it.'

Harriet realized there seemed to be something about the experience of prisoners which allows them to relate very strongly to the experience of horses. Horses are, after all, whether we like to admit it or not, our prisoners when they live all their lives with us locked in fields and stables. After her experience with John Thompson, Harriet decided that she needed to be much, much softer with Flower than she had thought. She realized if she asked less of her, she would get so much more. From then on Harriet softened and softened and softened her approach. She got to the point where even just a very slight feeling of preference for being somewhere or doing something would translate to Flower and she would go there with her. Harriet eventually found that she could do almost anything and Flower would be right there with her, whether it was turning a sharp corner, coming to a halt or rocking back and forth. There was this extraordinary kind of magnetic connection between them. Her huge head was right by Harriet's shoulder. Her feet were in line with Harriet's feet. Flower would synchronize with her movements as if there was an invisible umbilical cord between them. It was the most remarkable feeling to be with this beautiful great big shiny, glossy, gloriously dramatic horse, who could, if she chose to, do the most amazing movements and leaps, and yet she chose to stick to Harriet.

Harriet's job at the time was as a designer and marketing consultant. She worked from home and her life was just fine. Then one summer she was persuaded to give the horse thing a go at Portland Prison in Dorset. She agreed to do it on the condition that they record some actual data in order to see if it really worked. The data the prison currently had came in the form of a big book in which they kept a note of prisoners' behaviour. They would mark it up with green ticks and red crosses, a bit like in school. They also logged things called adjudications. That's when a prisoner behaves really badly and they have to go up before the governor or, if it's really serious, in front of a judge like a little court case in the prison. This could prolong their sentence. With the data Harriet hoped she would be able to tell whether her work with the horses was having a real impact. In 2010 she took Flower and Stormy through the huge gates of Portland Prison and they marched together down a narrow corridor. On either side of them were all the inmates in the workshops. It was such a novelty for them to see these two horses trotting by and they all started banging on the windows. Harriet kept going and they made their way to the prison rugby pitch where the course was to take place.

When it came to the men on her course, rather like when she had first found Flower, she had said to the governor, 'Don't give me the good ones. Give me the prisoners who aren't responding to anything else.' So the first eight young men she worked with were all violent offenders and all of them had been deemed to have a high risk of reoffending. None of them had responded to any of the talk-based programmes at the prison. What Harriet did was similar to what she had already been doing with those women and their horses: basically a series of exercises with the horses through which you learn different skills. So Harriet would say something like, 'Let's see if we can pick up the horse's feet.' This is naturally going to bring up a little bit of anxiety even in the bravest of us. If you're not calm, a sensitive horse won't want you to pick up its foot because it won't feel safe. So the horse will start to move and go 'No thanks.' So Harriet's coaching might begin with, 'Let's take a big breath out. Feel the wind. Count the leaves on that tree.' Basically anything to bring emotions down and calm the mind, to try to stop the inmates worrying about what had happened that morning or who they got into a fight with in the breakfast queue, or what's going to happen later on because their visits have been cancelled. Over a number of days the inmates gradually learned to connect with Flower and Stormy through various challenges. They would try to get the horse to kick a ball or to get up on a pedestal. Or they would get Flower to run alongside them and weave in and out of cones. While the horses are trained to respond, they're also very carefully trained to not tolerate any tugging or aggressive behaviour from people. The most powerful thing is that it wasn't about talking; it was about doing, and then the horses give you feedback. Everything with the horses was an opportunity for Harriet to also coach useful human skills like calmness, kindness, having clear boundaries and being able to assert yourself without aggression. The horse tells you right away through body language and behaviour if you're not calm or assertive enough.

Harriet had asked for the most difficult prisoners and they took her at her word. There was one guy in particular who, just like Flower, had been written off as completely uncontrollable. He was constantly assaulting staff and the other prisoners. He was also very smart and entrepreneurial, selling all manner of things that he shouldn't be in prison. In the end he had become so dangerous he was effectively segregated all the time by being shipped to one prison after another. Perhaps with a little bit of wickedness, they had decided to send him to Harriet to see if this horse business was all it was cracked up to be. When Harriet introduced him to the horses she realized she might need to work with him one on one, so they set about the course together doing all the exercises. At one point the guy was backing Stormy up and Harriet saw that the horse was looking absolutely terrified. Stormy's eyes were big and bulgy and he was snorting away. Harriet grabbed the rope and said, 'No, no. We can't do that. Can you see how you've made him feel?' When the guy saw how frightened Stormy was, this man, who was the most feared person in the prison, immediately burst into tears right there in front of her. He had previously shown no remorse for some really horrendous crimes. He was on an indefinite sentence. He had been written off as being incapable of feeling. But there he was in floods of tears. He was only nineteen. It turned out that he had been incarcerated since he was fifteen. He had been brought up in care and been abused as a child. He was almost a cliché of how people can end up becoming violent and unpleasant when everyone has given up on them. There had been no judgement or harsh words needed from Harriet to get through to him, just the realization of the effect he had on Stormy and that they needed to work together to rectify it. By the end Harriet was also in tears. After a few days she was able to have a really candid conversation with this guy. 'If things carry on like this, you'll just be in prison for the rest of your life,' she said. 'Yes, you may have some infamy for being the most aggressive person here and everyone will be scared of you. But ultimately that's pretty boring, isn't it? Because they'll be leaving and you won't.' She went on, 'You've got such a good brain. You're so bright and you're so energetic. You might as well use it. Get an education here. Just get what you can. Try to keep your nose clean. Then get out into the real world and play a bigger game. Do something really fantastic and make loads of money.' The guy seemed to like that idea. It wasn't like he went from being a devil to an angel overnight, of course. But instead of being involved daily in violent incidents, after working with the horses those incidents went down to weekly, then monthly. He signed up for education and stopped mucking about. He even helped Harriet teach the next group of prisoners on the horse course. He kept his nose clean and he eventually got parole.

I've seen Flower and Harriet work their magic with my own eyes at Portland Prison. A guy in his late teens was being encouraged to ask the horse to walk nicely at his shoulder, not in front and not behind. As I was watching, his caseworker leaned forward and told me that it was the first time she'd seen him smile; he'd been there for six years – his sentence constantly lengthening due to behavioural issues. I saw him smile a dozen times as Flower allowed him to ask things of her, but only when he presented himself appropriately. An amazingly powerful impact on a young man who had been let down by everyone until Harriet and Flower turned up.

Once the course had been running for a while they looked at the data for all prisoners. Remarkably they found that adjudications had gone down by 70% in the horse group. The red crosses in the book also went down by 70%. It really did work. That's when Harriet decided to give up her job and start a charity, TheHorseCourse. She felt it was incumbent on her to continue this work as it really did seem to be having an impact. She carried on working in prisons for the next few years. She trained people to go into other prisons and they started collecting more and more data, finding that reoffending rates basically halved. This was all the more extraordinary since they were among a cohort of really hard to reach young men, many of whom had been deemed untreatable.

Sadly Harriet was not able to continue her work officially in prisons. She faced obstruction from within the prison system and despite ministerial support it was made impossible to continue. But she didn't give up. Instead she started working in communities directly. She is now commissioned by local authorities and the NHS to work with adults, children and adolescent mental health, in social services, domestic abuse and drug and alcohol services, homelessness services and with veterans. She works right across the board, from eight years old to adults and even with whole families. It's a shame they are no longer able to go into prisons because it so obviously has a huge benefit, but at least they now have a much broader remit. Hopefully it means they can get the horses to people before they even end up in prison in the first place. TheHorseCourse has ten other hubs around the UK now doing the same programme.

Flower and Stormy have worked with so many people

now. From the most violent young men in prison to the most vulnerable and traumatized, even little tiny tots come and work with the horses. Harriet has had social workers in tears at the change they see in the kids they bring in to see her. Flower, in particular, is always so tuned in to the little kids, walking at their speed, prancing around them and being stunningly beautiful with it. Sometimes someone starts off really shut down and anxious and then you see them open up and start smiling like never before. It's incredible to see how kids will literally unfurl with Flower and become like little superheroes. Harriet remembers one day seeing Flower with a little girl, who had started off really all over the place, totally fizzy and unable to calm down. Then all of a sudden she just pulled herself together and said, 'I'm going to walk around these cones and head for that blooming ball and I'm going to get Flower to get it in that goal if it kills me.' The little girl braced herself and went, 'Come on, Flower. Let's do it.' And this huge great horse went 'Yes, ma'am. You're the boss.' Then Flower and this tiny little tot went marching towards the ball and Flower kicked it straight in the goal. Moments like that and so many others are absolute pure gold.

One of those whose lives have been transformed by meeting Flower is Pablo. He was referred by the Veterans Hub to help reduce stress and anxiety. Pablo describes how, without any halter or ropes, completely free, he was able to weave in and out of the cones with Flower and move together in total synchronicity. When he stopped running, Flower stopped running. She even kicked a ball for him and he got her to stand up on a podium. As Pablo stood with his hand on her side he could feel how Flower's breathing and his breathing matched. He felt perfectly calm and happy. Even to this day he has a picture of Flower on his phone, which he uses all the time to calm his breathing and relax. Pablo now volunteers at TheHorseCourse, cutting hedges, strimming and doing jobs on the quad. He always loves a chance to see Flower and have a cuddle when he needs one. She may be a big horse but to Pablo she's his Little Flower and his darling and he says Flower literally saved his life.

Flower is now twenty-one. She doesn't work as much any more. She hangs out with her mates in the field or in the barn next to the little tearoom where the horses have their hay. Sometimes if she hasn't worked for a while, Flower will come swaggering in and put her head over the railing into the tearoom as if to say, 'Excuse me, have you forgotten me? What the hell's going on here?' Harriet finds it reassuring that she'll always tell them when she wants to work. She will also tell them when she doesn't.

They now have fifteen horses across two herds at TheHorseCourse. Naturally Flower is the lead mare in her group and everyone follows her. She's fair but firm. She definitely gives the other horses the look if they don't move out of the way. But what's also great about horses is that it's very soon all forgotten and everything's fine again. Horses don't hold a grudge. Another remarkable thing about Flower is that, while most horses are afraid of pigs, whenever she comes across them she will always rush over and say hello. She then makes these funny snorty noises as if, after once being in a herd with Thelma and Louise, she can actually speak Pig and is having a chat with them.

Quite often these days you'll find Flower lying flat out in the barn. She isn't remotely bothered by the clattering of the tearoom making lunch next door. It's incredible to see this huge horse that at one point nobody could touch and everyone had given up on looking so obviously relaxed and happy. She has helped so many people in her long life. Now she can afford to lie about a bit. She flops out on a bed of shavings and hay snoring really loudly, her big tummy moving in and out and her back feet and hooves tucked together neatly. It's adorable to see and she's one in a million. Flower isn't the only horse who has been busy transforming people's lives. Across the Atlantic there are some other remarkable stories of horse therapy in action.

Angels with Four Legs

In the late 1960s in the East Bay Area of northern California in a small town called El Sobrante, Mrs Rabak took a visit to the doctors. She was feeling unwell. She thought she had the flu but when the doctor took a look at her he joked that she must have a nine-month flu because she was pregnant. She was thirty-nine. She and her husband already had children; the oldest was now sixteen and they had not been planning any more. But the news was welcome. She gave birth to a boy and they named him Anthony. For the first few years he was a happy-go-lucky kid. The couple ran a hardware and appliance store selling and servicing fridges, ovens and washing machines, while she helped run the business side from the office, little Anthony could join his mother during the day. When he was five years old and had just started school, he began to get very sick and was diagnosed with leukaemia. The doctors at the hospital told them the devastating news, that their son had no more than five years to live. Anthony had entered their lives unexpectedly and now they couldn't imagine life without him. Anthony's parents asked the doctors if there was anything they could do. They were told about a new kind of treatment, an experimental form of radiation. They were desperate for anything to save him, so in 1974 Anthony began a combination of chemotherapy and radiotherapy.

His life for the next three years revolved around tough and painful hospital visits. At one point he underwent a course of radiation which lasted for thirty-six days. Radiation therapy today is much more targeted, but this was something called 'neuraxis radiation'. It was prolonged and covered his entire central nervous system, brain, abdomen and internal organs. Miraculously by the end of the treatment, although it had been extremely painful, Anthony's prognosis had vastly improved. The leukaemia had gone and the family no longer had a death sentence hanging over them.

With their child well again, Anthony's parents felt they had been given a second chance. They spoiled him just a little bit. Anthony loved cowboy movies and when they discovered there was a horse on a piece of land nearby which was co-owned by some of their neighbours, they jumped at the chance for him to ride the horse. Out in the field was a tan-coloured mare called Mama. As soon as Anthony was plonked on her back he felt a sense of huge freedom. After years of medical treatments and hushed conversations he only half understood, Anthony finally felt alive again. Even though he was so small and fragile after all his treatment, Mama was gentle and calm; she seemed to know just how to handle him, as though he was something precious. I remember when my own daughter Emily first rode a horse it was remarkable to see how such a large, powerful animal can treat a child with such sensitivity, as though handling something fragile. After a few weeks of riding Mama, Anthony gained more and more confidence. In spite of his small size he was able to trot around the field confidently. He felt like he was in the Wild West, riding into town. He was the most relaxed and calm he could ever remember being.

One day when he was being lifted on to Mama's back he realized he'd forgotten his cowboy hat. He asked his mother if she could fetch it for him. When she returned she came round the side of the horse to hand it to him. Mama didn't see her coming and all of a sudden she reared up, her front legs rising up, her flank arching backwards. Anthony lost his grip and was thrown into the air, landing in the dirt beneath her. As he lay there in the shadow of her huge body, time seemed to slow down. Anthony watched Mama's large hooves about to come down on top of him. At the last moment the horse spread her front legs outwards a fraction, just enough so her hooves hit the ground on either side of him. *Thud.* She had avoided him by a matter of inches. Anthony felt sure Mama had intentionally reacted at the last second in order not to hurt him. He could tell that, even though she was spooked, she had acted with compassion to protect him.

This may not be so far-fetched. I have heard several stories of shire horses or Clydesdales – big horses – with their owners trying to whip them to get a move on and the horses standing stock-still because there's a baby cuddling their legs that nobody's seen and the horse will take the whip to avoid disturbing or damaging the baby. I also know how easily a horse can get spooked but mean no harm at all. Like with our old mare Bee. One day I was getting her in from the fields and she snagged her rug on the gate. I was trying to get her to back up so I could unhook it but she was starting to panic and panic and panic. I knew she was about to go right through me so I threw myself over a fence because I knew she would have taken me out. But I also know that that horse loved me. She was spooked and all that musculature and skeleton had been sparked by adrenaline and fear. That makes it all the more remarkable to think that a horse could still act with compassion in such a case as Anthony's. Whether Mama was being compassionate or not, for Anthony's mother it didn't matter. She scooped up her son, relieved to see that he was uninjured even if he was shaken. She had nearly lost him once and she wasn't about to risk him getting injured or worse again. So that was that. It was the last time Anthony ever rode Mama the horse.

For weeks afterwards he longed for that freedom of being on her back with the wind in his hair. He missed talking to Mama and the way his spirit lifted as soon as he saw her. The memories soon began to fade, though. Eventually he moved on with his life. As he got older he was more preoccupied with the trials and tribulations of being a teenager and school. Ever since his time in hospital, Anthony had been nurturing an ambition. He had spent so much time in hospital and around medical people, he knew he wanted to help people and give something back. He felt the best way he could do that was to become a doctor. He talked about it so much at school that Anthony's friends began to joke whenever they saw him, saying, 'What's up, doc?' While he was trying to get the grades to get into college and study medicine, he also began to help his parents in the shop. He dealt with customers and stocked the warehouse when the appliances were delivered. When he got his driving licence he started delivering the appliances to the customers. Anthony is a little guy, only five foot two, so you can imagine how people would be when he showed up at their houses on his own, how they'd look behind him and ask, 'Where's the crew?' He'd smile and reply, 'I am the crew. Where do you want this refrigerator, ma'am?' Then he would wrangle the large fridge singlehandedly up the steps and into the house.

Anthony eventually got the grades he needed for college and was on course to study medicine. But one day he began to feel numbness and tingling in the bottom part of his hand. He couldn't exactly explain it but it didn't sit right with him. Anthony completed his first year of college but the numbness and tingling kept returning. Sometimes it felt like it wasn't ever going to go away. He didn't know what was wrong, but something told him he needed to change direction in life and he decided to become a youth pastor. Perhaps he could help people that way instead. He joined a local ministry school and, although his focus was on his work and becoming a pastor, he met a young woman named Valerie who piqued his interest. They became good friends along with a bunch of other students, but Anthony's mind kept drifting back to Valerie. He didn't say anything to her and then it was too late; she had become engaged to someone else. Anthony thought all hope was lost. But after a while Valerie confided in the group of friends that she was having doubts about her upcoming marriage. She called off the engagement, but to Anthony's dismay she also decided to move several hours away to San Jose. He had never told her how he felt and now he was heartbroken.

After a year Anthony moved to Sacramento and, to his amazement and delight, he discovered Valerie was now living there, not San Jose. He wasn't going to make the same mistake again. He immediately told her how he felt. After all that, it turned out that she felt the same way. In 1993 they got married. People joked that the Capital Bible Institute where they had studied should have been renamed the Capital Bridal Institute.

Anthony and Valerie began to build their life together. As well as working with his local church community he also started his own business detailing, or cleaning up, cars. He also travelled overseas with his father around Europe and became a motivational speaker, talking about his recovery from leukaemia as a child. He enjoyed speaking to people about what he had learned through his own challenges and tried to inspire others to find new purpose in life. In spite of all the newfound happiness for the couple, there was a lingering fear in the back of Anthony's mind. The tingling and numbness in his limbs was not going away and he still didn't know what was causing it. On one trip to Poland with his father Anthony was walking down a cobblestone stone street when he tripped and started to lose his balance. He felt like he was drunk, but they had only just had breakfast. Everyone was looking at him as if to say, 'It's a little early to be boozing, isn't it?' It was scary and distressing.

When he and his father got back to the hotel Anthony began to join the dots. The numbness in his hands and now this loss of balance. He wondered whether it could be something neurological. As soon as he got home he sought medical advice. Every doctor he went to said, 'This must be radiation damage from when you were a kid.' But they didn't know what it was exactly. He couldn't understand why something which happened to him decades ago, when he was only five years old, would be impacting him as an adult. After a few more years of testing he was finally diagnosed with Multiple Sclerosis. It had been triggered by the cancer treatments he had as a child. What had at first been an occasional numbness was progressing into something much more debilitating and unpredictable. He was finding it difficult to walk and having recurring problems with balance and strength.

The doctors had told him he was his own worst enemy, because while he continued to work he was falling and putting himself in danger. Although his car detailing business was doing really well, Anthony began to understand that he would not be physically able to continue for much longer. Eventually he was advised by his doctors to take it easy and he reluctantly gave up his business. While Anthony was trying to come to terms with his new normal, the disease began to progress. He was losing his mobility. He began to grieve for the things he used to be able to do. It was frustrating to push himself to do something that he used to manage without a second thought. It was a tangible loss.

Anthony had regular physiotherapy to help with his motor skills. He also read about a programme of therapeutic horse riding, something called hippotherapy. He had heard that riding horses could work many of the same muscles as walking. Human locomotion is not that dissimilar to the gait of horses when they walk. Anthony found out there was a hippotherapy centre not far away from his home town, so he put his name down on the list and waited and waited. He waited a year: still no space. As the months passed he and Valerie decided to move away from the busy university town of Davis where they lived to a more quaint, affordable community further north called Grass Valley. They had literally packed their bags, when Anthony got a call from the hippotherapy centre; two years after he had applied they had a place. But it was too late to cancel the move and he had to turn down the place, but as soon as they settled into their new home, top of his list was to find another horse therapy centre. Pretty soon he discovered one just twenty-five minutes down the road. It was a little more casual, not a certified medical hippotherapy centre, but they did their own kind of horse therapy there and, best of all, there were no waiting lists. They said, 'Come right on down.'

Other than riding Mama when he was a little kid, Anthony had no experience of horses. His mobility was more restricted because of his MS but he was still able to drive to the centre himself. When the day came he got in the car and made his way along the highway towards the small ranch where they were based. He had no idea what to expect, but the first thing that hit him as soon as he turned off the main highway on to the country lane was the quiet. Away from the hustle and bustle of the town he immediately felt his mind relaxing, the troubles of daily life falling away. He pulled into a gate and parked up. As he got out of the car, the second thing to hit him was the smell. It's maybe not to everyone's taste – the heady mix of sweet, slightly rotting hay, with fresh horse muck, along with the crisp country air – but it immediately energized him. It was exciting but as he made his way to the stables he also had a feeling of trepidation. He may have been older than when he rode Mama, but he was still only five foot two. At the stables he was greeted by a group of staff and he could see other people milling about, some climbing down from their horses, others trotting around in the distance and people packing away their gear. The team met him and led him over to meet the horses. There was one horse named Lily. He reached out to touch her soft nose and she nuzzled into his hand. Her tail was lightly swishing. There was another horse called Odi. Anthony wondered whether it would all come back to him or whether he would have to learn it all again. Luckily he discovered the centre had a ramp in the stables which helped you get more easily to the height of the horse's saddle. With the help of one of the staff he lifted his foot into the stirrup and swung himself over and up on to Lily's back. He wobbled a little and she shifted her feet and shook her head as he found his position. Then she settled and he held on to the reins and relaxed his shoulders. He could hear her breathing gently as he patted her flank. He said quietly, 'Good horse, good girl, Lily.' He had forgotten how good it felt to be this high up on a living, breathing animal and he already felt safe. The first thing the staff did was get him to do some physical exercises, basic moving and balancing, stretches, holding his arms out and so on, almost like callisthenics on a horse. Next they began to lead him and Lily around the paddock. For a moment he forgot all his problems and all his pain. After the session, which seemed to end all too soon, Anthony felt his whole body tingling. It wasn't that different in a way to the exercises he had done in physiotherapy, but this had been outside in the fresh air with another living creature. It didn't feel like physiotherapy; it felt like living.

Anthony returned the following week, and the week after, and each time he got more confident on the horses. One day, after his usual exercises, a member of staff said, 'OK, you're ready.' Anthony couldn't believe they were telling him to trot round the arena completely on his own. He took a deep breath and they turned him and Lily loose. It was almost as if she knew they had been given a little bit more freedom and she picked up her pace. From a distance the staff member began to call out instructions: 'Turn left.' Anthony led Lily to the left and she followed. 'Go round that barrel.' Anthony made his way around the course. 'Turn round, back her up.' It felt so liberating to be working with a horse and her trusting him so completely. It was also a lot of fun.

Eventually he was able to back up the horse without somebody holding the halter, do figures of eight, turn and go this way and that in harmony with Lily. As his MS had worsened he had been losing his ability to multitask, and it was also affecting his short-term memory and his cognition, so being able to remember and get Lily to move through these instructions without assistance felt like a real accomplishment. It was also a joy to see the other people around him, kids with autism who had huge smiles on their faces, sitting tall and proud in the saddle. There was one little girl who was non-responsive until she started the programme, then she started talking to the horse and being around them broke down so many barriers for her. To see this girl and all the other people getting so much from it and to have that camaraderie and social interaction was a big boost for Anthony.

With MS, though, you can experience sudden and extreme physical setbacks. In Anthony's case he began, out of the blue, to experience almost total paralysis. He could control his head and move his arms but he had no coordination and was unable to stand. Having come so far with the horses and been physically independent, it was a massive disappointment to now be unable to do so much again. He didn't know if or when he would ever regain his physical movement and strength. While he was in recovery at a physical rehabilitation centre he met a woman who was missing an arm. When they got talking it turned out she had experienced a horsing accident. She had been leading a horse and someone had knocked a hornets' nest from a tree. It had swarmed and the horse had freaked out and taken off. Because she had her arm wrapped round the lead, it had ripped her arm off. That was something you're not supposed to do, but she loved the horses and she knew it wasn't the horse's fault. She told Anthony how it had reminded her of how much power these huge animals have and how you have to respect that, but she knew in their hearts they are kind, gentle creatures, not aggressive or out to hurt us. Anthony was amazed that she had no animosity at all towards the horse. He told her about his horse therapy and when she got out she went along, to get back on the horse so to speak. Her own horse, a beautiful Haflinger, even ended up joining the programme.

Eventually, after a year of recovery, Anthony found he was fit enough to go back to horse riding himself. He was now in a wheelchair, but this didn't stop him. They had a ramp to allow access. For him the horses were now his legs; they melded and became one. While his wheelchair helped him get around, he couldn't connect with it like he could connect with a horse. To him they were now his angels, angels with four legs. It felt like being back home. He had been away for a year but it was like being back with old friends. After a while they got him back to the point where they could trust that he could be on his own again and Anthony walked out into the arena on the Haflinger. He backed the horse up and did a figure of eight. He was free again. Before he left he went to the corner of the arena and stopped. He looked into the Haflinger's eyes and whispered to him, thanking her for spending this time with him and for helping him.

A Horse Called Willow

Anthony had got so much mentally and physically from riding horses. But there's another kind of horse therapy with no saddles or equipment at all.

Ever since she had first seen them at the age of four, Kristen de Marco had wanted to be around horses. When she was eight years old she was finally allowed riding lessons. Her mum was born and raised in Puerto Rico and had grown up with horses, so she loved watching her daughters ride and compete. Kristen had never known such a sense of peace and freedom. But it wasn't just in the saddle. It was also in those quiet moments in the barn or out in the field when she was just with the horses – alongside them, not on their backs. For the first time in her life Kristen felt she didn't have to be the perfect daughter or student or friend. She was just able to be herself. Although her mum supported her interest, the family told her she could never make a living from working with horses; she needed to go to university and get a real job. So at eighteen Kristen stepped away from her equine life.

She went to university and started a career in the fashion industry. She got married and had a baby. Then things started to go wrong. She was having trouble with her marriage. She was beginning to question her life and her career choices. What did she really want? What really mattered? Her mind started to drift back to her childhood. She heard about people who were working with horses in mental health. But it wasn't about horsemanship. There were no large arenas or saddles. It was about just being with the horses as a form of therapy in itself. Kristen went on a training course in equine-assisted psycho-therapy. She got up the courage to leave her marriage and decided to completely change her life. She rented space at a local therapeutic-riding stable, rented horses by the hour and started her own equine-therapy company. Kristen soon found that many of the people who wanted and needed this kind of therapy couldn't afford to pay for it. She joked that she would never turn anyone away, but this turned out not to be a great business model, so she decided to set up a non-profit for all the mental health work and make it accessible to those who needed it. They called it Gateway HorseWorks. As they worked with more clients, Kristen and a couple of other women at the centre became really attached to one horse in particular.

He was called Disney. He was a red-and-white-painted horse with unusually sky-blue eyes. He had tons of personality and kindness. Kristen could tell that he genuinely loved people.

As they attracted more clients, they were beginning to outgrow their space, so they rented a little farm across the street. But this meant they needed to get some horses of their own. The thought of leaving Disney behind was heartbreaking for Kristen. Then on her fortieth birthday, one of the board members had a surprise. They had purchased Disney from the riding centre. He was their first official therapy horse. They also took in another horse who was lame and needed a lot of physical rehabilitation. This horse instantly became buddies with Disney. Soon after they were settled into their new place, Kristen got a call from the top vet at a large equine hospital. They had a surrogate mare programme, an embryo-transplant programme for breeding horses. Sadly when mares can't have foals any more they're often put down. They had heard about Kristen's work and were offering her two mares who were going to be euthanized, to give them a chance at a longer life. Of course Kristen couldn't say no and along came Rimtiana and Fanny. They weren't exactly feral, but as broodmares who had only ever really been handled for reproduction or been out to pasture, they hadn't had much contact with people. Finally Kristen found another horse, a little pony called Nova, at a slaughterhouse auction. They discovered she was deeply attached to an old Standardbred mare called Willow, who had been in the racing industry, so they decided to adopt them both together. Nova and Willow were both in very poor body condition; they'd had no recent vaccines and they were clearly very distrustful of people. But they joined the gang anyway. With their motley crew of six outcasts and misfits, they got to work.

Although Kristen was starting an equine-therapy centre to give therapy to humans, she soon found that the horses themselves were also going through a kind of therapy. There was a lot of work to do not only to get them healthy again but also to gain their trust. One of the most damaged of all was Willow. Every time Kristen touched or went near her, even just to put a blanket on her, it was obvious she had never been treated with any care. She had clearly been mishandled on the racetrack, then she had been used as a broodmare over and over, and finally discarded and bound for slaughter. Who wouldn't find that a little bit irksome? Even when someone came in to clean her stall, Willow would pin her ears down and grind her teeth at them. She would turn her back on people really quickly and then kick out. This wasn't anger or aggression; it was fear. Willow kicked Kristen more times than she can count. She even broke her hand once.

Kristen's job was to help Willow understand that they were no threat to her and that she was safe. At first Willow wanted nothing to do with anyone, staff or clients. Then Kristen realized that this damaged horse was in a way a mirror for what a lot of the people who went there for therapy were also feeling. She didn't trust anybody; very often neither did they. Just like her, they might be unable to make connections in life; they might feel like it was safer to be alone than to take a risk and be vulnerable. Bit by bit Kristen began introducing Willow to some of the clients. At first when they approached her and put their hands out to her, she would immediately move away. After about a year and a half, slowly but surely, she began to improve. Kristen noticed that some of the most traumatized clients were beginning to connect with Willow really quickly. It would be small signs at first, like not moving away from someone but instead moving towards them and pricking her ears. Or she would put her head low and simply be still. Willow seemed drawn to some of their clients more even than to her, the one taking care of that damn horse. Kristen didn't mind, though. She didn't need Willow to like her. She just wanted her to not kick her. That would be a start. Then she wanted Willow to realize that she was respected and she was loved.

As Willow began connecting more and more deeply with more of the clients, it was remarkable to see how she and the other horses began to transform from scared, damaged creatures to trusting calm animals, just as the people there were also transforming themselves. On one particular occasion, Kristen had a group of inpatients from a drug and alcohol centre over to meet the horses. The men were talking about wanting to rebuild and gain the trust of their families and about all the ways addiction can fracture a family. Kristen took them out into the pasture where Willow was grazing. As soon as they walked into the field, Willow picked her head up. She was looking at the guys from a couple of acres away, assessing the situation. The men walked over, quickly at first, then they stopped when they got near her. They calmly and slowly put their hands out. Willow made a snorting noise and backed away. The men turned to Kristen and said, 'She doesn't like us.'

Kristen used this as a way to tap into some of the men's deeper feelings. She asked, 'What is it about you that she doesn't like?'

They came up with all kinds of ideas, like 'She doesn't know us,' 'She doesn't like our smell,' 'She has issues with men,' so on.

Kristen then asked them, 'What would it take for her to trust you?' Then she left the guys in the field with Willow to see what happened next.

The men began to work together. They decided to approach Willow one at a time. First they would try it head on. She did the same thing and backed off. So they decided to approach her from the side where she could see them better. One guy slowly approached her and eventually she kept her head down, eating away at the grass. When the man was able to put his hand on her side without her moving away he turned to the group with a huge smile on his face. One by one the others did the same and Willow remained calm, head down, grazing away.

Afterwards Kristen gathered them together and asked what they thought had happened out there. Their responses were that they had learned that when gaining the trust of others the approach matters. We can control our actions and how to approach someone, then they have the choice whether to move towards us or move away. The men took from it that being the first one to reach out in a way that you might get hurt or rejected makes you vulnerable, but it can be worth it.

As Kristen realized how powerful people's experiences with these horses could be in their therapy, she wondered whether the horses could be used to help people stuck in the criminal justice system. Together with a local probation officer she began a pilot programme with thirty women who had just got out of prison. After doing therapy with the horses only one went on to have new charges. Kristen wanted to work with more probationers but she found that many of them had problems getting out to the farm. So she asked whether she could work with people before they were released, at a lower security pre-release centre where inmates with good behaviour go towards the end of their sentence. The authorities agreed and for several years men and women were brought to the farm to work with the horses. The results continued to be really positive. Eventually, though, the cost, transport and manpower of getting them all over there was becoming too much. Kristen said, 'Why don't we build a pasture on site at the prison then?' After much eye rolling and laughter, when they began to look properly at the results, it was undeniable that this therapy was helping to reduce reoffending. They tracked the results for five years and found that only 8% had new charges. The national standard in the US after five years is about 79% of people being returned to prison. It was truly remarkable. To appease the bean counters she also pointed out that this was saving taxpayers on average $154,000 a year. Not only that but in the prisons where people had done therapy with the horses, just as Harriet Laurie had experienced in Dorset, there was less fighting, fewer people being sent back to the main facility for bad behaviour and it was changing the whole environment for the better. With all this data, Kristen raised the money and got approval to build a permanent pasture and horse shelter right next to one of the pre-release centres in Chester County, Pennsylvania. Every week they would transport the horses there and invite the inmates for therapy. While the prospect of meeting horses might seem like a draw, in fact, for many inmates it was really just the possibility of getting outside for a bit which appealed to them. There was also free food, which helped. Sometimes the inmates could be quite distant. One, Enzo, didn't want to touch any of the horses at first. On their second session, though, Kristen looked over and saw that Enzo was in tears with his hands on Willow. Afterwards she asked if he was OK. He nodded and she asked if he wanted to talk about it. He told her quietly and calmly no. But what happened out there would change his life completely.

Enzo

Lorenzo 'Enzo' Trout was adopted from Peru by a Christian missionary woman in America called Cheryl. Enzo was actually about to be adopted by a British family, but that fell through so they told Cheryl, who was looking for a child, she could adopt the baby. When he was thirteen Enzo told his mum he was transgender, and that while he had been born a girl he was really a boy. For a Christian missionary woman living on her own, this might have been quite a shock, but from day one Cheryl was 100% supportive and accepting of Enzo. When he asked his mum how she felt, she replied, 'Even if you wanted to be a dolphin, I'd love you no matter what.' It was the sweetest thing she could have said and it gave him the encouragement to be himself no matter what the world thought.

Cheryl was a single mum, but she was a top real estate agent and they had a pretty comfortable life. When he was a child, though, Enzo had experienced a difficult trauma. He didn't know how to handle it or talk about it and, as a result, layers of anger built up. He was a free-spirited and fun-loving kid and he always loved a bit of danger and spontaneity, but as an adolescent he was also filled with rage and did some stuff which didn't always go down well with law enforcement. The more he got cast as the mean kid, the more he thought, *I might as well play the villain then, and I'm going to do it to the fullest extent.* When he was fourteen he stole a car and drove down to Florida to talk to a girl he'd met online. When his mum found out she wasn't exactly angry. She just told him to stay there and think about what he'd done.

Throughout his teenage life Enzo was in and out of

probation and in and out of jail. The whole time his mum never turned her back on him. When he was eighteen, Cheryl had a stroke and she moved to live with her parents in the mountains. Enzo moved to the city on his own. He struggled to find somewhere to live and used drugs a lot to cope. Once, when he kind of blacked out on Xanax, he went on a binge with a BB gun, a gun firing blanks. He admits he was a complete menace and for this he was looking at five to ten years in prison. It was his first real serious trouble. When she found out his mum was in tears. He couldn't imagine going away for five years and leaving her. To make matters worse, she had found out she had a tumour in her stomach. Enzo was scared that if he went away it might be the last time he ever saw her on the outside.

While he was in prison, he got the opportunity to go to a trauma group. It was the first time he had ever seen a therapist or talked to anyone about the trauma he had experienced as a child. It helped him to quit drugs and he was on the path to turning his whole life round. The only problem was that when he was released on probation the paperwork he thought meant he could drive again was wrong. When he was caught driving with this faulty paperwork the judge wasn't happy. To them it looked like a relapse. Because he was still on probation, this fairly minor offence meant he was sent back to prison for a whole year. His mum continued to visit him every weekend. He had been in and out of prison more than twenty times by now and she had been there every step of the way. This time being in prison was particularly tough. Enzo had been finding a way out of it, but now it felt like he had slipped right back down even further. To make matters worse, when the Covid pandemic hit, there were fewer staff at the prison. Enzo was supposed to be in the processing section for about three or four days but due to staff shortages and general chaos he was in there for forty-five days. Because there were not a lot of correctional officers on staff, once in the main prison, the inmates were pretty much locked down in their cells for twenty-three hours of the day. It felt like being doubly punished. Then, after nearly a year, lockdowns started to lift and Enzo heard about a horse programme they were introducing for people who were close to release. At first he was sceptical. He wasn't really a horse guy. But he did love animals, so he thought why not? At least they'd be given some free food and get to go outside for a bit. At first Enzo kept his distance. He watched them bring the horses off the trucks and put them in the paddock. Then everyone sat down at a picnic table and Kristen and the team would always bring the inmates breakfast. After having jail food for a year this food seemed glorious. Then they would be allowed to walk out to the field and be with the horses. There were toys and things if the horses wanted to play, and combs and stuff like that for grooming them. You couldn't ride them, though, and definitely not stand behind them, but people were always pretty sensible. Enzo watched as the others went around to meet the horses. For now he was keeping his distance.

In their second session, Kristen asked him if he wanted to go into the field. He couldn't believe he was free to roam without a correctional officer. Looking up at the sky, it was the first time that entire year that Enzo had felt any freedom. It was summer. Someone had just cut the grass around the perimeter and he could smell it sweet and freshly cut. Again he thought why not? As soon as he entered the field it filled him with unexpected nostalgia. He could feel the sun on his face and a slight breeze. It took him right back to summers with his grandmother who lived in the mountains. When he closed his eyes he could hear his grandma singing a song she used to sing to him when he was little. This was before the trauma he had suffered as a kid. It was the happiest he had ever felt. Instinctively, without really meaning to, he started humming the song too. All these emotions came flooding over him. Then all of a sudden he could feel Willow's big nose right near his face. It was such a warm, comforting feeling. It felt in some weird way like his grandmother was also right there with him. When he opened his eyes and saw Willow standing there, her gentle eyes looked back at him. He began to cry. It felt so profound but he didn't know why or what was happening to him. Then quietly and calmly, Willow walked away.

After that, every Thursday it was like church for Enzo going to see the horses. Strangely no one at the prison would fight that day. There would usually be arguments almost every day but not on horse day. Everyone was focused on and looking forward to seeing the horses. On Wednesday nights Enzo couldn't sleep because he was so excited. Having previously been the one to hang back, now he was the first one going up to them. He wanted to hug them and be near them as much as possible. After what had happened with Willow, something had changed deep inside him. Enzo realized that he didn't need to keep messing up and he was going to do something about it. Just as Willow had walked away, he could walk away from his old life and start a new one. Enzo loved all the horses, but he was not used to any kind of really spiritual stuff. He wasn't into yoga or anything like that. So when one day they had a kind of meditation session holding hands in a circle, he found it all a bit weird. It all felt too witchy for him. As they were all closing their eyes and breathing deeply and stuff, he wasn't really buying it.

Then, right in the middle of this total silence, a fox ran through the circle. Everyone stopped and looked at each other. In that moment, even though he had been pretty sceptical, he found that encounter oddly spiritual and meaningful. They say foxes are good luck, so maybe that's what they all needed.

Enzo was given a choice before he went to prison. He could go into a male prison and be separated for protection – a male prison would mean being with a lot of very hard criminals, like sex offenders and murderers. His other choice was to be in a women's prison in his own cell. This was because although he had transitioned to being gendered male, anatomically he was still female. He decided he would prefer to be in his own cell in a women's prison than with a bunch of high-risk male prisoners. Among the women he was with were some older ladies who had never been to prison before. Among them was a woman called Miss Emily. That's not her real name but it's what we'll call her for her privacy. She was super sweet, with paper-white hair and old-fashioned glasses. She was in prison for the first time, for basically being in the wrong place at the wrong time. She had no experience of crime or prison or anything like that before and she was having a really hard time adjusting to prison life. It was quite common for some of the girls to beat up each other and stuff like that. While Enzo was used to it, Miss Emily had never experienced anything like this. She was really timid and not used to seeing violence at all. She would cry in her cell every night. Enzo decided to take her under his wing a bit. They ended up having deep talks outside in the yard about their lives. Miss Emily also came along on horse days. She would look up at the sky and there'd be these hawks flying around. Miss Emily would know what each kind of hawk was and she would tell Enzo. She knew all about birds and described how at her house she had a lot of bird feeders. Enzo loved to picture her in her garden filled with bushes and flowers and hummingbirds, a jungle of light and life. When she first met Enzo Miss Emily told him he was the first transgender person she had ever met. She came with no judgement and in the end she became like a kind of grandma to him in prison. She had no children of her own and he became like a kind of grandson to her too. After his experience with Willow, Enzo began to put together a plan to stay out of prison and get his life on track. Miss Emily talked it all through with him and finally his release day came.

The rule at Gateway HorseWorks is that you have to wait a year once you are out before you can go and see the horses again. This is tough but it's so you can focus on your own life first. Enzo started to build his life plan. He got a job at the hospital and stayed out of trouble. As soon as he could he called up Gateway HorseWorks and said, 'Yo, the year is up. When can I get out there?' Then he and Miss Emily went up there together to see the horses again. They said hello to Disney with his sky-blue eyes, the little horse Nova and another horse called Dallas, a very cute black-and-white thing with spots almost like a zebra. Then there was Willow, strong and calm and just as Enzo remembered her.

The parole system in America is quite draconian. He's now been eight years sober and not been in any trouble again but Enzo still has two more years left on parole before he's truly free. Having been what they call 'on papers' since he was fifteen, now at the age of thirty-four it will have been a long time coming. His life has been completely transformed by his experience with the horses, so much so that he now takes part in panel discussions talking about his life and the impact it has had on him. It's been quite a ride and very surreal at times. Like the time he found himself talking at an event next to the old district attorney for Chester County. He had only ever seen him before across the courthouse; now he was sitting there side by side with this guy as equals. Enzo's mum Cheryl is now in her seventies. Despite all they've been through, she's still his best friend. She has stuck by him through it all.

As for Miss Emily? She lives not that far from Enzo. They meet for lunch sometimes and chat on the phone. She says she probably wouldn't have made it through her time in prison if it wasn't for their friendship. She's still like a surrogate grandma to him. They talk together about Enzo's new girlfriend, his job and all his plans in life. Miss Emily gives him all her insights and wisdom. She still feeds all the animals in her garden. And, best of all, she's not 'on papers' or beholden to any probation officers. She's as free as a bird.

It's hard to pin down why animals, and horses in particular, can have such a profound and healing effect on us. Of all the horses Enzo has ever met, Willow was the most exquisitely sensitive. Kristen says her ability to read people and situations with such precision and then seemingly mirror that back, has helped many other people too, even if it's not what Willow intends or knows she's doing. Willow herself has also gradually become more trusting and more curious about the world around her. She can often be found in her field now, head low, ears forward, relaxed and happy as she's eating grass, while people put their hands on her, brush her and chat to her. At twenty-seven years old she looks amazing. She's strong and powerful. She may be an old lady but she's big and muscley. She has the kind of physique Enzo says he would love but knows he'll never have because he's not a horse. Best of all,

Willow lives life on her own terms. She knows when she's had enough of being with humans and she walks away, until the next time.

We seem instinctively drawn to horses, to the sheer pleasure of gaining their trust and companionship. I know I've fallen in love with a few over the years. When I was in Arizona filming for a documentary, I got to sit in on a horse-therapy session. I went out in the field and met one of the horses. I did Join-Up with it as I had been taught by the horse trainer Monty Roberts with my own horse Chester. To feel how this huge horse went from being fairly uninterested in me at first, to following me and sticking right by my side, gave me quite a belt in the solar plexus emotionally. It was moving and profound to interact with this powerful animal who was clearly also so sensitive. They were once our prey, but when the conditions are right still will trust us completely. A lot of people say they feel they're able to be truly themselves when they're with horses. Perhaps it's because they seem to come to us with no judgement or expectations. Of all the animals I've interacted or bonded with over the years, it seems to me that horses have the greatest power to change something in us at a really profound level. Perhaps it has to do with their own deep instincts, often, against all the odds, to connect with the world in order to survive. When we get the chance to tap into that, in some magical way it seems to help us to survive too.

Postscript

In June 2009 things got extra exciting on our farm. We had all sorts of cameras rigged up in the stables. Bee, Philippa's mare, was having her first foal. We were all very excited and also very anxious. As the due date got closer we rented an alarm which we strapped to Bee's chest to monitor her heart; if it raised it would send a signal to us in the house that she was in labour. But we were in and out of the yard so much at that time that I spotted her craning her neck and pulling hysterical faces at me with her lips before she set the alarm off so we'd never have missed it. It was the middle of the night. Emily had a friend on a sleepover and they were in their pyjamas. It was really exciting. Bee was quite old to be having her first foal so we were anxious that everything should go well for her. The foal's head and front legs had appeared but Bee was starting to struggle, we thought. My experience of lambing was not to wait too long if they look like they're in trouble so I slipped into the stall with them and gently started to pull and little by little it flopped out and started waving those lengthy, wobbly limbs. It was a filly and she was standing, albeit with a bit of a sway, in under half an hour. We called her Alice Marie.

Once they're up there is a lovely process that needs to be seen through before you can go to bed. The foal needs to drink that all-important first milk or colostrum. With gentle encouragement from Bee, Alice has to find her mother's teat. We've had another foal since and watching them gently banging the soft side of their mouths against every bit of the mother's warm body until they find that life-giving tap, you realize why nuzzling, when they rub the side of their face against another, is a thing in mammals that gives comfort. Cats, dogs, horses and donkeys, I know I've done it too. I'd have a foal every year if we could.

Another day of huge personal joy was when my beautiful boys Ronnie and Bruce came to Dorset from Fife in Scotland. They were eight months old when they came off the lorry. I'd met them at six months old up in Scotland with their breeder Ronnie Black. I'd only intended to buy one when I went up there. While I was filming *Horsepower*, a series about horses as a global and historical subject, travelling to the US, France and Mongolia, it seemed that wherever we went there was another horse in the background, never the horse we were filming, but the distinctive shape of a Clydesdale, tall, hairy with huge heads and feathered legs. It was like they were calling to me from the future. When it came time for me to retire my beloved Chester I asked a vet that I'd met in Glasgow making the *Horsepower* series, Patrick Pollock, if he knew who bred the nicest Clydesdales? Patrick made a few calls and looked to see who had been winning most at the shows and he came back with Ronnie Black's name. Originally when we went as a family to Scotland to meet them, Ronnie had put one aside that he thought would suit me best; he'd provisionally called it Martin, which was weird, and he was in a field with his half-brother. They shared a father in the multi-award-winning American Ben Franklin. They were both six months old, gangly and curious. It seemed a shame to split them up, so I bought them both but I had to change the name to Bruce, which I thought sounded suitably Scottish, and the other I named Ronnie after the breeder because they were both equally handsome.

Ronnie the horse is a real machine, a bit bolshy on occasion but in harness he's an absolute machine, especially going up hills – he just puts his head down and digs in. When a horse learns a job it gives them an ambition to do that job and Ronnie definitely liked his work. Bruce is the more thoughtful of the two. He's incredibly sweet-natured and biddable, though not as fast or strong as Ronnie, but as Robert Sampson who taught them both to work said, 'He'll get you out of the trouble that the other one gets you into.' He's also the one I take to our local hospice for a visit. Both the patients and the nurses love to see him and just want to reach out and touch him, which he's more than happy with because he likes to eat their beautifully kept lawn.

When you open your heart to an animal it's inevitable that once in a while your heart will get broken. Our stockman recently lost his sheepdog and he was devastated. It may have been a smelly outdoor dog but it was his smelly outdoor dog. They'd been together every day for seventeen years, working side by side through rain and shine. I believe that the death of an animal that we have been close to brings with it a grief that we sometimes don't allow ourselves to show when our grandparents or elderly relatives die. When the dog goes you can unravel as if there's a free grief pass, and sometimes I've felt that all those people I lost when I was young, when the advice was to put on a brave face and be grown-up, get folded into the grieving for a lost pet.

When a farm animal dies it will be taken away as 'fallen stock', which means it's basically fed to the hounds and a lot of hunter people will have their horses disposed of in this way too. But I know a posh landed farmer near us who hunted and loved his horse so much that when it died, instead of having it taken away, he had it buried on his grounds. The vicar even came up and said a few words at the graveside – the man was inconsolable. The first horse we lost was Philippa's mare Bee. She'd been retired from work for a few years like Chester and the two of them lived the life of the duke and duchess of our farm, sharing a field and coming in every day for food and care. She had been lame for a while and we didn't think it was kind to let her go into another winter, so with heavy hearts we made the decision to have her put down. She was a special horse for us giving us our first foal Alice and she had bonded really closely with us over the years and with the old boy Chester. When she was dead I took Chester down to the field to see her body. I felt it was important that he knew she was dead so he wasn't wondering where she had gone. I led him out of his stable and into the field where she was. I unclipped him some distance away and let him go. At first he strolled down and just looked at her. Then almost immediately he put his head up and ran around the field. He shot past me and went straight out and back to the yard. I didn't think he had fully dealt with it, so I went and got him back again. I led him up to Bee and stood there with him. He had a sniff and a look at her and when it seemed like he'd finished and his attention had wandered, we walked back to the top of the paddock. Just as we were leaving, Chester turned and looked back towards Bee and whinnied. I got a gut punch of emotion. I don't know what he thought or felt at that moment. We had hired a digger to dig a very big hole for Bee's grave and she was gently lifted in. We are lucky that we have the space to bury our horses and they don't have to go as fallen stock to the kennels.

I remember when I was in Amboseli in Kenya staying at the camp of Cynthia Moss, who basically wrote the book on elephant social behaviour, there were the sun-bleached bones of a poached elephant which had been a part of a herd that hadn't been to the camp for some time. One morning they all came to the camp, young and old, and without exception they all stopped and played their trunks over the remains of their old passed buddy. It was quiet and solemn as they moved through and it was a great privilege to witness it. There are some things about our animals we will never know and that's as it should be.

When Chester was nineteen years old he became very weak. I knew in my heart he was close but he would still eat a carrot, so there was some life in him. His hips were very bad and he was obviously getting weaker, so in the end we took the tough decision to put him out of his pain. If I'm honest, I may have left it a month or so too long, but it's an awesome responsibility and sometimes an emotional decision isn't always the kindest. He was out in the field when the vet came. I was talking to him and stroking his nose and he had a whole packet of peppermints. Then the vet gave him an injection and down he went. I think this is altogether more gentle and humane than the traditional method of shooting a horse in the head. Chester was buried alongside his old friend Bee and whenever I go down there I say hello to them both and think of all the time we shared together and all the trust and love and fun and how he helped me find new joy with my family, galloping together over the fields.

A few other animals have since joined Bee and Chester. One of the toughest for me was Jim my Jack Russell. Despite having 'sod' written right through him like a stick of rock, he'd always been my number two. He was at my side during every job around the farm. He even sat on my lap in the tractor. Jim made it to fourteen, which is the oldest we've managed to get a dog to so far. He was diagnosed with liver cancer a while ago so we knew it was coming. I made his coffin in advance because I wanted to be prepared to give him the best send off. I'm so glad we managed to help him drift off quietly and calmly before he started to suffer. When he died I filled his coffin with the tiny squeaky tennis balls that he loved for his journey. Then, in a tragic double blow, two weeks later we lost our funny, mad old Jackahuahua, Penny. She died from a brain tumour behind her eye that we knew nothing of; it was very sudden and unexpected and really sad. Even more unexpected was how the rest of the animal kingdom realized that without any terriers on the plot it was a free-for-all. There are deer wandering around the garden like it's theirs, the squirrels are plundering my bird feeders and a fox came and took our hens. Who knew that just the presence of two small dogs could keep the masses back? With two now blind cockers and a retired guide dog I knew that introducing a single puppy would be hard, even if it was a terrier, and the thought of returning to five dogs from three would be difficult. Quite by chance Philippa was on the train reading a magazine that had an ad at the back for Jack Russell puppies in Dorset. She sent me a photo of the ad and two days later we brought home two tiny little Jims, John and Murray; we haven't settled on their middle names yet.

Ronnie and Bruce, my two superstar Clydesdales, have now retired to life in the field and have half our old lambing shed that they can let themselves in and out of as they please. In my mind they live a life of retirement in smoking jackets watching Sky Sports with no one asking anything of them, and they are very happy horses with Bruce still on hospice duty. But I'm too old to give up yet myself and have been looking for at least one more horse for a couple of years. When you buy a horse, before parting with any cash you get a vet to take a good look at it. Ronnie had suffered from side bones in his feet, which is something that heavy horses are prone to. It's not a condition that has much bearing if the horse is just for showing but with our hills and my carriage to pull it's an issue. Three or four times I found a horse that looked likely and I'd have their feet X-rayed and send the pictures up to Patrick Pollock (my vet friend in Glasgow, working on the Scottish vet for a Scottish breed idea) and each time he'd spot a sign of problems in the future and I didn't want to hurt another horse.

Philippa and I went to visit a dealer in Yorkshire who had a couple of fillies that I liked the look of and in the back of my mind I was thinking, *Ooohh foals*. We weren't that taken by the fillies, but there at the back of the yard was a very nice two-year-old gelding who was very nicely put together. Cue the vet and cue the X-rays, which I sent up to Patrick, saying that if he liked this one, I'd name it after him. And that's how I got Patrick, who at three now is very much a project but he is an absolute dream, taking everything we ask of him in his quite considerable stride. I even had a little ride on him the other day and he made no objection at all. I think we are going to get up to great things together.

One of the most miraculous things about our bond with animals is perhaps how over all the thousands of years we've been connecting with them, with the exception of the odd parrot, they have never answered us back, at least not with words. When Chester turned and whinnied at Bee, I really had no idea what he was thinking at all. They communicate with us all the time in lots of ways and we just have to try to work out what they mean. They talk to us when they seem happy and they talk to us when they seem sad, with their eyes and their tails, in the way they look at us, often when we have a toy or a sausage. Unless something truly miraculous happens I suppose that's how it will always be and that's just fine. From the soldier behind enemy lines releasing his trusty pigeon, to the guide dog who is both friend and freedom, it's a connection which goes far beyond spoken language and words. For me, the most joyful moments are the tiny things which come and go. Like Jim sitting on my lap in the tractor, front paws up, ears pricked, tongue out. He always looked so happy, living purely in that moment. Or when I'm out with Patrick, whatever we're doing together, he's alive and I'm alive, and it's a feeling of pure companionship, pure trust, pure love and a partnership.

Further Reading and Acknowledgements

Thor Heyerdahl, *The Kon-Tiki Expedition: By Raft Across the Seas,* George Allen and Unwin, 1950

Michael Hingson with Susy Flory, *Thunder Dog: The True Story of a Blind Man, His Guide Dog & the Triumph of Trust,* Nelson Books, 2011

Michael Hingson and Kerry Wyatt Kent, *Live Like a Guide Dog,* Tyndale Momentum, 2024

Melody Horrill, *The Dolphin Who Saved Me: How an Extraordinary Friendship Helped Me Overcome Trauma and Find Hope,* Greystone Books, 2023 (originally published in Australia as *A Dolphin Called Jock: An Injured Dolphin, A Lost Young Woman, A Story of Hope,* by Allen & Unwin, 2022)

Garry McCafferty, *They Had No Choice: Racing Pigeons at War,* Tempus, 2002

Michael Morpurgo, *War Horse,* Kaye and Ward, 1982 (adapted for the stage by Nick Stafford, 2007)

General Jack Seely, *Warrior: The Amazing Story of a Real War Horse,* Racing Post, 2011

Special thanks to:

Dr Cindy Fast at APOPO, Jaina Mistry, Jade Heaney, Dr Claire Guest OBE and everyone at Medical Detection Dogs, Rob Howe, Melody Horrill, Sonia Turner, John Gilkey, John Dean at Arizona Search Dogs, Dr Cindy Otto at the Penn Vet Working Center, Denise Sanders at the National Disaster Search Dog Foundation, Michael Hingson, Phil Wells and Emma Dignam at London Retired Police Dogs Trust, Harriet Laurie at TheHorseCourse, Anthony Rabak, Kristen de Marco at Gateway HorseWorks, Lorenzo Trout, Valeria Rocca and to Sister Mary Joy Langdon at the Wormwood Scrubs Pony Center for being an inspiration.

Picture and Text Credits

Chapter openers: images via author or in public domain apart from page viii, © Jaina Mistry; page 46, © APOPO; page 66, © Jaina Mistry; page 116, © Dr Mike Bossley; page 168, © Cindy Otto, page 222, © Harriet Laurie.

Inset: Images via author or in public domain apart from page 1, bottom left, © Charlotte Eccles; page 2, top, © Chris Ware/Keystone Features/Hulton Archive/Getty Images; middle right, © Wikimedia Commons; bottom right © PDSA; page 3, top left, © Jaina Mistry; top right, © Guide Dogs UK; bottom right, © Jaina Mistry; page 4, top and middle, © Dr Mike Bossley; page 5, top left and bottom left, © Wikimedia Commons; page 6, top left © Michael Hingson; top right and bottom, © Cindy Otto; page 7, top, © Cindy Otto; page 8, top, © Mike Summers; middle and bottom, © Harriet Laurie.

Page 96, quotation from *They Had No Choice: Racing Pigeons at War,* by Garry McCafferty. Published by Tempus, The History Press, 2002.

Every attempt has been made to contact copyright holders of material reproduced in this book. We would be pleased to rectify any omissions in subsequent editions.